Nigeria's Soft Power in Anglophone West Africa

This book investigates Nigeria's soft power capabilities in West Africa, demonstrating the extent to which the power of attraction may serve the country's foreign policy interests.

With the increasing popularity of internationally acclaimed cultural outputs, including afrobeat, Nollywood, and charismatic Pentecostalism, and a foreign policy disposition that is altruistic and sparsely transactional, there is increasing interest in how these soft power attributes influence perceptions of Nigeria in Africa. Drawing on extensive original research in Ghana and Liberia, this book highlights the attractive and unattractive elements of Nigeria's soft power potential. In so far as it makes the case for Nigeria's soft power in West Africa, it also discusses the challenges encumbering the effective deployment of the full range of Nigeria's soft power capabilities in the operationalization of its African policy.

This book is a timely contribution to prevailing scholarly discussions about the nature and utility of soft power in Africa. It will be of interest to both Africanists and researchers of international relations, foreign policy, and political science more broadly.

Fidel Abowei is a visiting lecturer at the Centre for Security and Intelligence Studies, University of Buckingham, United Kingdom.

African Governance

For more information about this series, please visit: www.routledge.com/Routledge-Contemporary-Africa/book-series/AFRGOV

Nigeria's Soft Power in Anglophone West Africa

Insights from Ghana and Liberia

Fidel Abowei

Routledge
Taylor & Francis Group

LONDON AND NEW YORK

First published 2024
by Routledge
4 Park Square, Milton Park, Abingdon, Oxon OX14 4RN

and by Routledge
605 Third Avenue, New York, NY 10158

Routledge is an imprint of the Taylor & Francis Group, an informa business

British Library Cataloguing-in-Publication Data
A catalogue record for this book is available from the British Library

ISBN: 9781032500362 (hbk)
ISBN: 9781032500379 (pbk)
ISBN: 9781003396628 (ebk)

DOI: 10.4324/9781003396628

Typeset in Sabon
by Newgen Publishing UK

To Jamila, Mignonne, and Renee – for everything.

Contents

Figures

Tables

Foreword

Fidel Abowei's book, *Nigeria's Soft Power in Anglophone West Africa: Insights from Ghana and Liberia*, is the transformation of his doctoral dissertation into a readable treatise about one of the intriguing, yet interesting subjects in the current theory and practice of international relations.

The book explains the evolution of soft power within the contexts of liberalists, constructivist, and realist scholarship to provide a system dynamic conceptualization of the practice based on empirical evidence on three states in West Africa: Nigeria, Ghana, and Liberia. It questions the evolution of soft power and its substantive ontological and dynamic perspectives by examining what is attractive and unattractive about Nigeria in Liberia and Ghana. The three states are founding members of ECOWAS, one of the five Regional Economic Communities (RECs) to which the African Union (AU) has devolved responsibilities under the principle of subsidiarity. Together they have addressed issues of peace and security bedevilling West African and Sahelian States, including insurgencies and terrorism.

To bring to light the soft bases of power between a regional hegemon and its neighbouring states, the book moves beyond the limits of realism to neatly unpack the additional attributes of states that make them central or peripheral in the dynamics of global politics and the various means available to them to co-transmit ideas and values within their spheres of influence. Nigeria's classic Afrocentric foreign policy, driven by the concentric circle paradigm, is used to examine what elite perception reveals about the attractiveness of these attributes and their ability to translate into foreign policy outcomes.

The book finds that the elite perception of Nigeria's disposition in West Africa is driven to some extent by its hegemonic role in West Africa, across the political, social, and economic spheres. This finding is borne out by the current realities in the ECOWAS region where Nigeria's vanguard role in waging peace and security is substantial. For example, Nigeria's military intervention through the Economic Community of West African States Monitoring Group (ECOMOG) in Liberia (and Sierra Leone) established the "Thank God for ECOMOG" mantra in Liberian public consciousness – at home and the diaspora. Nigeria's commitment to technical cooperation in post-conflict security sector reforms have created dynamic feedbacks that make its attractiveness in Liberia a reality. Nigeria's liberal values in international affairs intersect with Liberia's foreign policy, which is steeped in liberalism allowing for the seamless transmission of Nigeria's soft power. That is why the votes of Liberia and Nigeria on burning international issues are, to a large extent, congruent.

It should also be noted that Nigeria and Liberia were members of the Monrovia Group of nations as opposed to the Casablanca Group where Ghana was a leading member in the debates prior to the formation of Organization of African Union (now AU) in 1963. Nevertheless, Nigeria and Ghana collaborate on many regional and technical matters in West Africa and globally, despite some aspects of competitiveness and of tense relations as regional collaborators. These contrasting examples make the issue of soft power discursive and recursive and goes beyond the realist's dismissal of the soft power as a possibility both in theory and practice.

Nigeria, Ghana, and Liberia are today jointly active members of ECOWAS, the AU, the United Nations, and many other international organizations where the ontological evolution of Nigeria's soft power has created a union in the resolutions of matters relating to peace and security. For example, the Ghana-led Accra Peace Initiative to combat terrorism is supported by Nigeria as complementary to its counterterrorism stance in the Lake Chad Basin Commission and the ECOWAS fund to combat terrorism to which Nigeria and Ghana have made substantial financial contributions.

The theoretical and methodological possibilities of soft power as a concept in understanding the relations between Nigeria and Liberia on the one hand and the former and Ghana on the other is therefore innovative in bringing to light the role of these states in world affairs with reference to their distinctions as ECOWAS Member States. The book provides a basis for further studies on the soft power of regional leaders across the globe in the spheres of influence.

I commend Dr. Fidel Abowei for this substantial scholarly contribution to the intriguing subject of soft power in the conduct of international relations.

Scholars, practitioners, and students of international relations and its related social science fields, including international politics, history, development economics, and regional studies as well as diplomats and government functionaries, will find this book a valuable guide to unlocking what makes the foreign policy of regional powers tick in their relations to states in their spheres of influence. I therefore recommend it highly for their work, reading pleasure and repertoire.

Al-Hassan Conteh, PhD
Liberian Ambassador to Nigeria
Abuja, January 30, 2023

Acknowledgements

Although the contents of this book reflect the efforts of a single author, this is not without the support of many. I cannot acknowledge everyone, but I remain mindful of their immeasurable contribution to the successful completion of this book.

Dr Vassilis Kappis deserves my deepest appreciation for his support and guidance throughout this project. Professor Julian Richards, the Director of the Centre for Security and Intelligence Studies, at the University of Buckingham, also deserves my gratitude for his support.

This research benefitted from the financial support of the Dennison Personal Research Grant and the Department of Economics and International Relations, University of Buckingham, without which the fieldwork in Liberia wouldn't have been conducted.

Finally, I can't be more grateful to my family.

Abbreviations

ACP	African, Caribbean, and Pacific
AfCFTA	Africa Continental Free Trade Area
AFCSC	Armed Forces Command and Staff College
AfDB	African Development Bank
AFL	Armed Forces of Liberia
AFN	Armed Forces of Nigeria
AFRICOM	United States Africa Command
AMISOM	African Union Mission in Somalia
ANC	African National Congress
AQIM	Al Qaeda in the Islamic Maghreb
AU	African Union
AUC	African Union Commission
BBC	British Broadcasting Corporation
BP	British Petroleum
CEAO	Communauté Economique de L'Afrique de Ouest
CEN-SAD	Community of Sahel-Saharan States
CET	Common External Tariff
CFA	Communauté Financière Africaine
DSS	Department of State Services
DTAC	Directorate of Technical Aid Corps
ECOMIB	ECOWAS Mission in Bissau
ECOMIG	ECOWAS Mission in the Gambia
ECOMIL	ECOWAS Mission in Liberia
ECOMOG	ECOWAS Monitoring Group
ECOWAS	Economic Community of West African States
EEC	European Economic Community
EU	European Union
FACCIA	Federation of African Chambers of Commerce, Industry, and Agriculture
FDI	Foreign Direct Investment
FPU	Formed Police Units
FRN	Federal Republic of Nigeria
GAFCSC	Ghana Armed Forces Command and Staff College

GDP	Gross domestic product
GIPC	Ghana Investment Promotion Centre
GTB	Guarantee Trust Bank
GUTA	Ghana Union of Traders Association
HRW	Human Rights Watch
ICAO	International Civil Aviation Organization
ICG	International Crisis Group
IPO	Individual Police Officers
LFCW	Living Faith Church Worldwide
MFA	Ministry of Foreign Affairs
MNCs	Multinational corporations
MNJTF	Multinational Joint Task Force
MODEL	Movement for Democracy in Liberia
MPLA	Movement for the Liberation of Angola
NBI	Nation Brands Index
NCAC	National Council for Arts and Culture
NCCIMA	Nigerian Chamber of Commerce, Industry, Mines, and Agriculture
NDA	Nigerian Defence Academy
NDC	National Defence College
NEPAD	New Partnership for African Development
NIDCOM	Nigerians in the Diaspora Commission
NNDP	Nigerian National Defence Policy
NPFL	National Patriotic Front of Liberia
NTAC	Nigerian Technical Aid Corps
NTCF	Nigerian Technical Cooperation Fund
NTF	Nigerian Trust Fund
OAU	Organization of African Unity
OCHA	United Nations Office for the Coordination of Humanitarian Affairs
ONUC	United Nations Operation in the Congo
PSO	Peace Support Operations
PWC	PricewaterhouseCoopers
QCA	Qualitative content analysis
RCCG	Redeemed Christian Church of God
RMCs	Regional member countries
RUF	Revolutionary United Front
SALW	Small Arms and Light Weapons
SCOAN	Synagogue Church of All Nations
SIPRI	Stockholm International Peace Research Institute
SP30	Soft Power 30 index
TCA	Technical Cooperation Agreement
UBA	United Bank for Africa
UEMOA	Union Économique et Monétaire Ouest-Africaine
UK	United Kingdom

UN	United Nations
UNGA	United Nations General Assembly
UNHCR	United Nations High commissioner for Refugees
UNMIL	United Nations Mission in Liberia
UNODC	United Nations Office of Drugs and Crime
UNSC	United Nations Security Council
US	United States
VON	Voice of Nigeria
WAEC	West African Economic Community
WAMZ	West African Monetary Zone
WEF	World Economic Forum
WTO	World Trade Organization

1 Introduction

Soft Power in a Changing Global Environment

The latter half of the 20th century and early 21st century saw the field of international relations witness important changes occasioned by the acceleration of the process that has come to be encapsulated by the term globalization. These changes range from the diffusion of power from states to non-state actors,[1] shifts in the global balance of power, to evolutions in the means of influence, especially with the emergence of new forms of communication networks and advancements in information technology. Non-state actors such as terrorist organizations and secessionist movements have also become relevant players in global politics by disrupting the traditional hierarchies of power once dominated by nation-states. Equally important is that challenges such as terrorism, financial crimes, climate change, and cyber espionage transcend traditional state boundaries, creating broad implications for global peace and stability that require extensive collaboration between states. Consequently, states have sought to advance their strategic objectives by building and sustaining complex, interdependent, and multilevel networks.

Accompanying these changes is the acknowledgement that intersubjective elements of power are increasingly important. It is not that military and economic power have lost their relevance, even if there is a growing disaffection with the human and economic cost of war, it is that soft forms of power have become useful tools for the expansion of influence and building of alliances necessary to navigate an increasingly complex global system. Soft power explains the increasing role of foreign publics in driving political change, as well as the influence of transnational cultural interactions and the flow of news on foreign policy outcomes.[2] The idea of soft power provides a basis to explain foreign policies and programmes that leverage attractive assets, and a justification for the reallocation of resources to initiatives associated with public diplomacy and international broadcasting (Hayden, 2012).

Over the past decades, countries such as China, Brazil, Turkey, and India have shown keen interest in improving their ability to achieve outcomes in international politics through the cultivation of attraction. Even the Russian government, which is commonly understood to favour realpolitik, has in the

DOI: 10.4324/9781003396628-1

past few years embraced the idea of soft power, if anything, to combat negative perceptions resulting from the annexation of Crimea (Ambrosetti, 2020). Perhaps, Russia's soft power may have even been applied to obscure its domestic economic challenges or even portray itself as an unbridled opponent of US global dominance and normative imperialism. By coming to the aid of others, and spreading culture, values, language, and economic models, through sporting events, cultural institutes, and joint infrastructural projects, states boost their reputation, expand their global economic footprints, and augment their hard power capabilities.

In the face of this geopolitical reality, the concept of soft power, coined by American political scientist, Joseph Nye, in *Bound to Lead: The Changing Nature of American Power*, has assumed a prominent place in international relations scholarship (1990a). Embracing Lukes' (1974/2005) three-dimensional view of power, Nye (1990a, 1990b, 2004) argues that the widespread application of Dahl's (1957) decision-making power (first face of power), especially in power politics, does not erode the fact that it provides an insufficient account of power relationships. This is because it does not account for structural aspects of power situated in the second (agenda-setting power) and third (ideological power) faces of power associated with the work of Bachrach and Baratz (1962) and Lukes (1974/2005), respectively.[3] In *The Future of Power* published in 2011, Nye makes a case for a behaviour-based understanding of power that accounts for the three faces of power, although he tends to overemphasize non-decision-making expressions of power situated in the second and third faces.

Accordingly, Nye (2011) defines soft power as the ability of a state to get others to do what it wants through the co-optive means of setting the agenda, persuasion, and cultivating attraction. This stands in contrast to hard power – the use of threats and financial inducements to obtain preferred outcomes – that Nye (2011) associates with the first face of power. To Nye (1990a), soft and hard power are of equal importance, not just because they can be mutually reinforcing, but also, because they can be used independently to meet specific outcomes in foreign policy. However, like the broader concept of power, soft power's meaning, application, and effectiveness are heavily contested within the discipline, furthering the refinement and application of the concept.

In Search of an African Perspective on Soft Power

Since Nye's initial submission, scholars and policymakers alike have developed the concept of soft power to explain the foreign policy behaviours of great and emerging powers alike, including the United States (US), United Kingdom (UK), China, Brazil, Russia, and India. Except for South Africa, there appears to be a general misappreciation, both at scholarly and policy levels, for the potency of soft power as a tool of statecraft in Africa.[4] This is despite the apparent avoidance of brazenly coercive posturing in intra-African relations.

Even more, African states share a common colonial experience, transborder cultural linkages, and a relatively high level of cooperative engagement – all of which are permissive or antecedent conditions for the exercise of soft power.

Nigeria, the presumed "giant" of Africa, embodies this empirical deficiency. Despite its superior material and ideational capabilities – a gross domestic product (GDP) of $409 billion that dwarfs of all West African states put together (African Development Bank, 2019), a relatively superior military, and a budding cultural influence from its movies, music, and literary icons – scholars of African studies or specifically Nigerian foreign policy have paid insufficient attention to Nigeria's soft power capabilities in Africa.

The last few years witnessed the emergence of exploratory accounts of Nigeria's soft power (see Ogunnubi & Isike, 2015, 2017; T. Ojo, 2017; Tella, 2017; Idowu & Ogunnubi, 2018; Ogbonna & Ogunnubi, 2018). These scholars, to different extents, address three important questions, albeit insufficiently. These are what soft power resources Nigeria possesses, the extent of their use in the pursuit of the country's foreign policy, and the extent of soft power's effectiveness as a strategic approach in Nigeria's foreign policy. Not only do they assert that Nigeria has soft power resources, even with some contradictions at the domestic level, but they also share an optimistic view of the country's ability to cultivate attraction. This is due to the regional and even global appeal of Nigeria's cultural exports, rising cross-border economic interactions between Nigerians and their regional counterparts, and its African diplomacy. Nonetheless, they argue that the impact of these resources on foreign policy outcomes falls short of expectations.

While these studies offer important contributions to contemplations of Nigeria's soft power, they suffer deficiencies that warrant the writing of this book. First, these studies are agent-centred, that is, they infer or in some sense assume that Nigeria has soft power by appraising any seemingly attractive national attribute and exploring their instrumentalization in the pursuit of Nigeria's foreign policy. In other words, they confuse Nigeria's soft power capability with the finite resources lying within official and unofficial circles. Consequently, their determination of what is attractive and unattractive about Nigeria is solely based on objective indicators, which further informs their conclusions about the potency of these resources to determine political outcomes. This reflects a notable deficiency in the study of soft power where the capability of states is inferred or assumed by simply evaluating the resources that are likely to be attractive without recourse to the subject of power where attraction and aversion ultimately lie (see Nye, 2004; Rawnsley, 2012). This is in light of an increasingly complex international system where the actions and inactions of political actors engender reactions or consequences that can either increase their influence (positive feedback) or neutralize it (negative feedback).

Second, the agent-centred approach adopted by these studies implies that critical elements of the power conversion process are not specified and evaluated. Of notable importance is the lack of consideration for scope or context; that is, power with/over whom? And power to do what? These are in addition to a lack of consideration for the power conversion strategies of the Nigerian government, perceptions of Nigeria's resources and behaviour, and how favourable or unfavourable perceptions may have altered the behaviour of West African leaders towards Nigeria. Consequently, important dimensions of Nigeria's soft power are unclear. Not only are we unsure of Nigeria's soft power capability in Africa, and specifically West Africa, which is considered the country's sphere of influence, the full extent of its attractive capability, and by implication, influence, has not been appraised. In essence, we do not know what resources and behaviours are attractive; why they are attractive; who finds them attractive; and how they can serve the purpose of Nigeria's African policy.

These deficiencies need to be filled in light of prevailing assumptions that Nigeria is gaining far less than it invests in West Africa, thus, calling into question the effectiveness of its African policy. Also, they epitomize a broader debate on the theoretical underpinnings of soft power, in terms of what it means, its sources, the relationship between attraction and tangible foreign policy outcomes, and how changes in the behaviour of the subjects of power may be ascertained. In other words, the deficiencies highlighted in the context of Nigeria's soft power literature are not unique and may be tied to the absence of a theoretical core guiding conceptualizations and operationalizations of attractive forms of influence.

Liberalist approaches propound a Western-centric view of attractive resources that excludes alternative political and cultural systems (see Nye, 2004, pp. 33–72), while constructivists account for only intangible resources and their discursive transmission, which implies an understanding of soft power that differentiates between hard and soft from the tangibility of resources rather than the policies and actions of a state (see Hayden, 2012; Vyas, 2013; Mattern, 2005). This leaves out material elements of power that may be equally attractive as a result of the legitimacy of deliberate actions taken by states. Realists could fill this gap but espouse a nominal view of power associated with the accumulation of material resources and, as a result, dismiss the idea of power being soft (Layne, 2010; Gelb, 2010; Wang & Lu, 2008). This suggests that soft power does not neatly fit into prevailing theoretical approaches.

The inadequacies of prevailing theoretical approaches to soft power reflect on the conceptual and methodological debates in the literature. For instance, liberalists' approach to soft power leads scholars towards a "resourcist route" where the soft power of a state is inferred by evaluating the conformity of its resources with liberal values (see Tella, 2017; Rawnsley, 2012), while constructivists evaluate intangible resources – ideas, norms, and values – of a state and account for their discursive transmission through diplomatic and communication-centric policies (Hayden, 2012; Vyas, 2013). However, there is a need to also consider the effects of soft power on political outcomes to estimate a state's soft power capability. Not only does this allow for the evaluation of the strategies states adopt to meet their desired objectives, but it also places the subject of power at the heart of deliberating why and where states are attractive. Equally notable is that it allows for the examination of soft power's effectiveness as a strategic approach and provides useful pointers for policymakers to understand the effects their power has on others and evaluate the need for strategic adjustment when goals are not being met.

Given the foregoing, this book aims to assess the potency of soft power as a tool of statecraft in intra-African relations. Following this objective, it interrogates what Ghanaian and Liberian political and academic elites may be willing to accept in terms of Nigeria's soft power and the extent to which outcomes may be obtained in foreign policy as a result of it. It proceeds under the assumption that within favourable contexts, defined by compatibility of interests, geographic proximity, and historical ties, Nigeria's use of its power resources through persuasive and attractive behaviours may likely cause changes in the behaviour of the Ghanaian and Liberian elites. It further assumes that where favourable perceptions of Nigeria exist amongst these elites, they are likely to support Nigeria's foreign policy objectives, suggesting that Nigeria has soft power.

Drawing from classical realist insights, specifically Morgenthau's (1948/ 1993) relational power, to advance a theoretical framework that accounts for material and intersubjective elements of power, this book evaluates the interconnectedness of the different variables that link the mobilization of soft power resources and tangible foreign policy outcomes. These are the context and pattern of relations between Nigeria and West African states, Nigeria's foreign policy objectives, the strategies underlying the pursuit of these objectives, and perceptions of Nigeria by Liberians and Ghanaians. It does not simply attempt to fill an empirical deficiency in the study of soft power. It equally makes the case for a classical realist approach to soft power that accounts for material and intersubjective elements of power and explains the translation of soft power resources into foreign policy outcomes.

The Purpose of This Book: Why Nigerian Soft Power?

This book reflects an attempt to move towards a theory-based assessment of soft power that accounts for intersubjective as well as material expressions of power. In so doing it redresses some of the theoretical, conceptual, and methodological inadequacies in contemplations of soft power. This is evident in its attempt to draw from classical realist insights to develop a conceptual and analytical framework that provides a holistic account of Nigeria's soft power capability in Anglophone West Africa. Conceptually, it accentuates Nye's behavioural approach to soft power where the attractiveness or unattractiveness of Nigeria's power resources and foreign policy behaviour are inferred from the perceptive disposition of Ghanaians and Liberians, specifically, the political and academic elites who are known to possess some form of influence over their country's foreign policy. Essentially, it attempts to determine the soft power capability of Nigeria by evaluating the extent to which favourable perceptions of Nigeria's resources and behaviour have amounted to support for its foreign policy objectives.

While the importance of the foregoing cannot be overemphasized, the empirical rationale of this book holds equal importance, if not more. This is because, true to their presumed peripheral significance in the global system, few studies have contemplated the soft power capabilities of African states or the utility of attractive forms of influence in interactions between states in the region, despite a growing body of research on the soft power of developing states. By assessing the soft power capabilities of Nigeria in West Africa, this book demonstrates that African states possess unique experiences that allow for the development of international relations concepts and theories with implications beyond the continent. This, I presume, opens up the discipline to more inclusive theorizing and may even give rise to important questions that could enhance existing scholarship on the workings of attractive forms of influence.

The purpose here is not to argue for an assessment of the soft power capabilities of African states because the same has been done with other developing countries. Rather, it is to make the case for the inclusion of an African perspective in contemplations of attractive forms of influence. This is because, unlike the great power competition that animates the prevailing global order, African states are bounded by shared colonial experiences, cross-border cultural ties, and to a large extent, respect for the integrity of sovereign territories that sustain a climate of cooperativeness between them. Even more, the behaviour of African states towards each other is more or less conditioned by intrastate rather than interstate wrangling, and military capabilities are rather instruments of internal and regional security than of coercive interactions. This geopolitical context necessitates an understanding of not just the workings of influence, but also the nature of power relations that animate prevailing interactions between African states. Soft power captures a distinct aspect of this power relationship that this book discusses. In a way, it challenges the very foundations of soft power, especially its universalistic or Western-centric assumptions on what it means to be attractive.

In a similar vein, the African continent offers peculiar political, economic, and strategic circumstances. With the end of the Cold War, the interest of the superpowers in the continent waned considerably. Except for China, whose Belt and Road Initiative is giving the capital cities of some African states some much-needed facelift, African states are fending for themselves, both in economic and security terms. Today, Africa maintains a position of low economic status, dependence, and rising poverty levels. While the spate of civil wars has abated to some extent, new forms of security threats such as the rise of Jihadist movements, the proliferation of Small Arms and Light Weapons (SALW), and drug trafficking are assuming transnational dimensions. Equally challenging is the deterioration of democratic practice, leading up to electoral disputes and the aggravation of grievances along ethnic and sometimes religious lines. That these challenges require a collaborative framework towards their resolution, which the African Union (AU) defers to sub-regional organizations, puts the spotlight on sub-regional leaders like Nigeria to mobilize consensus towards their resolution. This ultimately hinges on their ability to influence.

However, the extent of Nigeria's influence in West Africa has not been adequately scrutinized as existing accounts of its soft power are devoid of context and do not account for perceptions of the West African public or even elites. This is even though since independence Africa has been the centre-piece of Nigeria's foreign policy, with the West African sub-region being its traditional sphere of influence. By emphasizing outcomes as a measure of influence, this book not only addresses this deficiency but also provides an empirically backed account of the full range of Nigeria's soft power resources that may be instrumental to its African policy. As is the case with Nigeria, governments are not only unaware of resources at their disposal that can gen-erate soft power, they are sometimes unable to incorporate these resources into national strategies in a pointed, coordinated, and effective manner. This heightens the importance of accounting for or providing a clear picture of the attractive and unattractive components of Nigeria's soft power resources. That way the country can look towards a strategic and more effective approach to foreign policy that takes advantage of the full range of resources at its disposal while also addressing those challenges dragging down its inter-national reputation.

The fact that this book extends beyond the appraisal of Nigeria's soft power resources to also include an assessment of the nature of its interaction with West African states reflects an important step in holistically appraising Nigeria's African policy. In so doing, it puts to rest prevailing assumptions that the country has done so much for West African states without tangible benefits, as the arguments expatiated herein suggest that West African states are open to Nigeria's leadership and acknowledge its influence.

The Plan of the Book

The rest of this book is structured around chapters providing contributions that advance the objectives identified earlier. Following this introductory chapter are two theoretically focused chapters that precede the five core chapters of this book, the first of which – Chapter 2 – provides an exten-sive discussion on the state of knowledge on soft power. Because the the-oretical insights scholars bring to the concept of soft power affect how it is conceptualized and operationalized, the chapter analyses realist, construct-ivist, and liberalist approaches to soft power. It then proceeds to review contemplations of soft power, in terms of what it means, what its sources are, how it operates, and how its effects are ascertained. Given the objectives of this book, the chapter also revisits existing debates about Nigeria's soft power. In Chapter 3 I attempt to propose a theoretical refinement of soft power by drawing from realists' assumptions on power, specifically Morgenthau's relational understanding of power, to explain the operationalization of soft power in international relations

In Chapter 4, I seek to clarify the extent to which soft power can be an effective tool of statecraft in West Africa by exploring the relational dynamics and nature of historical and contemporary political, economic, and cultural relations between states in the sub-region. I argue in favour of the existence of cooperative relations, amidst subtle rivalries and disputes that provide a permissive environment for the use of soft power as a strategic device. I also analyse the specific nature of relations between Nigeria and Ghana on the one hand and Nigeria and Liberia on the other, which similarly reveals long periods of cooperation, albeit with intermittent political disputes.

In Chapter 5, I evaluate Nigeria's soft power potential, that is, those power resources that demonstrate a capacity to be attractive, both in their latent and manifest forms, across economic, military, cultural, and political/diplomatic power categories. I demonstrate the existence of potential soft power resources within the purview of state and non-state actors – with most of these residing with the latter. While Nigeria's economic, cultural, and military resources tend to dominate the sub-region, the country still suffers from the looming threat of terrorism and rising poverty. As the chapter demonstrates, these challenges have their roots in an internal political dynamic that suffers from the flaws of a federalist political system that has entrenched a democratic system that is at best flawed, both in the practice of elections and governance.

Consequently, Chapter 6 questions the deliberate translation of these potential soft power resources into capabilities in the conduct of Nigeria's African policy. I first evaluate the evolution of Nigeria's foreign policy objectives since independence, before proceeding to argue that Nigeria's economic, military, and human capital has served a national interest that prioritizes national security and the welfare of its citizens but garbed under commitments to value objectives such as good neighbourliness, racial equality, cooperation, regional democratic consolidation, and peaceful coexistence.

In Chapter 7 I turn to the assessment of elite attitudes in Ghana and Liberia towards Nigeria. Here, I demonstrate what is attractive and unattractive about Nigeria's power resources and foreign policy behaviour in Africa, as I also shed some light on the reasons for these prevailing attitudes. While these discussions provide a basis to evaluate the relationship between attraction and foreign policy outcomes, the fact that they also reveal the unattractive dimensions of Nigeria provides a basis to discuss the challenges Abuja confronts in projecting soft power and how such challenges may be mitigated in light of changing regional and global political dynamics. Chapter 8 builds on these discussions. In as much as I assess the extent to which the attractive components of Nigeria's influence have engendered tangible foreign policy outcomes, I also engage with the challenges affecting the projection of soft power by the Nigerian state and how these challenges may be mitigated.

I conclude the book with a brief synopsis that summarizes the main themes and discusses some theoretical and practical implications of the analysis.

Notes

1 The term, non-state actors, is used interchangeably with non-government actors in this book.
2 The notion of foreign publics derives from an understanding of "publics" in public relations and diplomacy as a group of people who share similar views on specific transnational issues, deliberate on these issues, and agree on steps to address them. Tam and Nam-Kim (2018, p. 30) define foreign publics "as the global constituents with whom a country builds relationships through public diplomacy."
3 Whereas Bachrach and Baratz (1962) make the case for power exercised when "a person or group, consciously or unconsciously, creates barriers to the public airing of policy conflict" (p. 949), Lukes (1974/2005) notes that governments exert control over people not only through the power of decision-making but also through ideological power, the formation and alteration of public preferences by shaping their ideas, beliefs, and desires.
4 Africa and sub-Saharan Africa are used interchangeably to refer to countries south of the Sahara. This is because the Arab-speaking North African states are mostly associated with their Middle Eastern counterparts under the aegis of Middle East and North African states.

References

African Development Bank. (2019). *Nigeria economic outlook*. Retrieved February 17, 2020, from www.afdb.org/en/countries-west-africa-nigeria/nigeria-economic-outlook

Ambrosetti, E. T. (2020, December 15). *Go West: Russia's soft power in Europe*. ISPI. Retrieved December 28, 2020, from www.ispionline.it/en/publication/go-west-russias-soft-power-europe-28703

Bachrach, P., & Baratz, M. (1962). Two faces of power. *The American Political Science Review*, 56(4), 947–952. doi:10.2307/1952796

Dahl, R. A. (1957). The concept of power. *Behavioural Science*, 2(3), 201–215.

Gelb, L. H. (2010). *Power rules: How common sense can rescue American foreign policy*. Harper Collins.

Hayden, C. (2012). *The rhetoric of soft power: Public diplomacy in global contexts*. Lexington Books.

Idowu, A. O., & Ogunnubi, O. (2018). Nigeria's soft power and economic diplomacy in Africa. *Journal of African Foreign Affairs*, 5(2), 189–206.

Layne, C. (2010). The unbearable lightness of soft power. In I. Parmar and M. Cox (Eds.), *Soft power and US foreign policy: Theoretical, historical and contemporary perspectives* (pp. 51–82). Routledge.

Lukes, S. (2005). *Power: A radical view* (2nd ed.). Palgrave Macmillan (Original work published in 1974).

Mattern, J. B. (2005). Why 'soft power' isn't so soft: Representational force and the sociolinguistic construction of attraction in world politics. *Millennium: Journal of International Studies*, *33*(3), 583–612. http://journals.sagepub.com/doi/pdf/10.1177/03058298050330031601

Morgenthau, H. J. (1993). *Politics among nations: The struggle for power and peace.* (K. W. Thompson, Ed.). McGraw-Hill (Original work published in 1948).

Nye, J. S. (1990a). *Bound to lead: The changing nature of American power.* Basic Books.

Nye, J. S. (1990b). Soft power. *Foreign Policy*, *80*, 153–171. https://doi.org/10.2307/1148580

Nye, J. S. (2004). *Soft power: A means to success in world politics.* Public Affairs Books.

Nye, J. S. (2011). *The future of power.* Public Affairs Books.

Ogbonna, N. C., & Ogunnubi, O. (2018). Rethinking the role of Nigeria's technical aid corps as soft power: Rough diamond or fools' gold. *African Journal of Peace and Conflict Studies*, *7*(2), 121–141.

Ogunnubi, O., & Isike C. (2015). Regional hegemonic contention and the asymmetry of soft power: A comparative analysis of South Africa and Nigeria. *Strategic Review for Southern Africa*, *37*(1), 152–177.

Ogunnubi, O., & Isike C. (2017). Nigeria's soft power sources: Between potential and illusion. *International Journal of Politics, Culture, and Society*, *31*(1), 49–67.

Ojo, T. (2017). Nigeria, public diplomacy and soft power. In N. Chitty, L. Ji, G. D. Rawnsley, and C. Hayden (Eds.), *The Routledge handbook of soft power* (pp. 315–325). Routledge.

Rawnsley, G. (2012). Approaches to soft power and public diplomacy in China and Taiwan. *Journal of International Communication*, *18*(2), 121–135. https://doi.org/10.1080/13216597.2012.695744

Tam, L., & Kim, J. N. (2018). Who are publics in public diplomacy? Proposing a taxonomy of foreign publics as an intersection between symbolic environment and behavioral experiences. *Place Branding and Public Diplomacy*, *15*(1), 28–37. https://doi.org/10.1057/s41254-018-0104-z

Tella, O. (2017). Attractions and limitations of Nigeria's soft power. *Journal of Global Analysis*, *7*(2), 109–128.

Vyas, U. (2013). *Soft power in Japan-China relations: State, sub-state and non-state relations.* Routledge.

Wang, H., & Lu, Y. C. (2008). The conception of soft power and its policy implications: A comparative study of China and Taiwan. *Journal of Contemporary China*, *17*(56), 425–447. http://dx.doi.org/10.1080/10670560802000191

2 Soft Power
Theoretical, Conceptual, and Methodological Perspectives

Introduction

The ideas underpinning the concept of soft power are not new to IR scholarship as they are drawn from Gramsci's (1971) hegemony, Weber's (1968) authority, Bourdieu's (1984) symbolic power, and other classical works. However, the origin of the term "soft power" is found in Joseph Nye's *Bound to Lead*, emerging at a moment in America's history when scholarly contentions revolved around notions of "imperial overstretch" and the likely decline in US global influence and leadership in the face of challenges from China and Japan (Kennedy, 1987). Making the case for America's continuous global dominance, Nye argues that assumptions about its global influence should extend beyond material capabilities to also account for intangible aspects of power located in American culture, values, and foreign policy. Nye (1990) calls these expressions of influence soft power.

Although conceived and elaborated within the context of US foreign policy, soft power has assumed wide application, evolving to become a term frequently used by scholars and international actors evoking non-coercive forms of influence. As Hayden (2012) captures correctly, within scholarly circles, soft power "has been appropriated, critiqued, and equivocated in a variety of ways; perhaps [indicating] that it is difficult to reduce into a statement of theory" (p. 24). Notwithstanding the volume of engagement with the concept, it presents issues across contextual, theoretical, conceptual, and methodological categories of analysis that this chapter attempts to unpack.

This chapter provides a starting point for this book by discussing the theoretical and conceptual approaches, as well as the methodological pluralities that animate existing debates on the soft power resources and programmes of international actors. I start by discussing prevailing theoretical approaches to the concept of soft power across liberalist, constructivist, and realist perspectives. This is particularly important because the theoretical insights scholars bring to the concept of soft power derive from their view on the role of power in international interactions. Subsequently, I focus on existing scholarly contentions of soft power – how it is defined, what it constitutes,

DOI: 10.4324/9781003396628-2

what its operational mechanisms entail, and how its main components determine foreign policy outcomes. This is necessary to situate the main themes of this book within the broader context of existing debates.

Theoretical Approaches to Soft Power

This section discusses ideas embedded in liberalist, constructivist, and realist theoretical approaches to soft power by evoking their main points and limitations. In a way, it serves as a prelude to discussions in Chapter 3, where the case for a classical realist approach to soft power is made.

Liberalism and Soft Power

Liberalist scholars have found soft power appealing, even if liberalism does not explicitly address the concept of power, save for the role of economic, institutional, and consensus power on state preferences (Moravcsik, 2010). Perhaps, this may be because Nye's conceptualization of soft power, in terms of its sources and operational context, is embedded in liberal values and steeped in liberalism. Even the idea of complex interdependence, which talks up the emergence of issues amenable to a positive-sum game where the exercise of soft power is likely to be effective, is firmly embedded in liberal internationalism (see Keohane & Nye, 1977/2011; Walker, 2013). This is not only because of the role it accords non-governmental actors or global institutions in international relations, but also the emphasis it places on cooperative ideals of interdependence and the relationship between trade, peace, relations of cordiality, and the declining utility of military force. To a large extent, liberalism may also account for China's rising influence, especially in developing countries, built against the backdrop of growing economic interactions in the form of development aid, trade, and investments.

Going back to the origins of the concept, Nye (1990) associates soft power with free-market economics, "universal" values such as human rights, and liberal democratic politics. In his view, these values are shared and universal, making any state that absorbs them an attractive partner. Accordingly, Nye (2004) notes that if a state's culture and political practice espouse universal values such as democracy, individual liberties, and human rights, the more likely other states will follow it. The fact that the concept was coined within the context of the global neoliberal economic revolution and academic debates about the future of US global leadership shaped Nye's assumptions about the sources of attraction, which are firmly embedded in Western political values.

This poses a problem for liberalist approaches to soft power, as alternative systems of political practice and values can also constitute attraction, especially within contexts where they are shared (Fan, 2008). A well-known example lies in the fact that China's one-party political system of government has certainly not turned African governments or even the people away from it. If anything, research demonstrates that China's soft power is growing exponentially in the continent (Cloke, 2020). Given the foregoing, scholars of China's soft power acknowledge the need for a soft power theory better acclimated to the Chinese experience (Holyk, 2011; Fan, 2008; Cho & Jeong, 2008). This is evident in their portrayal of Confucianism as a religious practice likely to generate positive sentiments or proposition of Marxist and socialist principles as functioning political values alternate to Western capitalism and liberal democracy.

Beyond scholars of China's soft power, Eriksson and Norman (2011) argue that Nye's understanding of culture and values is consistent with American values and as a result problematic because he assumes a certain universalism in the "liberal conception of the rational individual, unconstrained by culture and religion" (p. 427). To Hudson (2014), Nye's description of attractive values and culture through the "prism of American hegemony" means that states with alternative values and culture "would in principle be advancing an inferior product" (p. 11). This is as Hudson equally argues that Nye has opened himself to charges of "ethnocentrism [by] implying an essentially universal definition of 'attraction' along American lines" (2014, p. 11). This constitutes a challenge for liberal approaches to soft power as it limits the utility of soft power in exploring alternative systems.

Another implication of a liberalist approach to soft power is that it leads scholars towards the "resourcist route" in their assessment of soft power. What this implies is that states that uphold culture and values that appear in conformity with what is practised in the West are assumed to have soft power while those who uphold contrary values are deemed not to have soft power. Scholars who assess Nigeria's soft power potential have fallen into this trap. This is evident in the fact that Nigeria's political practices are completely ruled out as a potential source of attraction because they suffer from certain vices, including electoral malpractices and corruption, that contradict the Western model (Ogunnubi & Isike, 2015, 2017). This is not to suggest that Nigeria's model of democratic practice may be worthy of emulation. Rather, it is to suggest that within the African context, where states are at different levels of democratic consolidation, the ability of a state to consistently transition from one "democratically" elected government to another may be perceived favourably in states where these expressions of liberal principles are rare.

Constructivism and Soft Power

Constructivists approach soft power as a communicative and argumentative process that entails the use of symbolic resources, associated with culture to alter the perceptions of foreign audiences (see Vyas, 2013; Hayden, 2012). Although Utpal Vyas and Craig Hayden have differing goals, they are unified by the argument that ideational factors should be incorporated into traditional understandings of power because actors affect the behaviours of others through ideas, ways of thinking, and culture. As such, constructivists espouse a view of soft power that suggests the transmission of ideas, norms, and culture through discursive or communicative-centric policies like public diplomacy and international broadcasting to influence foreign attitudes. Unlike realists who assume that states are unitary actors, constructivists, and to a lesser extent, liberalists, emphasize the internal composition of states, which include multiple actors interacting intersubjectively both within and across boundaries, based on shared ideas, interests, and identities (see Vyas, 2013).

This approach is evident in Hayden's (2012) use of Japan, America, Venezuela, and China as case studies to examine the relationship between discourse and practice, and by extension, the various ways states apply soft power in their strategic communications and public diplomacy strategies to alter the subjectivities of foreign publics. Mattern (2005) takes a different route by developing a constructivist theory of soft power wherein attraction is specified as a "sociolinguistic construct" produced through communicative exchanges characterized by "verbal fighting" or "representational force." In Mattern's view, soft power is not so different from hard power because the communicative exchange between agents and subjects of power is a coercive process. Emphasizing the social construction of identity and its role in the formation of interests, Tella (2017) explores the cultural appeal of Nollywood and Nigeria's use of technical cooperation to play the dual role of combatting its negative image, while also enhancing its image as a benign regional hegemon.

While these studies do not paint an exhaustive profile of constructivist approaches to soft power, as we can also include Vyas' (2013) study on the use of soft power in Japan–China relations at the state, sub-state, and non-state levels, they illustrate a penchant for constructivist epistemology and methodology in the study of soft power. To Vyas (2013), the fact that constructivists acknowledge important sources of power associated with realist and liberalist scholarship, including coercive power, structural power, and institutional power, even if explained in constructivist language, makes it a suitable tool to explore attractive forms of influence.

No doubt, in emphasizing the performative aspects of power, especially its operationalization, constructivists make important contributions towards a theory-based study of attractive forms of influence and their transmission to foreign audiences. However, their limitation of the sources of attraction to intangible resources is a significant deficiency, as material resources are excluded as potential sources of attraction (Hayden, 2012, p. 28). This makes for a narrow conception of soft power that is synonymized with intangible resources even though ideas, norms, and culture can have constraining effects on actors. Also, constructivists mostly approach soft power as a narrative-based phenomenon, which seems to exclude those expressions of influence that are equally attractive but are not conveyed through discourse.

For instance, the practice of states contributing to peacekeeping efforts or disaster relief are not ideas communicated through discourse, but actions purposively taken by state actors based on their material capability.

Realism and Soft Power

Expectedly, realists scoff at the idea of power being "soft." This is in no small way due to their competitive outlook of international interactions as anarchic and defined by rationalism and material structures. To a large extent, all realists agree on these. Also, the state is a unitary actor, security is paramount, and little room is accorded to the possibility of non-state actors influencing the relationship between states. Beyond these is the fact that prevailing assumptions about soft power tend to suggest that intersubjective realities somehow trump material realities in altering the behaviour of states, which realists deem contrary to their worldview. Consequently, they challenge assumptions that attraction, a critical determinant of outcomes in the operationalization of soft power, can alter the national interest of a state in foreign policy decision-making or that public opinion should be taken into account in foreign policy decision-making (Gelb, 2010; Layne, 2010; Lock, 2010; Wang & Lu, 2008).

Realists also argue that instruments of soft power are by themselves insufficient to make foreign leaders decide against their national interest (see Layne, 2010; Gelb, 2010). As Layne (2010) notes, there is hardly any evidence to suggest that states "make decisions because they like another state or its leaders" (p. 53). On their part, Wang and Lu (2008) argue that the assumption that a link exists between attractiveness and the ability to influence and persuade others in international politics is a fundamental limitation of soft power. Also, Layne (2010) is at odds with Nye's assumption that policymakers can be swayed by public opinion – the direct recipients of public diplomacy efforts of influencing states – in the realm of foreign policy decision-making. In his words, "public opinion does not make foreign policy [...] decision-makers do and there is little reason to believe that public opinion affects their calculations significantly" (2010, p. 53).

One can assume that much of the criticism realists throw at soft power may be due to the importance Nye accords to intersubjective elements of power, especially when much of the logic of soft power derives from realists' insights. When Nye (1990) developed his arguments on soft power, he noted how variables like technology, economic growth, and education are gaining prominence in estimations of influence, whereas geography, population, and natural resources are losing importance. In *Bound to Lead*, Nye acknowledges anarchy and the imperative of security in the interest of states. Using the logic of the balance of power theory, Nye (1990) notes that soft power reflects another layer of this balance that is equally important, even if more difficult to use as a strategic device. In other words, hard power is important and so are the interests underlying its utility, but the level of cooperation between states can be enhanced and undermined by the degree of attraction or repulsion between them (Nye, 2004). Also, Nye admits that states are rarely constrained by public opinion but argues that within specific contexts public opinion may engender direct or indirect effects depending on the goals states pursue, their degree of importance, and how issues overlap or interact (Nye, 2010).

Given the foregoing, it may be suggested that Nye does not provide a new ontological explanation for power in international relations, but simply acknowledges the growing importance of intangible forms of power. In the words of Hayden (2012) soft power is no more than a "complementary dimension to strategic assumptions of realist politics" (p. 9). Despite this, realists are reluctant to consider soft forms of influence, even though classical realists have long acknowledged the importance of prestige, ideas, and reputation to statesmen. This is an important deficiency. Also, realists' bias for great power politics and the little interest they accord to smaller states in a way obscures the fact that these states increasingly rely on softer forms of influence to advance their interests.

Conceptualizations of Soft Power

In IR scholarship, soft power is a contested concept but this is not because of its meaning *per se*. Rather, it is because of how the meaning of the concept relates to its sources and operationalization. Nye (2004) defines soft power as a state's ability to get others to desire the same political outcomes through the co-optive means of attraction, persuasion, and agenda-setting. This contrasts with the ability to coerce or bribe other states to comply with one's instructions, which Nye (1990) refers to as command or hard power. For Nye, soft power stems from the attractiveness of a country's culture, political values (when they don't appear duplicitous), and the legitimacy of its foreign policy. Nye's conception of soft power has since gained prominence in policy and scholarly circles, with Lock (2010) remarking that "if the value of a concept were to be measured by the breadth and frequency of its use," soft power may be deemed a success (p. 32).

This does not, however, erode the fact that for some scholars Nye's submission is "protean and arguably imprecise" (Geiger, 2010, p. 86) or that it "lacks rigour, its use is problematic and uncertain, making a strict definition of the concept hard to obtain" (Geraldo & Ramos, 2010, p. 16). Fan (2008) even goes as far as labelling it as the "power of confusion" for the multiple meanings associated with the concept (p. 147). In this section, I engage with existing debates on the conceptualization of soft power along two thematic lines – soft power as resources and soft power as behaviour. I also shed some light on the fact that even the ideal-typical behaviour – attraction – associated with the operationalization of soft power is without consensus.

Competing Conceptions of Soft Power

Two competing conceptions of soft power exist in IR scholarship, which derives from how scholars approach the causes of attraction. While a group of scholars see soft power as a derivative of the resources a state possesses, others attribute the cause of attraction to the behaviour of a state.

Soft Power as Resources

Because hard power stems from physical and material elements such as military and economic resources, scholars often associate the sources of soft power with intangible resources. While this practice portends to resolve some of the definitional problems associated with soft power, it provides a narrow understanding of a concept whose sources include much more. Two variants of this view of soft power exist – one, which synonymizes soft power with cultural power (see Fan, 2008; Hudson, 2014; Tharoor, 2012) because culture appears "soft," while an expansive understanding synonymizes soft power with intangible or soft resources such as ideas, global symbols, images, culture, and discourses (Lee, 2009; Hayden, 2012).

According to Fan (2008), soft power is simply "cultural power" (p. 149). Fan argues that foreign policy is antonymic to the idea of soft power because it substantially reflects hard power. In other words, even if a state's foreign policy appears legitimate, it cannot be a source of attraction. As such, what is left of soft power are the values and institutions of a state, which as Fan contends draws from its culture, thus making soft power a derivative of culture. Similarly, Hudson (2014) asserts that soft power reflects "the cultural facet of international leadership" (p. 6), while Tharoor (2012) associates it with the cultural values of states, which can be consciously or unconsciously projected to global audiences.

Alternative perspectives associate soft power with intangible resources. Lee (2009), who sought to develop a theory of soft power argues that hard power entails material resources – military and financial, while soft power relies on "soft resources" (p. 209). His list of soft resources includes any intangible asset that may be influential, including ideas, know-how, culture, national symbols, discourses, education, theories, etc. He is no different from Hall (2010) who notes that soft power "captures assets less tangible than bombs or chequebooks such as culture and values" (p. 1). Similarly, Hayden (2012) argues that soft power encompasses intangible assets that get political actors to want the same objectives and share the same normative view of the international arena. These resources, Hayden argues, entail "influence," "the force of an actor's argument," and "the attractiveness of an actor's culture and institutions" (2012, p. 8). This is suggestive of the view that soft power captures the roles of ideas, norms, and culture on the ability of states to cause a change in the behaviour of others. Vyas (2013) shares the same view as he ascribes the sources of attraction to ideas and information, which when transmitted may alter the values, norms, and ideas of the recipient state.

Soft Power as Behaviour

Nye (2011) argues that soft power stems from both resources and behaviour. That is, attraction may emanate from the quality of a state's resources, as it can also emanate from their exercise. Conversely, command power stems from coercive behaviour. Intangible and structural as the sources of attraction appear, Nye (2011) notes that tangible resources like military and economic resources may also produce soft power, and as such, soft power is more about the behaviour of the state than the resources it possesses. Put differently, soft power is a behaviour that draws from all dimensions of power resources, as long as they are attractive.

In as much as Hayden (2012) defines the sources of attraction in intangible terms, he nonetheless embraces the notion of soft power being the result of attractive behaviour. Where Hayden (2012) differs from Nye is in limiting the sources of attractive behaviours to only intangible resources such as ideas, norms, and values. While this is because he approaches soft power from a constructivist perspective, attributing the sources of attraction to intangible soft power potential alone is insufficient, as it suggests that military and economic resources only engender coercive behaviours of threat and inducement. It ignores the fact that foreign policy entails the use of material resources for political ends and the legitimacy of this practice can be attractive. Even more, the limitation of soft power to intangible resources excludes aspects of statecraft that involve the non-coercive use of military and economic power resources in the form of military cooperation, peacekeeping, disaster relief operations, and development assistance (Brown, 2017). It also ignores the fact that intangible resources like culture, ideology, and norms that are assumed to be soft may not necessarily be attractive, especially when they contradict prevailing societal norms, and are perceived as instruments of instability (Mingjiang, 2009).[1] For instance, Nye (2004, p. 52) notes how Iranian mullahs find US popular culture offensive as it tends to contradict the tenets of Sharia.

Operationalizing Soft Power: The Problem of Attraction

Soft power has been applied variously to assess the capabilities and foreign policies of middle powers and superpowers (see Wilson, 2008; Smith, 2006; Kurlantzick, 2007; Ogunnubi & Okeke-Uzodike, 2015; Valença & Carvalho, 2014). These studies are mostly approached in line with Nye's (2004) assertion that the concept reflects an analytical device used to fill a deficiency in how power is understood. However, scholars such as Hall (2010) and Angey-Sentuc and Molho (2015) argue that soft power is not suitable as an analytical device. Whereas, Angey-Sentuc and Molho (2015) argue that its application "blurs the line between political discourse and scientific observation" when used as an analytical device (p. 1), Hall (2010) is rather more detailed in his submission as he contends that the widespread use of soft power does not make it a suitable category of analysis because attraction, which reflects the core of the concept, is not a suitable basis for a category of analysis.

According to Hall (2010), not only are there methodological difficulties in parsing out what attraction entails but "the concept of attraction itself makes for an unwieldy theoretical tool" (pp. 18–19). In addition, Hall notes that it is unclear "whether or not it takes different forms or is transferable across categories, [how it translates] into support, and how permanent an asset's attraction [...] is" (2010, p. 19). This is not so different from Mattern (2005) and Kōse et al. (2016) who assert that soft power, and by implication attraction, lacks theoretical clarity and presents ambiguities that render the concept deficient. Mattern (2005) even goes further to assert that attraction is inimical to the logic of global politics, whether we see it as a natural occurrence or the result of persuasive arguments. Accordingly, she argues that attraction should be conceived as a "non-physical" but coercive form of power constructed through representational force and exercised through language (p. 583).

Nye did not necessarily present a clear-cut theory of soft power, which may explain why attraction and its mechanism are not clearly specified, despite being central to the operationalization of soft power. As Hayden (2012) notes, attraction is the "archetypical soft power behaviour," but its ability to determine foreign policy outcomes and how it relates to the national interest remains unclear (p. 29). These deficiencies in the explanations of the attractive mechanisms of soft power and their attendant effects on outcomes may not be unconnected with the fact that prevailing approaches, including Nye's, to soft power, are agent-centred. That is, the soft power of a state is inferred from examining the quality of resources and their instrumentalization in foreign policy.

Competing Methodological Approaches to Soft Power

Despite the conceptual development of soft power, a unified approach to measuring the capability of states remains elusive. This may be because the operationalization and effects mostly exist as a nascent potential that is rarely obvious to the mind or eye (Hudson, 2014). While Mukherjee (2014) blames the intangibility of soft power sources and impact, its diffused nature, and the long-term nature of its effects, McClory (2015) notes its inherent subjectivity, the reliance on the subject of power to determine effects, the ephemeral nature of attraction, and the plurality of soft power resources, which defies simple categorization and quantification. This section discusses several attempts at this fraught enterprise by grouping existing scholarly contributions into three loose categories – agent-centred, subject-centred, and outcomes-based approaches.

Agent-Centred Approaches to Soft Power

A prevailing approach to soft power is the *resourcist* or agent-centred approach, where the qualities and activities of a state (agent of power) are evaluated, and their association with possible outcomes is implied based on the credibility of resources (see Nye, 2011; Tella, 2018; Rawnsley, 2012). Where a state appears politically stable, has an effective government, and has rich cultural values, it is presumed that other states will perceive it favourably or be attracted to it. For instance, Rawnsley (2012) used this approach to compare China and Taiwan's soft power resources and their application in the public diplomacy strategies of both countries. This is also the case with Nye's (2011) study on the use of soft power in US foreign policy.

As discussed previously, this methodological approach to measuring soft power suffers several deficiencies that are worth noting. First, the emphasis on the credibility of resources, which draws mostly from the prism of American or Western values, contradicts the fact that credibility is dynamic, culture-bound, and context-specific (Grass & Seiter, 2009). Second, an agent-centred approach excludes the insights, interpretations, and behaviour of the subjects of power. Third, it does not account for the compatibility of interests and values between the agent and subject of power (Ji, 2017). Fourth, not only does it confuse resources with power, it does not account for critical variables in the power conversion process. Finally, the absence of consideration for perceptions of the subject of power limits the path towards policy formulation, implementation, and evaluation.

Subject-Centred Approaches to Soft Power

Another approach to measuring soft power turns the table around by assessing subject perceptions and attitudes towards the agent. Two approaches exist in the literature. One emphasizes media images – visibility and valence – to estimate perceptions of a country (Manheim, 1994), while the other uses factor analysis to explore the features of a country's brand and soft power. Examples of the latter are indexes such as the Anholt-Ipsos NBI and Soft Power 30 (SP30) Index (Ipsos Public Affairs, 2019; McClory, 2019). With a country's image and brand an important determinant of positive and negative perceptions, these approaches evaluate the brand, image, and reputation of a country. For instance, Manheim (1994) assesses the representation of countries in media discourses within the US by examining the quantity of coverage (visibility), and the degree of favourability of the coverage (valence). These are in addition to examining how these images influence the policy disposition of US policymakers.

While Manheim (1994) emphasizes the image management of a state through public diplomacy and public relations initiatives, the Anholt-Ipsos NBI and SP30 reduce the number of variables gathered from country B (subject) about Country A (agent) into a smaller number of factors, or in this case dimension or categories of soft power sources. For instance, the Anholt-Ipsos NBI contained seven dimensions – exports, culture, people, tourism, immigration, investment, and governance – with the common score of each dimension used to highlight the performance of a state. In the case of SP30, a composite index combining both objective metrics (government, digital, culture, enterprise, engagement, and education) and subjective or international polling data on variables such as cuisine, tech products, friendliness, culture, luxury goods, foreign policy, and liveability is used to assess and compare the soft power resources of the most influential countries in the world, while also attempting to account for their potential to influence foreign policy outcomes.

These studies contain certain deficiencies that are worth noting. Manheim's visibility-valence model only reveals whether the public relations campaign of foreign governments is effective in favourably altering the perceptions of policymakers in the US. In other words, how "media emotions" or valence affect the policy disposition of policymakers. In so far as it does not account for variations in media emotions and also provides insights into why a nation is represented favourably or unfavourably, or what can be done to alter negative perceptions towards a specific country, its policy implications are limited (Ji, 2017). On their part, the SP30 and Anholt-Ipsos NBI operate under a generic global context that makes it impossible to compare country-specific conditions that may alter the effectiveness of soft power in bilateral contexts. Also, they do not evaluate the policies of states. In a way, they share similar deficiencies with the visibility-valence model in the sense that the reasons behind favourable or unfavourable sentiment are unknown and they do not reveal how these emotions may have altered the behaviour of the subject towards the agent of power.

Outcomes-Based Approaches to Soft Power

Outcomes-based approaches account for agents' resources and subject perception in a measurement process that culminates in the determination of the effects or outcomes of attraction, understood as behavioural change. While Singh and MacDonald (2017) introduced a statistical approach to assessing the relationship between soft power resources and foreign policy outcomes, Hayden (2012), Gürsoy (2020), and Ji (2017) approach the measurement of effects qualitatively.

Singh and MacDonald (2017) measure the effects of soft power by assessing the relationship between soft power assets – political values, levels of prosperity, culture, and citizen communication – and tangible outcomes such as social attractions (number of international students a country recruits), cultural attractions (number of incoming international tourists and cultural institutes), economic attractions (levels of Foreign Direct Investment (FDI) and levels of prosperity), and political attraction (United Nations (UN) General Assembly (UNGA) voting close to the average "ideal point" of voting for all states). Their study finds bivariate relationships between pairs of independent and dependent variables to be statistically significant, suggesting a positive correlation between soft power assets and foreign policy outcomes. Although the findings of this study speak to the value of soft power assets and their propensity to draw strategic advantages, it does not take into consideration the opinions of the subject of soft power, leaving little room to isolate, for instance, what specific aspects of a country's culture are the cause of attraction.

Accordingly, Hayden (2012) argues that soft power functions as a communicative process in a global system characterized by communication networks. It is within these networks that soft power resources are mobilized and deployed in a dialogical approach that engenders shared meanings and understanding. As such, Hayden (2012) makes the case for the use of discourse analysis in examining perceptions of soft power resources. This involves investigating the qualities and policies of the agent of power, as well as the relational context between the agent and subject, which then allows for an understanding of attraction as resources and behaviour. As Ji (2017) argues, this approach, which embraces the socially constructed nature of attraction and persuasion, does not fully account for the reactions of the subjects to the agent's resources and behaviour. For instance, narratives of cultural domination, which characterize soft power discourse, may just be discursive constructs that do not reflect the lived experiences of "subordinate" cultures (Iwabuchi, 2010).

Ji (2017) argues that investigations of soft power effects should be geared towards the subjects of power. As such, he advances a processual and subject-oriented approach that emphasizes two categories of outcomes (cognitive and behavioural) at three hierarchical levels – micro (individual actors), meso (institutional actors), and macro (state actors). Whereas the micro-level emphasizes public sentiments towards an agent's resources and activities which may be captured through opinion polls or survey questionnaires, the meso- and macro-levels emphasize how an agent's resources and activities, communicated through discourse, are interpreted, understood, and perceived by state actors. As Ji (2017) notes, the effects of the agent's soft power may be determined using analytical approaches in the positivist and interpretivist traditions, including textual, content, discourse, and framing analysis. Apart from the fact that this approach uncovers subject perceptions, it also exposes the reasons for negative and positive views. Equally, the meanings embedded in communicative discourse between the agent and subject can be unpacked, and the social context of their interaction examined.

Gürsoy (2020) puts this approach into practice in his assessment of the UK's soft power in Turkey. Drawing from records of parliamentary proceedings between 2011 and 2018, he investigates the views of Turkish political elites to ascertain the attractive and unattractive components of the UK's soft power. Gürsoy (2020) uses qualitative content analysis (QCA) as a methodological approach to unpacking references to the UK in Turkish parliamentary proceedings, which are then textually analysed and coded according to positive and negative references. While an important contribution, his analysis falls short of measuring outcomes and this is because Britain's relationship with Turkey was not sufficiently explored to reveal the UK's interests in Turkey, and how attraction or aversion towards the UK may have affected these interests. In other words, the extent to which the views or opinions of the collectivity within an institution or a country may in turn shape institutional policies, foreign policies, and policy-related interactions is unclear.

Contextualizing Soft Power: The Case of Nigeria

Studies demonstrate that the sources of soft power vary across cultures and contexts. This is evident in the number of publications assessing the place of soft power in the rising influence of emerging and regional powers such as India (Malone, 2011; Mukherjee, 2014; Tharoor, 2012), Russia (Feklyunina, 2015), Brazil (Valenca & Carvalho, 2014), and South Africa (Tella & Ogunnubi, 2014; Ogunnubi & Okeke-Uzodike, 2015; Sidiropoulos, 2014).

Consistent with this development, the last few years witnessed the emergence of scholarly works exploring notions of Nigeria's soft power, with questions ranging from what resources the country possesses, to the extent to which their instrumentalization has amounted to tangible gains. This scholarly endeavour began with Ogunnubi and Isike's (2015) comparative assessment of Nigeria and South Africa's soft power resources vis-à-vis their quest for hegemonic leadership in sub-Saharan Africa. The pair followed this with another study, *Nigeria's Soft Power Sources: Between Potential and Illusion*, which assessed the attractive potential of Nigeria's power resources as well as the domestic contradictions that may affect their effectiveness (Ogunnubi & Isike, 2017). While both studies differ in their objectives, they are similar in their use of Nye's (2004) sources of soft power as analytical categories to offer an exploratory account of Nigeria's soft power resources. Given the "resourcist" approach to their study, Nigeria's soft power resources include any seemingly "attractive" national attribute that falls within these analytical categories, notably Nollywood, music, iconic personalities, sporting accomplishments, participation in peacekeeping, conflict mediation role in Africa, the policy of development assistance, the policy of good neighbourliness, Nigerian churches, and the diaspora community.

With these studies highlighting a flurry of potentially attractive resources within official and unofficial circles, T. Ojo (2017) and Tella (2017) moved on to question their instrumentalization in Nigeria's foreign policy, albeit without consideration for scope or context. For instance, T. Ojo (2017) focused on Nollywood and Nigerian Pentecostal churches as attractive cultural resources and tools of public diplomacy that may serve the purpose of building transnational cultural relations and improving Nigeria's image around the world. In a similar vein, Tella (2017) examines Nollywood and the Nigerian Technical Aids Corps (NTAC) scheme – Nigeria's own international voluntary services modelled after the American Peace Corps – as instruments of cross-cultural dialogue. Given Tella's (2017) interest in the challenges to Nigeria's attractiveness, he also explores the negative effects of Boko Haram's activities and endemic corruption within official circles on Nigeria's image and political values.

In a subsequent publication, Tella (2018) moved beyond the resources debate to examine Nigeria's soft power capability. Having examined some obvious attractive qualities that Nigeria possesses, including Nollywood, Pentecostal churches, and corporations, he concludes that these do not go beyond potential, as Abuja has been unable to deploy them effectively to achieve its foreign policy objectives. Although Tella (2018) adopts an approach to soft power that suggests an Outcomes-based study, his analysis fails to account for critical aspects of the measurement process this approach to the measurement of soft power requires, including the relational and contextual parameters of Nigeria's strategies, and perceptions of its behaviour.

While these scholarly contributions to the knowledge base of Nigeria's foreign policy cannot be overemphasized, their determination of what is attractive and unattractive based solely on objective indicators, which further informs their conclusions about the potency of these resources to determine political outcomes, reflects a notable deficiency in the study of power relationships. Put differently, their approach to soft power determines the capacity of a state to attract by simply evaluating its potential soft power resources. For instance, Tella's (2017) assertion that corruption and terrorism have undermined Nigeria's influence speaks to a pattern in these studies where the impacts of Nigeria's attractive potential and contradictions on foreign policy are simply assumed and not backed by empirical evidence drawn from the perceptions of the subjects of power where attraction and aversion ultimately lie. Similarly, Ogunnbi and Isike (2017) claim that "there is little soft power claim [Nigeria] can make from its political ethos" based on a human rights profile that is tainted with allegations of extra-judicial killings by security forces (p. 13). While this assumption may be correct, it remains unclear if Africans, especially the political elites who determine the foreign policy dispositions of their states, feel this way and are consequently averse to cooperating with Nigeria.

In a bid to remedy these gaps, Idowu and Ogunnubi (2018) and Ogbonna and Ogunnubi (2018) sought to move beyond prevailing agent-centred approaches to examine the specific relationship between Nigeria's economic diplomacy and the changed behaviour of African states. While the former relies on opinion surveys conducted by Afrobarometer from 2002 to 2014 on the government's handling of the local economy to infer positive or negative outcomes, the latter explores the link between the NTAC scheme and voting coincidence in the AU. This was done by questioning the extent to which Nigeria's investment in the NTAC scheme has amounted to the support of African states for Nigerian citizens seeking elective offices in the AU. While these studies contribute to the study of Nigeria's soft power, they suffer certain limitations that emphasize the need for a more robust assessment of Nigeria's soft power.

First, Idowu and Ogunnubi's (2018) use of opinion survey data – gathered from domestic audiences – on the Nigerian government's handling of the domestic economy to infer a negative outcome for its economic diplomacy initiatives appears erroneous, given that these initiatives are geared towards enhancing the country's influence in Africa not necessarily to derive immediate domestic economic benefits. Also, their analysis ignores countervailing domestic factors like corruption and poor economic policies that may induce negative sentiments about the handling of the local economy. By drawing from the perception of Nigeria's domestic audience to assess the effectiveness of its economic diplomacy initiatives, they appear to conflate Nigeria's domestic economic goals with a diplomatic approach that involves the use of economic tools. Also, they highlight the focus of Nigeria's economic diplomacy to include promoting export, debt rescheduling, and encouraging FDI without specifying how they situate within the pursuit of Nigeria's strategic objectives. In addition, the study lacked context, as the targets of Nigeria's policies where economic benefits to the country are to be derived are not clearly stated.

In the case of Ogbonna and Ogunnubi (2018), they argue that Nigeria's investment in the NTAC has not amounted to tangible foreign policy gains because this initiative is not tied to the country's regional interests. In their view, Nigeria needs to attach conditionalities to the NTAC scheme to meet its strategic interests. This conclusion is based on the fact that in 2012 Nkosazana Dlamini-Zuma of South Africa defeated Nigerian-backed Jean Ping of Gabon and in 2017 two Nigerian-backed candidates also suffered defeats. The problems with this conclusion are threefold. First, their reliance on three negative electoral outcomes to infer the ineffectiveness of Nigeria's soft power is not only a small sample size but also ignores other instances where Nigerian-backed candidates were elected with the support of African states. Second, the lack of contextualization is again glaring, as these scholars assume that Nigeria's influence extends beyond West Africa to include other sub-regions in the continent, ignoring the influence of Egypt in North Africa, South Africa in the Southern part of Africa, and Ethiopia in Eastern Africa. Third, they ignore that soft power entails the willing support of others for one's objectives and does not in any way imply the complete abdication of the national interest.

Conclusion

Taking into consideration the nature of soft power and the implication this has on studies examining the relationship between attraction and foreign policy outcomes, it may not be foolhardy to assume that the impasse reached in conceptualizations of soft power may be difficult to break. One of the reasons for this is that, as a theory, soft power lacks parsimony and as an analytical concept it assumes multiple meanings. But this does not render it any less important as the flurry of engagement with the concept reveals. While the indispensability of softer forms of power in today's world is axiomatic, its application and evaluation have mostly focused on influential power blocs, while African states with attractive potential are ignored. While this may be due to the peripheral status of African states in international politics, it, nonetheless, reflects a significant limitation in the study of soft power.

As discussions in this chapter affirm, exploratory accounts of Nigeria's soft power began to emerge in 2015, offering important contributions that have shaped how we understand the soft power of Africa's proverbial giant. As preceding discussions demonstrate, these studies suffer deficiencies that subsequent discussions in this book will attempt to address. They adopt an agent-centred approach and, as a result, synonymize power with the finite resources Nigeria possesses, and by implication, overlook and underspecify critical elements of the power conversion process that clarifies the workings of political influence. Consequently, important dimensions of Nigeria's soft power are unclear. Specifically, what resources and behaviours are attractive, why they are attractive, who finds them attractive, and how they can serve the purpose of Nigeria's African policy? As discussions on the conceptual and theoretical engagement with soft power reveal, these deficiencies highlighted in the context of Nigeria's soft power literature are not unique and may be tied to the fact that the broader study of soft power lacks a theoretical core guiding its conceptualization and operationalization.

Thus, in Chapter 3, I propose a theoretical refinement of soft power that accounts for ideational and material power resources and their translation into foreign policy outcomes through the deliberate actions of policymakers. This is done by drawing from classical realist insights, specifically Morgenthau's relational understanding of power, and leaning on Nye's behaviour-based understanding of soft power.

Note

1 During Mao Zedong's reign China promoted its culture and communist ideology in Southeast Asia as a means of advancing its revolutionary goals; however, this was rebuffed by some countries through the institutionalization of measures to restrict Chinese culture (Mingjiang, 2009).

References

Angey-Sentuc, G., & Molho, J. (2015). A critical approach to soft power grasping contemporary Turkey's influence in the world. *European Journal of Turkish Studies*, 21. https://doi.org/10.4000/ejts.5287

Bourdieu, P. (1984). *Distinction: A social critique of the judgement of taste* (R. Nice, Trans.). Harvard University Press.

Brown, R. (2017). Influence in French and German cultural action. In N. Chitty, L. Ji, G. D. Rawnsley, and C. Hayden (Eds.), *The Routledge handbook of soft power* (pp. 37–48). Routledge.

Cho, Y. N., & Jeong, J. H. (2008). China's soft power: Discussions, resources, and prospects. *Asian Survey*, 48(3), 453–472. http://jstor.org/stable/10.1525/as.2008.48.3.453

Cloke, F. (2020). Soft power diplomacy on the African continent: The rise of China. *Journal of Social and Political Sciences*, 3(1), 268–276.

Eriksson, J., & Norman, L. (2011). Political utilisation of scholarly ideas: The 'clash of civilisations' vs. 'soft power' in US foreign policy. *Review of International Studies*, 37(1), 417–436. http://doi.org/10.1017/S0260210510000173

Fan, Y. (2008). Soft power: Power of attraction or confusion? *Place Branding and Public Diplomacy*, 4(2), 147–158.

Feklyunina, V. (2015). Soft power and identity: Russia, Ukraine and the 'Russian world(s)'. *European Journal of International Relations*, 22(4), 773–796.

Geiger, T. (2010). The power game, soft power, and the international historian. In I. Parmar and M. Cox (Eds.), *Soft power and US foreign policy: Theoretical, historical and contemporary perspectives* (pp. 83–102). Routledge.

Gelb, L. H. (2010). *Power rules: How common sense can rescue American foreign policy*. Harper Collins.

Geraldo, Z. & Ramos, L. (2010). From hegemony to soft power: Implication of a conceptual change. In I. Parmar and M. Cox (Eds.), *Soft power and US foreign policy: Theoretical, historical and contemporary perspectives* (pp. 12–31). Routledge.

Gramsci, A, (1971). *Selections from the prison notebooks*. International Publishers.

Grass, R. H., & Seiter, J. S. (2009). Credibility and public diplomacy. In N. Snow and P. M. Taylor (Eds.), *Routledge handbook of public diplomacy* (pp. 154–165). Routledge.

Gürsoy, Y. (2020). Reconsidering Britain's soft power: Lessons from the perceptions of the Turkish political elite. *Cambridge Review of International Affairs*, 36(1), 35–53. https://doi.org/10.1080/09557571.2020.1832959

Hall, T. (2010). An unclear attraction: A critical examination of soft power as an analytical category. *The Chinese Journal of International Politics*, 3(2), 189–211. https://doi.org/10.1093/cjip/poq005

Hayden, C. (2012). *The rhetoric of soft power: Public diplomacy in global contexts*. Lexington Books.

Holyk, G. G. (2011). Paper Tiger? Chinese soft power in East Asia. *Political Science Quarterly*, 126(6), 223–254. https://doi.org/10.1002/j.1538-165X.2011.tb00700.x

Hudson, V. (2014, July 21–25). *Questioning the applicability of Joseph Nye's soft power to the BRICS: Revealing the hard foundations of attraction,* [Paper presentation]. The XXIII IPSA World Congress of Political Science, Montreal, QC, Canada.

Idowu, A. O., & Ogunnubi, O. (2018). Nigeria's soft power and economic diplomacy in Africa. *Journal of African Foreign Affairs*, 5(2), 189–206.

Ipsos Public Affairs. (2019). *Anholt Ipsos Nation Brands Index (NBI)*. Paris: Ipsos.

Iwabuchi, K. (2010). Taking Japanization seriously: Cultural globalization reconsidered. In D. K. Thussu (Ed.), *International communication: A reader* (pp. 410–433). Routledge.

Ji, L. (2017). Measuring soft power (section overview). In N. Chitty, L. Ji, G. D. Rawnsley, and C. Hayden (Eds.), *The Routledge handbook of soft power* (pp. 75–92). Routledge.

Kennedy, P. (1987). *The rise, and fall of great powers: Economic change and military conflict from 1500 to 2000*. Random House.

Keohane, R. O., & Nye, J. S. (2011). *Power and interdependence* (4th ed.). Pearson.

Kōse, T., Özcan M., & Karakoc, E. (2016). A comparative analysis of soft power in the MENA region: The impact of ethnic sectarian and religious identity on soft power in Iraq and Egypt. *Foreign Policy Analysis, 12*(3), 1–20. https://doi.org/10.1093/fpa/orw003

Kurlantzick, J. (2007). *Charm offensive: How China's soft power is transforming the world*. Yale University Press.

Layne, C. (2010). The unbearable lightness of soft power. In I. Parmar and M. Cox (Eds.), *Soft power and US foreign policy: Theoretical, historical and contemporary perspectives* (pp. 51–82). Routledge.

Lee, G. (2009). A theory of soft power and Korea's soft power strategy. *Korean Journal of Defence Analysis, 21*(2), 205–218. https://doi.org/10.1080/10163270902913962

Lock, E. (2010). Soft power and strategy: Developing a 'strategic' concept of power. In I. Parmer and M. Cox (Eds.), *Soft power and US foreign policy: Theoretical, historical, and contemporary perspectives* (pp. 32–50). Routledge.

Malone, D. (2011). Soft power in Indian foreign policy. *Economic and Political Weekly, 46*(36), 35–39. www.jstor.org/stable/41719935

Manheim, J. B. (1994). *Strategic public diplomacy and American foreign policy: The evolution of influence*. Oxford University Press.

Mattern, J. B. (2005). Why 'soft power' isn't so soft: Representational force and the sociolinguistic construction of attraction in world politics. *Millennium: Journal of International Studies, 33*(3), 583–612. http://journals.sagepub.com/doi/pdf/10.1177/03058298050330031601

McClory, J. (2015). *The soft power 30: A global ranking of soft power*. Portland.

McClory, J. (2019). *The soft power 30: A global ranking of soft power*. Portland.

Mingjiang, L. (2009). Domestic sources of China's soft power approach. *China Security, 5*(2), 55–70.

Moravcsik, A. (2010). *Liberal theories of international relations: A primer*. Princeton University.

Mukherjee, R. (2014). The false promise of India's soft power. *Geopolitics, History and International Relations, 6*(1), 46–62.

Nye, J. S. (1990). *Bound to lead: The changing nature of American power*. Basic Books.

Nye, J. S. (2004). *Soft power: A means to success in world politics*. Public Affairs Books.

Nye, J. S. (2010). Responding to my critics and concluding thoughts. In I. Parmar and M. Cox (Eds.), *Soft power and US foreign policy: Theoretical, historical and contemporary perspectives* (pp. 215–227). Routledge.

Nye, J. S. (2011). *The future of power*. Public Affairs Books.

Ogbonna, N. C., & Ogunnubi, O. (2018). Rethinking the role of Nigeria's technical aid corps as soft power: Rough diamond or fools' gold. *African Journal of Peace and Conflict Studies, 7*(2), 121–141.

Ogunnubi, O., & Isike C. (2015). Regional hegemonic contention and the asymmetry of soft power: A comparative analysis of South Africa and Nigeria. *Strategic Review for Southern Africa, 37*(1), 152–177.

Ogunnubi, O., & Isike C. (2017). Nigeria's soft power sources: Between potential and illusion. *International Journal of Politics, Culture, and Society*, 31(1), 49–67.

Ogunnubi, O., & Okeke-Uzodike, U. (2015). South Africa's foreign policy and the strategy of soft power. *South African Journal of International Affairs*, 22(1), 1–19.

Ojo, T. (2017). Nigeria, public diplomacy and soft power. In N. Chitty, L. Ji, G. D. Rawnsley, and C. Hayden (Eds.), *The Routledge handbook of soft power* (pp. 315–325). Routledge.

Rawnsley, G. (2012). Approaches to soft power and public diplomacy in China and Taiwan. *Journal of International Communication*, 18(2), 121–135. https://doi.org/10.1080/13216597.2012.695744

Sidiropoulos, E. (2014). South Africa's emerging soft power. *Current History*, 113(763), 197–202.

Singh, J. P., & MacDonald, S. (2017). *Soft power today: Measuring the influences and effects*. Edinburgh: The Institute for International Cultural Relations, The University of Edinburgh.

Smith, P. M. (2006). Soft power rising: Romantic Europe in the service of practical Europe. *World Literature Today*, 80(1), 20–23. www.jstor.org/stable/40159018

Tella, O. (2017). Attractions and limitations of Nigeria's soft power. *Journal of Global Analysis*, 7(2), 109–128.

Tella, O. (2018). Is Nigeria a soft power state? *Social Dynamics*, 44(2), 376–394. https://doi.org/10.1080/02533952.2018.1492833

Tella, O., & Ogunnubi, O. (2014). Hegemony or survival: South Africa's soft power and the challenge of xenophobia. *Africa Insight*, 44(3), 145–163.

Tharoor, S. (2012). Bollywood vs. the terracotta army. *The World Today*, 68(4), 38–40. www.jstor.org/stable/41962788

Valença, M. M., & Carvalho, G. (2014). Soft power, hard aspirations: The shifting role of power in Brazilian foreign policy. *Journal of the Brazilian Political Science Association*, 8(3), 64–94. http://dx.doi.org/10.1590/1981-38212014000100021

Vyas, U. (2013). *Soft power in Japan-China relations: State, sub-state and non-state relations*. Routledge.

Walker, T. C. (2013). A circumspect revival of liberalism: Classics of international relations. In R. O. Keohane and J. S. Nye (Eds.), *Power and interdependence* (pp. 160–168). Routledge.

Wang, H., & Lu, Y. C. (2008). The conception of soft power and its policy implications: A comparative study of China and Taiwan. *Journal of Contemporary China*, 17(56), 425–447. http://dx.doi.org/10.1080/10670560802000191

Weber, M. (1968). *Economy and society: An outline of interpretive sociology*. Bedminster Press. (Originally published in 1922).

Wilson, E. J. (2008). Hard power, soft power, smart power. *The ANNALS of the American Academy of Political and Social Science*, 616(1), 110–124. https://doi.org/10.1177/0002716207312618

3 Classical Realism and Soft Power

Introduction

In this book, I assume that soft power reflects an analytic category or concept used to capture context-specific – historical, cultural, and political — *positive* reactions to expressions of influence associated with certain resources and political actions, and how these reactions translate to tangible favourable foreign policy outcomes. As the discussions in this chapter will demonstrate, the concept emerges from a theoretically driven understanding of international interactions where power assumes a central role. To a large extent, it reflects an assemblage or in some sense the intersection of theoretical assumptions on the requirements for attraction and/or persuasion in international relations, how the nature of relations between states affect different streams of influence, and the increasing role of public perceptions in shaping political outcomes.

As discussed in Chapter 2, liberalism and constructivism assume some role for power in interstate relations and have something to say about its nature, but it is the realist school of thought, with scholars such as Carr (1939/2016), Morgenthau (1948/1993), Waltz (1959), amongst others that sought to highlight the determining effects of power on the behaviour of states. As a result, this chapter makes the case for a realist approach to soft power, drawing specifically from classical realist insights. It moves beyond the narrow depiction of attraction as the result of communicative processes and compliance with liberal "universal" values associated with constructivist and liberalist approaches, respectively, to account for attractive behaviours resulting from the legitimate use of military or economic resources for political purposes. It explains how soft power derives from material and ideational resources through their instrumentalization in the foreign policies of states. I draw from Morgenthau's relational power to accentuate a behaviour-based understanding of soft power where attraction emerges from the operationalization of power resources in a two-way relationship to alter the behaviour of others. I specify the conditions under which Nigeria's use of its power resources may engender attraction by examining the operationalization of soft power in foreign policy.

DOI: 10.4324/9781003396628-3

The chapter is structured around three thematic questions that theorize the translation of power resources into attraction and foreign policy outcomes and how this translation process may be observed. What assumptions about realism explain the use of soft power as a strategic approach to foreign policy and how we understand soft power? What is soft power? And, how is soft power operationalized and observed?

Realism, Power, and International Relations

Traced to the works of early thinkers such as Sun Tzu (544–496 BC), Thucydides (460–395 BC), Machiavelli (1469–1527), and Thomas Hobbes (1588–1679), realists assume that states are mostly driven by the need to accumulate material resources to stave off threats posed by an unregulated or anarchic system of states. This threat, they assume, stems from their belief in human egotism and the absence of a higher authority to regulate the behaviour of states. They are similarly sceptical of the prospect of a peaceful world (Gilpin, 1981) and are of the view that moral and ethical considerations are secondary to material interests and power (Taliaferro et al., 2009). This brings to the fore the importance of security and the unpleasant reality of security competition and war in realist thinking, which they consider inescapable.

By and large, realists portray a gloomy view of interstate relations where states are primary actors – a view that unites all variants of this school of thought. However, much of the development of the theoretical basis of this book is grounded in classical realist thoughts. This is due to the emphasis they place on a relational understanding of power and their acknowledgement of the power of ideas. Classical realists dominated the study of international relations from the 1940s to the 1970s through Morgenthau's *Politics among Nations*, and E. H Carr's *Twenty Years Crisis*.[1] They attribute the struggle for power in interstate relations to man's unending quest and lust for power and his zeal to dominate others. It is this lust for power, an innate desire, that reflects in the egoistic tendencies of states.

What separates classical realists from structural realists or neorealists is the theoretical primacy the former accords to the nature of man and the individual himself in shaping the behaviour of states while relegating structural considerations to second-order determinants of state behaviour (Mearsheimer, 2001). Structural realists attempt to explain similar behavioural patterns in international politics. They assume that states are rational entities merely seeking survival and contrary to the assumptions of classical realists are not driven by a will to power motivated by their inherent aggressiveness. Waltz (1979) argues that systemic or structural constraints, imposed on states – especially the ones with significant capabilities– by anarchy, compel them to focus on the act of balancing so as to assure their security in a self-help system where everyone must fend for themselves.

Competition, conflict, and the absence of trust are due to the anarchical nature of the international system where states need to be sensitive to the capabilities of others. In other words, benevolence and trust are recipes for disaster in anarchic conditions, as trusting states risk being wiped out. Thus, the path to security and, more importantly, survival in a world where relative gains are more important than absolute gains is to maximize one's military resources by forming alliances and balancing others.

On the Concept of Power

In IR scholarship, realists place an important premium on the concept of power given its centrality to the security of states. In as much as their view of power rests on the capacity of an actor to alter the behaviour of another, they differ on where power is situated as a determining factor in the behaviour of states, which in turn affects their view on the sources and measurement of power. Contrary to classical realists who consider power the *ultima ratio*, structural realists see power solely as a means to an end, with the end being security. Waltz (1988) argues that states are not particularly concerned with power, but are rather focused on securing themselves, which informs their need to self-appropriate a good amount of power resources. In line with this view, structural realists such as Gilpin (1981) and Mearsheimer (2001) see the accumulation of power as the most important means to guarantee the survival of states. Thus, they define power mostly in terms of material capabilities.

By capability, Waltz refers to the "extent of one's power" but goes on to suggest that this "cannot be inferred from the results one may or may not get" (1959, p. 192). Waltz's submission implies that a state is not only powerful when it can control others, cause them to change their behaviours, and bring about desired outcomes but also when it fails to do so. From this logic, Waltz suggests that an actor has power over others if its ability to affect them supersedes theirs. In as much as I concede that power is not always effective and effectiveness should not be the ultimate determinant of a state's capabilities, Waltz's approach to power accounts for only tangible power resources that can be aggregated to infer the capability of a state, while ignoring equally important dimensions of power that are intangible. In a similar vein, Mearsheimer (2001) advances two kinds of power – latent and military power. While the former encompasses socio-economic factors such as the wealth of a country and the size of its population, the latter refers to the size and strength of a country's army.

Despite espousing structuralist views, Gilpin (1981) deviates from neo-realist notions of power, by incorporating intersubjective elements such as ideas in his conception of power. Gilpin (1981) refers to power as "the military, economic and technological capabilities of [a] state" (p. 13). Gilpin also acknowledges certain intangible and "incalculable," yet important aspects of power which he associates with the concept of prestige such as public morals, quality of leadership, and E. H Carr's power over opinion (1981, p. 13, 30). By prestige, Gilpin refers to a state's reputation for power, which derives from other states' perceptions of its capabilities and willingness to exercise them (p. 31). Gilpin goes further to allude to the power of religion and ideology, which he contends powerful states use to justify their dominance. These structural and intangible elements, largely ignored in mainstream neorealist accounts of power, are features of classical realist accounts of power that Nye alludes to when he talks about the sources of attraction.

For instance, E. H. Carr (1939/2016) argues that the effective control of any government depends on the source of its power. He proposes three inter-dependent categories of power resources – military power (armaments and manpower), economic power, and power over opinion. While Carr considers armament, manpower, and economic power as the most essential elements of power, he submits that "power over opinion [...] is not less essential for pol-itical purposes" than other elements of power especially when one considers that "the art of persuasion has always been a necessary part of the equipment of a political leader" (p. 120). As Carr further remarks, states increasingly exercise power over the opinion of the masses through the "modern weapon of propaganda" by relying on popular education, radio, film, and the press (p. 124). Through propaganda, ideas of ostensibly universal principles have been used to influence mankind. The propagation of ideas associated with the French Revolution, communism, free trade, and liberal democracies reflect instances where actors have sought to influence international opinion through propaganda. It is these expressions of power through ideas and shared meanings that have seen constructivists self-appropriate the concept of soft power, as discussed in Chapter 2.

Long before *Man, the State, and War*, Morgenthau (1948/1993) displayed an inclination for both a relational and elements of national power approach. Morgenthau captures the diversity of power resources by distinguishing between two groups of power elements that may be taken into consider-ation if the power of a state is to be determined – relatively stable elements and those subject to constant change (p. 124–160). While the former include geography, population, natural resources (food and raw materials), mili-tary preparedness, and industrial capacity (technology, leadership, and the quality and quantity of armed forces), the latter, which are intangible, include national character, quality of society, quality of government, and the quality of diplomacy. In Morgenthau's view, intangible elements of power are the most important due to their relevance in times of peace. Given the nature of these intangible elements, Morgenthau embraces a relational conception of power, which emphasizes how individuals or states induce change in others by exercising power.

Morgenthau's treatment of power provides a theoretical core for the con-ceptualization of soft power in this book because of its association of the exercise of power with "man's control over the minds and actions of other men" (1948/1993, p. 30). He defines political power first as relations of con-trol and second as a psychological relationship, both of which, he notes, differ from force or physical violence.[2] Thus, political power refers "to the mutual relations of control among the holders of public authority and between the latter and the people at large" and "a psychological relation between those who exercise it and those over whom it is exercised. It gives the former control over certain actions of the latter through the impact which the former exerts on the latter's mind" (1948/1993, p. 30). What this implies is that power is inherent in the social processes that constitute the actions of political actors at two levels of relationship – at the domestic level, where power reflects a means to an end, and at the international level, between statesmen who hold political authority, where power is sought as an ultimate objective.

This latter view of power is akin to Max Weber's (1922/1968) relational definition of power, which suggests that power is a social relationship where despite resistance an actor may still carry out his or her will. This presumes a relationship of power entailing an agent and subject where the assessment of power goes beyond accounting for the assets of the agent to include the nature of relations or patterns of interaction permeating the power relationship. Within this relationship, Morgenthau (1948/1993) submits that power may be exercised by relying on threats, command, and charisma. The impact of the agent on the subject of power emanates from three sources: "the expectation of benefits, the fear of disadvantages, and the respect or love for men or institutions" (Morgenthau, 1948/1993, p. 32). Here, the legitimacy of power is an important factor, especially in the conduct of foreign policy.

Morgenthau (1948/1993) defines legitimate power as "power whose exercise is morally or legally justified." This is in contrast to illegitimate or "naked" power, which is unjustifiable from a moral and legal perspective (p. 32). As he notes, an important aspect of foreign policy is to discern how the different elements of a state's power contribute to its overall power arsenal, and soft power reflects an important component. With this understanding of classical realism and power in mind, how does soft power fit into realism?

Bringing Soft Power in

It is sometimes assumed that soft power is an attempt to provide an alternative ontological explanation for power or that because the concept mostly reflects the use of intangible or intersubjective elements of power, it falls outside the purview of realism (see Gelb, 2009; Layne, 2010). With the way soft power is often presented as a moral element of power and even a replacement for material resources, these views are justified, but they are based on a narrow understanding of soft power. When Nye (1990a) developed his arguments on soft power, he situated his discussion within realists' assumptions on the balance of power by noting the deterministic effects of anarchy on the behaviour of states and the inclination of policymakers to act primarily towards "reducing risks to the independence of their states" (p. 35). What this implies is that Nye (1990a) simply explains the "softer" aspects of this balance that have long featured in classical realist writings, but are often ignored because realists devote more time to discussing the dangers that may accrue to states who dwell on ideas or utopia, than exploring the workings of intersubjective elements of power in the dynamics of global politics (Grix & Brannagan, 2016; Barkin, 2003).

Two important reasons exist for realist disinclination towards soft power. First, realism tends towards a materialist bias that emphasizes military and economic resources or visible expressions of power – the first face of power – over non-visible dimensions located in the second and third faces of power. To the exclusion of power expressed where there are no visible expressions of conflict (Bachrach & Baratz, 1962), and power expressed when A secures the compliance of B by shaping and influencing his beliefs and desires (Lukes, 1974/2005a), realists consider agents and sources of power as pre-constituted and as a result concern themselves with only expressions of power amenable to situations of conflict, where A gets B to do what B would otherwise not do (Bilgin & Elis, 2008). Realism need not limit itself to expressions of power where visible conflicts exist but should be open to other expressions of power such as the mobilization of bias, as well as the use of norms and values to affect human consciousness.

Second, realists tend to synonymize power with control, and expressions of compulsion. Although practical, this has the effect of limiting the scope of the paradigm to the coercive dimensions of power at the expense of other dimensions, which may emanate from a state's attractiveness. While seeing power as the possession of guns and money may not be completely out of place in contemporary global politics where great power rivalries persist, ideational resources, embedded in the culture and political values of states can also shape preferences in ways that action political outcomes.

With the expansion of foreign policy beyond the traditional concerns for competition, winning hearts and minds can be included in the realist framework without compromising the ontological assumptions of the paradigm (Bilgin & Elis, 2008). As Morgenthau (1948/1993) argues, "the power of a nation ... depends not only upon the skill of its diplomacy and the strength of its armed forces but also upon the attractiveness [of] other nations [to] its political philosophy, political institutions, and political policies" (p. 165). It is this aspect of power, which Nye (1990a) calls soft power that is conspicuously missing from realist power analysis. As Hayden (2012) notably remarks, soft power reflects a "complementary dimension to the strategic assumptions of realist politics – and justifies a reallocation of resources to policies like public diplomacy, international diplomacy, international broadcasting, and strategic communications" (pp. 9–10).

This is evident in the growing importance of the concept within policy circles as states are increasingly concerned with the transnational flow of culture, people, and businesses, transnational security threats from non-state actors, and the emergence of new forms of communication and information technologies. Contrary to the assumptions of scholars who situate soft power within the liberalist or constructivist scholarship, there is a theoretical space for soft power in realism but not without the help of some constructivist insights, specifically from an epistemological and methodological point of view (see Barkin, 2003). Without conceding that material capabilities are second to intersubjective elements in determining the behaviour of states, the latter can help drive the interests of states, especially when such interests involve shaping how other states define theirs or conditioning the environment for the exercise of influence. Even if states are driven by concerns for security and power, their conception of these interests and the strategies they adopt are products of their intersubjective understanding and expectations arising from recurrent patterns of practices amongst states.

Notions of prestige, which derive from a reputation of previous success and achievement, have long been featured in realist scholarship as a critical element of power. Cardinal Richelieu points to the importance of reputation in international politics when he remarked that "reputation is so very necessary to a prince that he of whom one has a good opinion does more with his name that those who are not esteemed to do with their armies" (cited in Church, 1972, p. 500). Traditional realists recognize the quality of a state's diplomacy, the attractiveness of its policies, and success in times of war as sources of power (see Morgenthau, 1993). Even ideas spread through mediums of education, movies, and radios, whether as deceptive devices or otherwise, have a theoretical space within realism at the unit level where state and society relations operate, and between states at the systemic level. Even Gilpin (1981) has talked about the promotion of religion and ideology by "dominant states," as a means of co-optation, to draw followers and expand their dominance (p. 30). This is akin to Barenskoetter and Quinn's (2012) argument that shared ideas and culture in the form of soft power can be used to explain the bandwagoning of the European Union (EU) with the US.

However, to explain the operationalization of soft power using realism, it is imperative to move beyond the tendency of analyzing power by simply counting guns and money to include a relational understanding of power where intersubjective elements are obvious. As Morgenthau (1948/1993) notes, power shouldn't necessarily be synonymous with the accumulation of resources, rather, what is relevant is the ability of a state to further its goal in a two-way relationship by leveraging its resources. From this view, "the measure of A's power [will] require an understanding of how A's presence, decisions, and actions affect others. It looks at streams of influence within a relationship" (Berenskoetter & Quinn, 2012, p. 217).

Conceptualizing Soft Power: A Relational Approach

Given the realist foundations of this study, what does soft power mean? What does attraction mean? And, what is it about a state's behaviour that causes attraction? These questions are addressed in this section by first offering a conceptualization of soft power that draws from Nye's development of the concept, before elaborating on what makes a state attractive.

What Is Soft Power?

To the central question of this section, it is important to start by elaborating on what soft power is not. Drawing from Chitty's language, this book advances a conceptualization of soft power that is not suggestive of a "modulated power, or a grade of intensity as in a spectrum ranging from very soft, through soft, medium intensity, to hard and very hard power" (2017, p. 10). Certainly, intangible elements of power may cause attraction, but soft power is not limited to these elements, as it also does not exclude material resources. What this implies is that soft power has less to do with the nature or tangibility of resources at a state's disposal, and more to do with the nature of behaviour a state exhibits in its transactions with others. Having clarified this, what does soft power mean?

From a qualitative standpoint, soft power stands on the attractive or co-optive end of a one-dimensional spectrum of power behaviours that includes coercion or command at the other end. Within this spectrum, a state can lean on hard and soft power – smart power – depending on its strategic objectives and the issues at stake. What this means is that both soft and hard power can be located in the three faces of power, with hard power assuming the use of inducement and/or coercion by A to forcibly change B's strategies (first face), truncate B's agenda (second face), and forcibly shape B's preferences (third face), while soft power assumes the use of attraction and/or persuasion by A to alter B's preferences (first face), the use of attraction within institutions to sway B on the legitimacy of A's agenda (second face), and to shape the early preferences of B (third face) (Nye, 2011, p. 91).

This book acknowledges the fuzzy nature of soft power as a concept and the limitations this engenders, and as such, adopts an approach that accentuates a behaviour-based understanding of soft power in line with the Weberian conceptualization of power (Weber, 1968). That is, soft power is understood to mean a state's ability to affect others by relying on the co-optive means of setting the agenda, using non-coercive and ethical persuasion, and eliciting positive attraction to obtain preferred outcomes (Nye, 2011). This implies a meaning of soft power that draws from its expression or what actors do and the effects that derive from their actions. However, effectiveness depends on the resources available to a state, the context – scope and domain – within which resources are applied, the foreign policy objectives of a state, the power conversion strategies it adopts, and, most importantly, perceptions of the subject.

From this view, various types of resources may contribute to soft power, but only attractive behaviours constitute soft power. Setting the agenda in a way that is co-optive and deemed legitimate by the subject of power, and the reliance on ethical and non-coercive persuasive tactics by the agent – both of which may be subsumed into the use of positive attraction – are behaviours that connote soft power.[3] Conversely, the use of coercion and payment-based agenda-setting, force, and payment connote hard power (Nye, 2011; Brown,

2017). Thus, this book operates under the assumption that what separates hard from soft power is not the resources states possess *per se*, but how their instrumentalization is perceived by subjects of power. This approach to soft power is behavioural or relational. It stands in contrast to the resource-based or "elements of national power" approach prevalent in IR scholarship that equates soft power with "soft" resources.

A resource-based approach equates power with resources or synonymizes power with the resources that may engender desired outcomes. From this perspective, the power of an object is reduced to the quality and quantity of its properties. In other words, power is confused with the vehicle that leads to outcomes or as Lukes (2005a) contends "whatever goes into operation when power is activated" (p. 478). Morriss (2002) is notable for calling this approach the "vehicle fallacy." This approach is widely held because power cannot be exercised without the use of some form of resources. Moreover, it makes power appear concrete, predictable, and measurable (Nye, 2011; Vuving, 2009). For policymakers, this "resourcist" route is preferable because it can guide political actions; however, this does not negate the fact that it offers a limited understanding of power relationships (Nye, 2011; Dowding, 2008; Morgenthau, 1993).

Morriss (2002) notes that the results of the application of resources cannot be measured easily and as such "we have to infer that things are resources by examining other people's reactions to them [and that] one cannot simply measure resources since the worth of a resource is determined by the effects it produces" (p. 139). Even if we assume that it can be observed directly, having the means of power does not necessarily mean one is powerful and as such theorists who adopt a resource-based approach are often confronted with the paradox that power does not always deliver desired outcomes (Waltz, 1979; Lukes, 2005b; Nye, 2011).[4]

While a resource-based approach portends to resolve some of the definitional problems associated with soft power, its understandings are at times too constricting, as it is likened to either cultural power or anything other than military or economic power. These limitations do not necessarily render a resources-based approach to power any less important, after all, power resources are the first approximation of a state's capabilities and provide clues to its distribution, but as Nye (2011) notes,

"power resources are simply the tangible and intangible raw materials or vehicles that underlie power relationships, and whether a given set of resources produces preferred outcomes or not depends upon behaviour in context. The vehicle is not the power relationship.

(p. 9)

It is against this backdrop that this book adopts a behavioural approach. This is particularly important because Africa, specifically its western sub-region, presents unique circumstances associated with the nature of relations between states, the nature of issues, and the resources available to influence others, that a resource-based approach may be unable to adequately capture. Even more, we can derive evidence of Nigeria's soft power not only from analysing how it exercises its power resources but also from the effects of its actions on political and academic elites in Ghana and Liberia.

Attraction and Persuasion as Soft Power Behaviours

To refer to attraction as behaviour is to evaluate the policies and actions adopted by an agent to cause the subject to identify with the agent's most compelling attributes. Vuving (2009) proposes three behaviours of an agent that may cause attraction – "benignity, brilliance, and beauty" (p. 8). These are qualities and actions of an agent that may generate positive reactions from the subject. A state is likely to be perceived as benign when it exhibits a positive attitude or a tendency of reciprocal altruism. This, in turn, generates trust, acquiescence, and credibility. Brilliance or competence refers to the *savoir-faire* of an agent. It connotes being successful and capable. This manifests in different forms, including strong economic growth, military invincibility, resplendent culture, and a well-run or governed society. In interstate relations, the promise of brilliance lies in the possibility of states embracing the successful practices, institutions, values, and policies of others because they are attracted to their success (Vuving, 2009). Finally, beauty refers to the "resonance that draws actors closer to each other through shared ideas, values, causes, or visions" (Vuving, 2009, p. 10). It derives from the sense of security or warmth actors feel by interacting with others and how compelling a state's adherence to its ideals, values, and visions is. This encourages friendship, confidence, and cooperation between states.

Nye (2011) proposes a psychological approach to attraction by arguing that it reflects an implicit desire to emulate the alluring qualities of the agent. This is as it remains unclear if psychological notions like allure and magnetism, which Nye uses, may readily apply to nation-states, given the complexity of institutional arrangements. What is clear is that people are often attracted to alluring physical characteristics and to those with whom they share similar qualities, attitudes, and beliefs. In the words of Byrne et al. (1986), "attitude similarity is as potent today as when Aristotle observed its effect on friendship" (p. 1167). And, depending on the issues at stake and their position in government, these people can make decisions that are favourable to the interests of other states. For practical purposes, this study defines attraction as positive reactions to an agent's compelling attributes. These reactions may take different forms, depending on who – decision-makers or the general public – finds the agent's behaviour attractive within a state. This may range from wanting to be like the agent, to supporting and promoting the objectives of the agent.

With respect to persuasion, the goal and means of persuasion need to be differentiated to resolve issues of ambiguity inherent in how it is understood in the context of soft power. While the goal of persuasion may depend on the objective of a state, the means could be either coercive or non-coercive or as Lebow (2005) suggests, ethical or unethical. What is of relevance to this book is not so much the goal but the means of persuasion. Drawing from Lukes (2005a), for persuasion to be non-coercive, an agent may secure the conviction of others through "freely exercised judgments" (p. 490). In other words, persuasion that is based upon non-rational means – bribes and threats – employed to produce assent would be coercive. Ethically, persuasive tactics are deceitful and unethical when they propound false logic or imbibe other forms of "verbal chicanery" (Lebow, 2005, p. 565). Conversely, persuasion characterized by sincerity, openness, honest dialogue, and the actualization of mutual interests is considered ethical. For soft power to be effective, persuasion needs to be non-coercive and ethical.

Operationalizing Soft Power: An Analytical Framework

To measure Nigeria's soft power capability in West Africa is to examine the various ways the Nigerian state, through its specialized agencies of government, translates available power resources into foreign policy strategies that may engender the willing cooperation of Ghanaian and Liberian elites, if perceived favourably. This derives from the assumption that soft power goes into exercise, sometimes over long periods, when a state, based on its strategic objectives and worldview, adopts strategies to convert attractive resources into operational power ability. By implication, for power to have desired effects in a two-way relationship between an agent and subject (s), it needs to be conveyed through the use of some form of power resources in a conversation process that culminates in cognitive and behavioural outcomes.

Notwithstanding the contested nature of soft power, some common elements constitute this dynamic process and, as such, form the analytical basis of the empirical discussions. These elements include an agent's power resources, its strategic objectives, the approach it adopts to meet these objectives, perceptions of the subject, and finally outcomes. In this section, I clarify what these elements suggest.

Context and Relationship

An understanding of an agent's power requires contextualization. Context, in this case, connotes the circumstances within which power relations are embedded. These circumstances entail the purpose, scope, and domain of power. This means we must clarify the purpose of power (power to do what), the scope of power (the actors involved in the power relationship), and the domain of power (the issue involved) within the West African context. As Nye (2011) notes, the scope and domain of power are important antecedent variables to consider in the operationalization of soft power. This is because attraction is inherently subjective, and, as such, its meaning stems from what people within and outside the government consider important and valuable.

In terms of scope, attraction is likely to occur in interactions between an agent and subjects where an air of friendliness, credibility, trust, and cooperativeness exists (Grix & Brannagan, 2016). Where animosity exists, governments are likely to block the flow of the agent's soft power into their territories. Scholars of political and social psychology have long assessed how patterns of relationship between states result in different images – ally and enemy images (see Alexander et al., 2005; Herrmann, 2013). These studies suggest that an ally image fosters the attractiveness of an agent's power resources and behaviour, especially where cooperative relations exist. However, where an adversarial relationship exists, suggesting the presence of an enemy image, the flow of attractive resources is likely to be disrupted. Ji (2017) puts this in clearer terms when he notes that if an agent is perceived as an enemy, "[subjects] normally distort ideology and political values of the counterpart as well as block the flow of soft power products to the market. Distortion and obstruction will inevitably catalyse hostile and suspicious perceptions" (p. 82). This makes accounting for the context of relations between the agent and subject of power an essential condition in ascertaining outcomes.

Equally important is the domain of power. The ontological foundations of this study suggest that states act based on the national interest, and where the interest of the agent and subject collide, it is difficult to envision a scenario where attraction causes the subject to abdicate what is in the interest of its people. Thus, a deliberate approach to foreign policy that seeks to rely on attraction for political outcomes may likely yield tangible benefits where there exists a certain level of shared interests between the agent and the subject, especially on contentious issues.

Beyond the compatibility of interests is that of resources. Culture and political values as instruments of influence are likely to generate resistance in cases of incompatibility despite prevailing assumptions of global cultural homogenization or universal values. Huntington (1993) notes the existence of different cultures across the globe and their propensity to lead to conflict in situations of incompatibility when he asserted that, "the great divisions among humankind and the dominating source of conflict will be cultural" (p. 22). In a world of cultural and value pluralism, an agent's culture and values may likely be attractive to the target, only to the extent that it is compatible or shared. This is where regional peculiarities come into play. The distinctiveness of the regions of the world – politically and culturally – engenders a global context where certain soft power resources are impenetrable unless they emanate from "physically and cognitively similar others or those belonging to the same group as oneself" (Chitty, 2017, p. 25). Thus, analyses of the exercise of soft power by states that fail to contemplate the relationship patterns and context within which the politics of attraction take place may paint an insufficient portrait of the workings of soft power.

Operational Categories of Soft Power Resources

Since a relational approach to soft power emphasizes a state's behaviour in context, the potential sources of attraction are varied. Soft power resources are national possessions with attractive potential that a state can wield to alter the preferences of others. For states to aspire to wield soft power, they simply need to possess those resources that are likely to alter subject perception within suitable contexts, while recognizing that with each resource comes different levels of receptivity. I propose four broad analytical categories of soft power potential – culture, military, economy, and political – all of which are dichotomized into their active and passive forms.

In its passive form, soft power emanates from "the exercise by a social object of an inherent attraction, before this being activated by symbolic, mercantile or military influentials" (Chitty, 2017, p. 22). This is akin to Lukes' (2005b) inactive power which does not derive from the actions of an agent, but from the inherent properties of its resources. This source of influence which includes relatively constant elements such as language, exemplary values, practices, ideas, artefacts, objects of symbolic interaction, and political narrative, in most cases, spontaneously created within the social fabric of a state (Blumer, 1969; Chitty, 2017). Conversely, soft power resources in their active form are more akin to a state's manifest action. They derive from the active effort of states to generate attraction through public diplomacy, military exchanges, development assistance, economic aid, educational exchanges, and international broadcasting (Nye, 2011). It is here that the rising influence of non-state actors, whether in the economic or cultural sector, with cross-border linkages, comes into play. These actors are increasingly influential in shaping foreign policies and as such states increasingly tap into their networks to meet self-interested and milieu goals.

Culture as a Source of Soft Power

Historically, states have relied on cultural forms for global dominance. Jacob (2017, p. 138) documents the projection of Hellenistic culture by the Greeks from 323 BCE across Europe, North Africa, and parts of Asia to sustain political and cultural dominance. At the heart of the Greek foreign expansion policy was the use of language, arts, music, theatre, poetry, mathematics, science, and philosophy to showcase an attractive side that other societies could imitate and identify with. Centuries later, culture remains an important source of influence, especially in an era of innovations in information technology, increased interconnectedness, and cultural contacts between people from different backgrounds. Through cultural exchange programmes, media, and online virtual spaces, lifestyles and values are easily experienced and shared.

Culture assumes different meanings. In *Culture: A Critical Review of Concepts and Definitions*, Kroeber and Kluckhohn (1952) document over

100 definitions of culture, which affirm the diversity of cultural encounters that shape the views of scholars. A popular view of culture is one held by Geertz (1973) who attributes culture to shared meaning or understanding of symbols. Since culture is variable, this popular understanding seems cumbersome, especially with societies divided along ethnic, social, and economic lines (see Jacob, 2017). Here, I approach culture as an instrument of power or hegemonic influence within a system of subordinate and dominant groupings. This is in line with Gramsci's concept of hegemony where groups of lesser power consent to and accept the leadership of the dominating group as well as its ideas and values not because they are induced or compelled to, but because they want to – for reasons of their own (Strinati, 1995; Jacob, 2017).

This

> presupposes a constantly readjusted and re-negotiated system that creates spontaneous consent for cultural transfer and indeed cultural dominance to the extent that reality (be it moral, conceptual, or logical) is seen through the lenses constructed by the dominant group or culture.
>
> (Jacob, 2017, p. 138)

From this view, culture is an instrument of ascendency that transcends the lived experiences of those at the receiving end of it. In other words, culture constitutes the norms, values, and practices that differentiate one society from another and can be wielded as an instrument of ascendancy to affect outcomes. However contextual factors and issues of complementarity or compatibility would have to be favourable for culture to achieve desired effects.

Culture, in its passive and active forms, is a core element of soft power and a fundamental source of attraction. Aspects of culture such as language, literature, artefacts, art, and even architecture are "the most enduring soft power capital" and tend to survive the longest (Chitty, 2017, p. 27). This explains why countries like the US, China, France, and Germany invest in promoting their culture abroad through language institutes, and other cultural initiatives. While emphasizing the importance of culture as a part and parcel of foreign policy, Federica Mogherini, the EU's High Representative for Foreign Affairs and Security Policy, points to the power of culture in bridging the gap amongst societies and engendering mutual understanding (cited in Singh & Macdonald, 2017, p. 13). Cultural resources in their passive forms include among others language, religion, education, arts, music, and entertainment, while in their active form, they include the active promotion of high and popular culture, through educational exchanges, international broadcasting, and sporting events. These activities do not necessarily produce direct effects, rather, they "promote understanding, nurture positive images, and propagate myths in favour of the source country" (Vuving, 2009, p. 12).

Political Sources of Soft Power

The political sources of soft power in their internal dimension derive from the nature of relations between a government and its citizens, the political values a society espouses, and the adequacies of internal governance mechanisms. The external dimension derives from the values and practices a state espouses in its interaction with other states and international institutions. In their passive form, the sources of political soft power are the political ideologies espoused within a state, the strength and efficacy of government institutions and agencies, the number and quality of diplomats, the spread and reach of diplomatic missions, and long-term diplomatic relations. The external dimension of a state's manifest action takes the form of multilateral agreements, active participation in international interactions, diplomatic cooperation, and the promotion of good governance.

Military Sources of Soft Power

When military power is evoked, it is often thought of in terms of soldiers, tanks, ships, and bombers – resources that underlie the hard power behaviour of coercion (Abowei, 2020). Scholars often confine military resources to command behaviour because they are often used to limit the choices available to others and can have constraining effects (see Rotham, 2011; Tella, 2018). However, military resources entail much more than a tool for threats, fighting, or winning wars.

Historical evidence abounds of military resources being used as instruments of soft power. When Mount Vesuvius erupted, affecting the cities of Stabiae, Pompeii, Herculaneum, and Oplontis in AD 79, the commander of the Roman fleet at Misenum – Pliny the Elder – led a humanitarian mission to Pompeii to rescue civilians imperilled by the eruption (Elleman & Paine, 2015). Similarly, the Greek anti-piracy operations by the US in the Aegean Sea to protect trade routes between 1825 and 1828 are well documented (see Elleman & Paine, 2015, p. v). More recent examples include the use of military resources for peace operations and humanitarian missions by countries like Brazil and Canada (United Nations, n.d.; Government of Canada, 2020).

Passively, attraction may derive from a state's military strength and invincibility (competence), historical security ties, and military alliance. Nye (2011) highlights how Hitler and Stalin attempted to develop a sense of invincibility based on their military accomplishments. A state's tendency to maintain a reputation for competence and success in the use of force can also generate attraction especially when its actions are considered legitimate or right. Military alliances and long-held security ties may create personal networks and even spur a "climate of attraction" (Nye, 2011, p. 46).

In their active form, attraction may derive from the use of military resources to protect and proffer assistance. Providing protection is an important feature of alliance relations, which when perceived as credible and trustworthy may generate goodwill and encourage other states to request membership

(Nye, 2011). The North Atlantic Treaty Organization represents an example of alliance relations where the US has successfully cultivated a favourable environment from its commitment to protect. States can also protect through peacekeeping operations and even by overthrowing tyrannies, which may generate attraction insofar as their actions are credible and legitimate. Equally, military resources can be used to assist others through training, military exercises, personnel exchanges, humanitarian assistance, and disaster relief. These acts can produce soft power especially when they are perceived as coming to the aid of others in times of need.

Economic Sources of Soft Power

Economic resources are also often viewed in coercive terms because of the constraining effects they may have on the behaviour of lesser, indigent, or dependent states (see Cooper, 2004; Campbell & O'Hanlon, 2006). However, this is not always the case. Depending on how they are used, economic resources can generate both hard and soft power. According to Nye (2011), "a successful economic model not only produces the [passive] military resources for the exercise of hard power, but it can also attract others to emulate its example" (p. 52). In addition, the use of economic resources for political ends, in the form of economic aid, development assistance, and even sanctions, can generate attraction when perceived as legitimate or done with benignity. A notable example is China's reliance on economic assets to enhance its soft power in South America, Africa, and some Eastern European States by investing in infrastructure, and providing low-interest loans (Hancock et al., 2018; Lekorwe et al., 2016).

Beyond the purview of the state are economic actors with global-scale influence capable of altering the dynamics of interstate relations. MNCs and diaspora entrepreneurs are increasingly instrumental in the exercise of influence by states in what is now dubbed "commercial diplomacy." Bell's (2016) study on the instrumentalization of corporate actors in the exercise of British soft power illustrates that corporations may be able to influence foreign governments and the public alike if they uphold values that demonstrate an appreciation not only for profit-making but also for humanitarian causes. The ties executives foment with host governments, at times stemming from the value of their investments, can afford them important access to decision-makers. Although not completely distinct from corporations, since most entrepreneurs operate within corporate bodies, diaspora entrepreneurs are mostly skilled people with transnational business networks who live outside their country of origin, even if on a part-time basis (Vemuri, 2014). Due to their transnational and trans-functional nature, they represent valuable assets to their home and host governments alike.

Economic resources have passive and active components. Passive economic resources provide the basis for economic power as well as all instruments of power. I classify GDP, natural and human resources, technological innovations, and high-level market institutions of a state as indicators of its economic competitiveness and success. Non-state actors also play a passive role in deriving attraction. To the extent that they contribute positively to the economy of their host country, they can be a source of influence that may be instrumental to the foreign policy objectives of their home country. The link between migration and entrepreneurship has long been a staple of trans-national studies in part due to the ascendency of business activities by dias-pora groups, facilitated by the global flow of goods and services (see Vemuri, 2014). To the extent that diaspora communities generate revenues, stimu-late innovation, and create businesses, their activities can arouse favourable sentiments in their host country.

In their active form, the sources of economic soft power may be understood in terms of sanctions. Sanctions entail the instrumentalization of economic relations for political purposes. Nye (2011) defines sanctions as "measures of encouragement or punishment designed to reinforce a decision or make a policy authoritative" (p. 71). Thus, sanctions may be positive when it is used to compensate or negative when it is used as punishment, however, this is largely dependent on perception. Baldwin (1985) provides examples of posi-tive and negative sanctions. While the former includes investment guaran-tees, tariff reduction, and the provision of aid and favourable market access, the latter consists of withholding aid, and freezing of assets. More recent examples of negative sanctions may include trade and arms embargos, and travel bans. This distinction proposed by Baldwin is quite fluid as negative sanctions may be perceived as positive in one context while the reverse may be the case in another. For the purpose of this book proving aid, granting favourable market access, and reducing tariffs for strategic purposes such as nation-building and democratization are actions that may generate attraction, whereas a decision to withdraw these for non-compliance may be deemed coercive and synonymous with hard power behaviour.

Power Conversion Process

Power conversion is a process that entails the articulation of the objectives a state seeks to achieve and the strategies underlying the pursuit of these objectives (Nye, 2011). It is a critical intervening variable in the conversion of resources into outcomes. The fact that power works when resources are converted into operational power ability through the implementation of strategies requires the evaluation of the power conversion process.

An important element that follows resources in the measurement of soft power is the foreign policy goals that states seek to achieve. Policy goals serve the dual role of stimulating the initial behaviour of states and providing a baseline for ascertaining the effectiveness of a particular course of action. These goals situate between resources and strategies in the analytical process of this book because first of all, a preferred course of action is determined by the goals a state seeks to achieve. Second, outcomes are better assessed when goals are clearly stated. Beyond their impact on the strategic choices of states, they are worth specifying because they reveal the targets of power, thus minimizing the methodological challenges of evaluating outcomes. Two types of goals are contemplated in this book – milieu and self-interested goals. The latter can be likened to Wolfers' (1962) "possession goal" because states often compete to gain an edge over one another, and can sometimes include objectives like the signing of trade agreements, ensuring access to resources, and membership in international organizations like the UN Security Council (UNSC). Milieu and self-interested goals are not mutually exclusive and can be pursued by a state simultaneously; however, the former is mostly associated with powerful states who seek to shore up their influence.

As Lee (2009) notes "becoming attractive [...] *per se* cannot be a goal of soft power" except if such a state is a hegemon that wants to maintain its dominance by creating an enabling environment (p. 216). This type of goal is known as a milieu goal. They entail what Nye (2011) called "value objectives" such as the promotion of human rights, democracy, and free markets. They are structural, rarely transactional, slow to produce outcomes, and tend to have indirect effects. They are intended to create a "framework of relationship within which transactions can take place" and thus can take years to manifest (Brown, 2017, p. 44). With this type of goal in mind, decision-makers operate under the assumption that their behaviour will condition other states to treat them as a trusted and familiar ally, as well as consider their interests and sensibilities (Brown, 2017). This does not mean that they may not disagree, but disagreements will be aired in the context of friendship, familiarity, and trust.

Self-interested goals are associated with all states. However, lesser powers tend to selectively focus on specific issues that are responsive to the instruments of soft power, given their lack of aspiration for preponderance. While these goals differ due to country-specific policy orientations, Lee (2009) suggests five broad categories of self-interested goals, which are the improvement of a state's security environment, mobilization of other countries' support for foreign and security policies, manipulation of other countries' preferences and behaviour, and maintenance of the unity of a committee of states (pp. 207–208). These goals may generate direct effects because they are mostly targeted at the ruling or governing elites, especially where they dispose of a certain degree of autonomy in foreign policy decision-making (Nye, 2011).

The implementation of these goals requires strategy. As with other aspects of public policy, the exercise of soft power is a political choice that stems from political argumentation and is put into action through institutions. For a strategy to take form, an "institutional framework for strategy development" needs to be put in place where modes of action can be deliberated (Singh & MacDonald, 2017, p. 26). This often involves the careful consideration of objectives, available resources, the intended targets, and, more importantly, the articulation of a clear implementation plan. Given the objectives of this book, it is important to capture the manifest actions of states, that is, their deliberate attempt to cultivate attraction through strategies. These strategies reflect the behaviour of agents and the means through which they seek to achieve their objectives.

However, it is important to note that contemplating a state's strategy or approach to soft power is a difficult exercise fraught with challenges especially when one considers that soft power's most potent instruments, in the form of culture, are situated within the purview of non-state actors, and are, at times, difficult to wield.

Target Perception

Agents apply soft power resources to change the preferences of the subject and, as such, it is important to go beyond assessing their resources and behaviour to evaluating the perceptive dispositions of the subjects when estimating the soft power capability of an agent. What this implies is that a two-directional approach is important in evaluating the soft power capability of states. Three reasons are particularly salient to buttress this point. First, the socially constructed and structural nature of attraction and persuasion renders the thinking of the targets important. Second, the measure of the credibility of resources lies within an evaluation of the perceptive dispositions of the target. Third, it offers insight into the distinctive features of the targets and by implication, the effectiveness of soft power approaches in reaching a given policy goal.

Who are the targets of soft power? It is important to recall that there are multiple actors within states, and the impact of soft power both at the cognitive and policy level will depend on which actor finds an agent's qualities and behaviour attractive and the level of control they have over policymaking (Fan, 2008). To answer the preceding question, I draw from Ji's (2017) proposition of three hierarchical levels of target audience where soft power is likely to produce desired effects: micro, meso, and macro. While individual actors are situated at the micro-level, institutional actors are situated at the meso-level, and finally, state actors are situated at the macro-level. Individual actors may be political, business, and academic elites, as well as private individuals, whereas institutional actors mostly operate in organizational, business, and administrative settings. State actors are those individuals who act on behalf of the state, especially in matters of foreign policy.

All three categories of target audiences are likely to be indirectly affected by milieu objectives pursued by the agent of power, however, self-interested goals are directed towards state actors given their direct involvement in foreign policy decision-making, and ability to shape foreign policy decisions in favour of the agent. Given the centrality of elite attitudes in estimating Nigeria's soft power capabilities, the book will focus, mainly on the meso- and macro-levels.

Foreign Policy Outcomes

Outcomes reflect the effectiveness of soft power. In the words of Hayden (2012) "Outcomes [...] capture the expected capacity of soft power to achieve influence of some sort. Outcomes [also] covey what soft power is supposed to strategically accomplish" (p. 42). Since this book is concerned with the measurement of soft power, determined through the effects attraction for a state has on the behaviour of others, it assumes that states will gear their strategies towards audiences relevant to their desired objectives. Thus, at any of the levels discussed previously, a change in the behaviour of the subjects is anticipated where there is an attraction to the agent.

As discussed in the previous section, the use of soft power may be geared towards milieu or self-interested goals. At the individual level where indirect effects manifest, attraction may reflect in the consumption of cultural products and favourable perception of the qualities and behaviour of the agent. At this level, changes in the behaviour of the subject towards the agent, expressed in terms of support for its foreign policies, reflect a positive outcome. At the institutional level, where relational goals drive the behaviour of the agent, attraction may engender change in group opinion and institutional policy or lead to policy-related outcomes. This book anticipates similar effects at the state level where attraction may engender voting coincidence and policy-related interactions such as trade agreements and alliance formation (see Ji, 2017).

However, one has to be mindful of the fact that soft power effects manifest in a very slow manner and over long periods. This is because the process of changing the "mindsets that have been fixed in the cognitive system requires [a] long-term cultivation process" (Ji, 2017, p. 82). Similarly, other factors might intervene during this process, making it difficult to determine whether attraction or persuasion is solely responsible for the changed behaviour.

Conclusion

The chapter set out to provide the theoretical basis of this book by drawing from Morgenthau's relational understanding of power to accentuate a behaviour-based conceptualization of soft power where attraction emerges from the operationalization of power resources by an agent to alter the behaviour of others. It specified the theoretical framework within which discussions in the empirical sections are embedded. This proceeded by first making the case for a classical realist approach to soft power that accounts for both material and ideational resources as instruments of influence before drawing from Nye (2011) to provide a conceptual and analytical framework for the rest of the analysis, beginning with Chapter 4.

Notes

1 While E. H. Carr and Morgenthau may be the most famous classical realists, other prominent classical realists who derive their view of international politics from the insatiable will to power of human beings are Reinhold Niebuhr (2021) (*Moral Man and Immoral Society*) and Friedrich Meinecke (1997) (*Machiavellism: The Doctrine of Raison d'Etat and Its Place in Modern History*).
2 Morgenthau argues that the "psychological relations between two minds" is the essence of political power and as a result should be distinguished from military force because when the latter is exercised or become actualized, it abdicates the usefulness of political power. That is, physical violence would have substituted psychological relationship thus rendering the latter useless (1948/1993, p. 31).
3 Ethical and non-coercive persuasion suggest a process where a state convinces another of the legitimacy of a course of action by drawing from previous knowledge of related circumstances or communicating unprejudiced assessments of the factors informing that particular course of action.
4 The failure of the US in Vietnam, Afghanistan, and Iraq reflects instances where states with superior power capabilities have failed to meet their desired objectives despite superior capabilities.

References

Abowei, F. (2020). The military and soft power: Assessing the case of Nigeria's security engagement in West Africa from the perceptions of Ghanaian and Liberian political elites. *Global Security and Intelligence Notes (GSIN)*, 2.

Alexander, M. G., Shana, L., & Henry, P. J. (2005). Image theory, social identity, and social dominance: Structural characteristics and individual motives underlying international images. *Political Psychology*, 26(1), 27–45. https://doi.org/10.1111/j.1467-9221.2005.00408.x

Bachrach, P., & Baratz, M. (1962). Two faces of power. *The American Political Science Review*, 56(4), 947–952. doi:10.2307/1952796

Baldwin, D. A. (1985). *Economic statecraft*. Princeton University Press.

Barkin, J. S. (2003). Realist constructivism. *International Studies Review*, 5(3), 325–342.

Bell, E. (2016). Soft power and corporate imperialism: Maintaining British influence. *Race & Class*, 57(4), 75–86.

Berenskoetter, F., & Quinn, A. (2012). Hegemony by invitation: Neoclassical realism, soft power, and US-European relations. In A. Toje and B. Kunz (Eds.), *Neoclassical realism in European politics: Bringing power back in* (pp. 214–233). Manchester University Press.

Bilgin, P., & Eliş, B. (2008). Hard power, soft power: Toward a more realistic power analysis. *Insight Turkey*, 10(5), 5–20.

Blumer, H. (1969). *Symbolic interactionism: Perspective and method*. Hall, Inc.

Brown, R. (2017). Influence in French and German cultural action. In N. Chitty, L. Ji, G. D. Rawnsley, & C. Hayden (Eds.), *The Routledge handbook of soft power* (pp. 37–48). Routledge.

Byrne, D., Clore, G. L., & Smeaton, G. (1986). The attraction hypothesis: Do similar attitudes affect anything? *Journal of Personality and Social Psychology*, 51(6), 1167–1170. https://doi.org/10.1037/0022-3514.51.6.1167

Campbell, K., & O'Hanlon, M. (2006). *Hard power: The new politics of national security*. Basic Books.

Carr, E. H. (2016). *The twenty years crisis, 1919–1939: Reissued with a preface from Michael Cox* (Ed.). Palgrave Macmillan (Original work published in 1939).

Chitty, N. (2017). Soft power, civic virtue, and world politics. In N. Chitty, L. Ji, G. D. Rawnsley, and C. Hayden (Eds.), *The Routledge handbook of soft power* (pp. 9–36). Routledge.

Church, W. F. (1972). *Richelieu and reason of state*. Princeton University Press.

Cooper, R. (2004). Hard power, soft power, and the goals of diplomacy. In D. Held and M. Koenig-Archibugi (Eds.), *American power in the 21st century* (pp. 167–180). Polity.

Dowding, K. (2008). Agency and structure: Interpreting power relationships. *Journal of Power*, 1(1), 21–36.

Elleman, B. A., & Paine, S. C. M. (2015). *Navies and soft power: Historical case studies of naval power and the non-use of military force*. Naval War College Press.

Fan, Y. (2008). Soft power: Power of attraction or confusion? *Place Branding and Public Diplomacy*, 4(2), 147–158.

Geertz, C. (1973). *The interpretation of culture: Selected essays*. Basic Books.

Gelb, L. H. (2009). *Power rules: How common sense can rescue American foreign policy*. Harper Collins.

Gilpin, R. (1981). *War and change in world politics*. Cambridge University Press.

Government of Canada. (2020, September 9). *Peace support operations (1954–present)*. Canada.ca. Retrieved April 10, 2022, from www.canada.ca/en/services/defence/caf/militaryhistory/wars-operations/peace-support.html

Grix, J., & Brannagan, P. M. (2016). Of mechanisms and myths: Conceptualising states' "soft power" strategies through sports mega-events. *Diplomacy & Statecraft*, 27(2), 251–272. https://doi.org/10.1080/09592296.2016.1169791

Hancock, T., Hornby, L., & Wildau, G. (2018, March 13). China revamps bureaucracies as Xi tightens grip. *Financial Times*. Retrieved October 1, 2019, from www.ft.com/content/3c0d4596-2666-11e8-b27e-cc62a39d57a0

Hayden, C. (2012). *The rhetoric of soft power: Public diplomacy in global contexts*. Lexington Books.

Herrmann, R. K. (2013). Perceptions and image theory in international relations, in Leonie Huddy, David O. Sears, and Jack S. Levy (Eds.), *The Oxford handbook of political psychology* (2nd ed.) (pp. 334–363). online edn, Oxford Academic. https://doi.org/10.1093/oxfordhb/9780199760107.013.0011

Huntington, S. P. (1993). The clash of civilizations? *Foreign Affairs*, 72(3), 22–49. www.jstor.org/stable/20045621

Jacob, U. J. (2017). Cultural approaches to soft power (section overview). In N. Chitty, L. Ji, G. D. Rawnsley, and C. Hayden (Eds.), *The Routledge handbook of soft power* (pp. 137–143). Routledge.

Ji, L. (2017). Measuring soft power (section overview). In N. Chitty, L. Ji, G. D. Rawnsley, and C. Hayden (Eds.), *The Routledge handbook of soft power* (pp. 75–92). Routledge.

Kroeber, A. L., & Kluckhohn C. (1952). Culture: A critical review of concepts and definitions. Peabody Museum of Archaeology & Ethnology, Harvard University, 47(1), 223.

Layne, C. (2010). The unbearable lightness of soft power. In I. Parmar and M. Cox (Eds.), *Soft power and US foreign policy: Theoretical, historical and contemporary perspectives* (pp. 51–82). Routledge.

Lebow, R. N. (2005). Power, persuasion and justice. *Millennium, 33*(3), 551–581.

Lee, G. (2009). A theory of soft power and Korea's soft power strategy. *Korean Journal of Defence Analysis, 21*(2), 205–218. https://doi.org/10.1080/1016327090 2913962

Lekorwe, M., Chingwete, A., Okuru, M., & Samson, R. (2016). *China's growing presence in Africa wins largely positive popular reviews* (No. 122). Afrobarometer. Retrieved June 2, 2019, from https://afrobarometer.org/publications/ad122-chinas-growing-presence-africa-wins-largely-positive-popular-reviews

Lukes, S. (2005a). Power and the battle for hearts and minds. *Millennium, 33*(3), 477–493.

Lukes, S. (2005b). *Power: A radical view* (2nd ed.). Palgrave Macmillan (Original work published in 1974).

Mearsheimer, J. J. (2001). *The tragedy of great power politics*. W.W. Norton & Company.

Meinecke, F. (1997). *Machiavellism: The doctrine of Raison d'Etat and its place in modern history*. Routledge (Original work published in 1957).

Morgenthau, H. J. (1993). *Politics among nations: The struggle for power and peace*. (K. W. Thompson, Ed.). McGraw-Hill (Original work published in 1948).

Morriss, P. (2002). *Power: A philosophical analysis* (2nd ed.). Manchester University Press.

Niebuhr, R. (2021). *Moral man and immoral society: A study in ethics and politics* (Later part. ed.). John Knox Press (Original work published in 1932).

Nye, J. S. (1990a). *Bound to lead: The changing nature of American power*. Basic Books.

Nye, J. S. (2004). *Soft power: A means to success in world politics*. Public Affairs Books.

Nye, J. S. (2011). *The future of power*. Public Affairs Books.

Rothman, S. B. (2011). Revising the soft power concept: What are the means and mechanisms of soft power? *Journal of Political Power, 4*(1), 49–64. https://doi.org/10.1080/2158379X.2011.556346

Singh, J. P., & MacDonald, S. (2017). *Soft power today: Measuring the influences and effects*. Edinburgh: The Institute for International Cultural Relations, The University of Edinburgh.

Strinati, D. (1995). *An introduction to theories of popular culture*. Routledge.

Taliaferro, J. W., Lobell, S. E., & Ripsman, N. M. (2009). Introduction. In S. E. Lobell, N. M. Ripsman, & J. W. Taliaferro (Eds.), *Neoclassical realism, the state, and foreign policy* (pp. 1–42). Cambridge University Press.

Tella, O. (2018). 'Is Nigeria a soft power state?' *Social Dynamics, 44*(2), 376–394. https://doi.org/10.1080/02533952.2018.1492833

United Nations. (n.d.). *Brazil's enduring contribution to UN Peacekeeping | UN News*. United Nations. Retrieved April 10, 2022, from https://news.un.org/en/gall ery/537202

Vemuri, S. R. (2014). Formation of diaspora entrepreneurs. *ZenTra Working Paper in Transnational Studies, 41*.

Vuving, A. L. (2009, September 3). *How soft power works [Paper presentation]*. American Political Science Association Annual Meeting, Toronto, ON, Canada.

Waltz, K. N. (1959). *Man, state and war: A theoretical analysis*. University Press.

Waltz, K. N. (1979). *Theory of international politics*. Addison-Wesley Publishing Company.

Waltz, K. N. (1988). The origins of war in neorealist theory. *Journal of Interdisciplinary History*, *18*(4), 615–628. www.jstor.org/stable/204817

Weber, M. (1968). *Economy and society: An outline of interpretive sociology.* Bedminister Press. (Originally published in 1922).

Wolfers, A. (1962). *Discord and collaboration: Essays on international politics.* The Johns Hopkins Press.

4 The West African Context

Introduction

It is impossible for any power analysis to suggest that a state has power over others without specifying the actors involved in the relationship, the issues in contention, and their historical patterns of interaction. This also applies to assessments of soft power, especially as the concept captures the attractive dimensions of economic, political, and cultural interactions between partners, who, based on the nature and context of their power relationships, adopt strategies to influence each other. Within this relationship, actors operating at different levels of a state consciously interpret the qualities and actions of one another, which, in turn, affects their actions and inactions towards each other – positively or negatively. As Chapter 3 hypothesizes, a positive impact is anticipated in the workings of soft power when interactions between the actors take place in a cordial and cooperative atmosphere.

This chapter subjects this reasoning to empirical scrutiny. It argues that the operationalization of Nigeria's soft power is likely to be visible when the broader patterns of interaction within the sub-region and the specific interactions between Nigeria and its sub-regional counterparts are observed. It also argues that the existence of bonds of alliances and cooperative relationships between Nigeria and its neighbours may have a facilitative and magnifying effect on the effectiveness of Nigeria's soft power. Conversely, the presence of cultural incongruity and a conflictual relational dynamic, amongst other variables of inhibiting effect explained previously, are likely to hinder the effectiveness of Nigeria's soft power, even where resources have attractive potential.

The aim here is to describe the West African context, drawing from Webber and Smith's (2002, p. 10) notion of the "foreign policy arena." This is understood as a terrain occupied by competing forces – actors, interests, and issues – wherein the problems or debates in contention and the actors involved influence how states leverage their contextual knowledge to apply resources towards specific outcomes (Webber & Smith, 2002; Hayden, 2012; Nye, 2004). It is also a terrain upon which power is manifested and exercised. It constrains and offers opportunities to states. Equally important

DOI: 10.4324/9781003396628-4

is that factors of economic, military, political, cultural, and geographical dimensions bolster this contextual landscape in different ways, which in turn engenders power and influence hierarchies (Webber & Smith, 2002). It is within this system that competitive tendencies are entrenched and patterns of conflictive and cooperative interactions emerge.

This chapter discusses the relational dynamics of West African states by questioning their historical and contemporary political, economic, and cultural framework of relations. It takes a historical approach by tracing the evolution of their relationship to highlight patterns of interaction, including the issues and actors involved, across economics, politics, and culture. These are in view of evaluating Nigeria's specific relationship with Liberia and Ghana. These discussions will proceed in two sections. The first provides an overview of the political, economic, security, and cultural context, before exploring the evolution of relations and the accompanying patterns of alliances that shaped political interactions between West African states. Here, the role of structural variables such as colonialism, Pan-Africanism, and *la Francophonie* in the dynamics of West African relations are addressed. It follows this by discussing the issues and actors shaping the present political realities of the sub-region. The second section focuses on the specific relationship between Nigeria and its West African counterparts, Ghana and Liberia.

Relational Dynamics of West African States

What factors influence the patterns of alliance between West African states? How have these alliances evolved to date? How have these evolving dynamics shaped the emergence of contemporary issues and actors in West African foreign policies? These questions are addressed in this section by assessing the historical, political, and cultural framework of relations between West African states. It makes the case for the compatibility of West African political and cultural values given the contiguity of West African borders, cross-border ethnic and religious ties, as well as similar socio-economic and political conditions. Also, it demonstrates the impact of colonialism and its accompanying ideas of *La Francophonie* and Pan-Africanism on the evolution of West African relations. Finally, it addresses the issues and actors at play within the sub-region.

West Africa: An Overview

With a population of just under 380 million people, West Africa follows East Africa as the most populous region in Africa. Although countries in the sub-region are often delineated by their membership of the Economic Community of West African States (ECOWAS), which currently comprises 15 states, geographic West Africa comprises 16 states – Nigeria, Benin, Cote d'Ivoire, Ghana, Senegal, Togo, Sierra Leone, Niger, Mali, Liberia, Cape Verde, Mauritania, Burkina Faso, Guinea, Guinea-Bissau, and The Gambia.

Except for Cape Verde, which sits off the coast of Senegal along the Pacific Ocean, all other states in the sub-region are geographically contiguous. These countries are separated by three official languages – English, French, and Portuguese – and range in size and population, with Niger and Mali leading the sub-region in landmass – 489.4 sqm and 478.8 sqm, respectively. Nigeria's population of about 200 million people leads the combined population of other West African states, which ranges from as high as 29 million in Ghana to as low as 543,000 in Cape Verde (World Bank, 2020a).

Although there is evidence that humans have inhabited the sub-region since 9400 BCE, West Africa's modern political history is tied to the Berlin Conference of 1884, which formally launched the scramble for Africa and the dispersion of homogenous ethnic groups into separate colonies. Thus, creating lines of possible fracture such as ethnic, religious, linguistic, and customary differences within clear-cut boundaries and central colonial authorities. With Ghana, the first to gain independence in 1957, and Cape Verde the last state to do so in 1975, all West African states are today made up of diverse ethnic groups and native languages with cross-border links. For instance, the Fulanis, numbering about 16 million in northern Nigeria, are equally settled in Guinea, Senegal, Niger, Ghana, Mauritania, Burkina Faso, Sierra Leone, The Gambia, and Cote d'Ivoire. This also applies to the Yorubas who are settled in southwest Nigeria, Benin, Togo, Ghana, Ivory Coast, and Sierra Leone, and the Mandingos who are spread across Liberia, Guinea, Sierra Leone, and Cote d'Ivoire (Sangare, 2019; Adebajo, 2002).

This imperial exercise, the negative consequences of which continue to haunt the sub-region in the form of ethno-religious conflicts, civil wars, and challenges to sovereignty that are often unresolved, nevertheless led to the emergence of culturally diverse societies with cross-border links, that are today the source of networks, cross-border cultural interactions, and alluring cultural outputs. From Nigeria and Ghana to Senegal and Cote d'Ivoire, these countries share similarities in culture, be it cuisine, native languages, music, religion, fashion, and the arts and crafts that are increasingly the basis of cross-cultural interactions. That these diverse cultural systems are compatible, even with different indigenous languages and religious practices, is evident in the ease at which cultural outputs from Nigeria are readily consumed or accepted in Ghana, Liberia, and the wider sub-region.

The reverse is also the case as Nigerian cultural actors often refer to the influence of their contemporaries in West African states. Take for instance Nigeria's legendary Afrobeat singer, Fela Anikulapo Kuti, whose variant of highlife was influenced by Ghanaian musicians such as E. T. Mensah. Beyond that, Fela built a formidable career as one of the best in Africa based on strong support from Ghanaians, even before his music became popular in Nigeria (see Collins, 2015). This "consummation" of cultural outputs is all the more facilitated by the emergence of technological innovations and modern forms of communication, especially digital communication channels such as Twitter, Facebook, and YouTube. As will be discussed in Chapters 5 and 7, Nigeria's music and movie industries are globally revered, thanks in part to a huge African diaspora.

Beyond the geographical and cultural implications of colonialism is its impact on the political philosophies, institutions, socio-economic structures, and security of West African states. To a large extent, all 16 states in the sub-region embrace a certain level of democratic governance system, modelled on the former colonial states' system. The relatively imperfect nature of this Western model of governance is exposed by the struggles of African states to build sustainable nations devoid of ethnic allegiance or fragmentation along ethnic lines and rooted in social cohesion, patriotism, and nationhood. While countries like Ghana, Senegal, Benin, and Cape Verde have been spared the negative security consequences of colonialism, Nigeria, Cote d'Ivoire, Liberia, and Sierra Leone have all experienced civil wars at various moments in their post-independence political history.

The triggers of these conflicts vary from political and economic marginal-ization and competition over resources to issues of land ownership. However, poor governance and contests for political power appear to be the most prominent of all. The Cold War era witnessed the involvement of the major powers in some of these conflicts, albeit through proxies, as were the former colonial powers. Although the current security context of the sub-region is markedly different from the 1980s and 1990s when political strife and civil wars were common occurrences, the sub-region faces new forms of security challenges, mostly posed by non-state actors, such as trans-border Islamic fundamentalist movements – Boko Haram and Al-Qaeda in the Islamic Maghreb (AQIM) – narcotics trafficking, the proliferation of SALW and maritime piracy (see Palik et al., 2020). Overall, the regional security profile marks a notable improvement from the immediate post-Cold War years, as West Africa has suffered fewer conflicts and fatalities than other sub-regions in the continent (see Marc et al., 2015 for more information on conflict cas-ualties in Africa).

This improved security context may not be unconnected with the fact that the last two decades witnessed increased levels of political inclusiveness and democratization in West African states, even if recent years have recorded varying degrees of regression as political instabilities in Mali, Burkina Faso, Guinea, and Cote d'Ivoire suggest. As the democracy index of 2019 by the Economist Intelligence Unit reveals, apart from Ghana and Cape Verde whose democracy is classified as flawed, all other states in the sub-region are hybrid regimes marred by electoral frauds, non-independent judiciary, corruption, and political repression (Economist Intelligence Unit, 2020, pp. 10–13). The implication is that West African governments are increasingly unable to govern effectively. As the Ibrahim Index of African Governance (IIAG) of 2020 reveals, apart from Cape Verde, Ghana, and Senegal, all other West African states feature outside the top ten states in the continent in terms of governance performance, with Nigeria, Guinea, and Guinea Bissau featuring amongst the least ranked states for their poor human rights record and disregard for the rule of law. The appearance of Ghana and Cape Verde at the top of both indexes reveals the extent to which the practice of democracy can positively impact governance.

West African states are at different stages of economic development; however, they remain amongst the least competitive economies in the world, with GDP per capita ranging from as low as $484 in Sierra Leone to as high as $3,064 in Cape Verde (World Bank, 2020b). Buoyed by rises in commodity prices, growth rates have been promising as nine countries, including Cote d'Ivoire, Senegal, and Ghana, experienced growth of about 5% between 2017 and 2018; however, the sub-region still harbours some of the poorest states in the world with over 30% of citizens living in extreme poverty, while unemployment remains high, and inflation remains a challenge, declining to about 9% after an uptick of 13% in 2017 (World Data Lab, 2020). Equally, the AfDB Economic Outlook of 2019 reports that in addition to depreciating currencies, the combination of expansionary fiscal policies and weak internal revenue mobilization has engendered souring external debts levels for most states. This bleak regional economic profile may not be unconnected with internal domestic challenges associated with political instability, weak state institutions, as well as the lack of transparency and accountability.

Forty-five years after the creation of ECOWAS with the specific aim of deepening integration, trade relations within the region remain protectionist and weak. Given the widespread reliance on extractive commodities for revenues, the volume and value of intra-regional trade pale in comparison to industrialized nations. Bearing in mind that over 75% of intra-ECOWAS trade is unaccounted for as a result of their informal and, at times, illicit character (see Torres & van Seters, 2016; Golub, 2015), figures from 2018 reveal that intra-ECOWAS trade accounted for only 11.9% of the total volume of trade in the region (AfDB, 2020).[1] The fact that Nigeria's top five commercial partners, whether in terms of import or export, feature no West African state is indicative of the low volume of formal trade between states in the sub-region (Chete & Adewuyi, 2012; Torres & van Seters, 2016). There is no single reason for this, as common issues affecting regional trade include the implementation of protectionist policies by West African governments, disparities in fiscal and monetary policies, lack of trade complementarity, issues of comparative advantage, and low levels of economic development (see AfDB, 2020).

The foregoing discussions demonstrate the context within which West African states have advanced their foreign policies as well as provides a basis for understanding the issues surrounding interactions between them, both bilaterally and within the framework of ECOWAS, which serves as the nucleus of interaction on issues of integration, democratization, and conflict management.

Nature of Relations and Patterns of Alliances

Historical relations between West African states can be best understood through the prism of the continent's colonial past. Not least because of the bonds and patterns of alliances engendered by their shared colonial experience but also the overbearing influence of extra-continental actors, which created lines of discord that, although not as pronounced as before, continue until today. On the one hand, colonialism influenced the mobilization of pan-Africanist sentiments in Anglophone West Africa to unite political elites, amidst subtle leadership and ideological rivalries, towards the struggle for independence and the subsequent integration processes that culminated in the formation of the Organization of African Unity (OAU) in 1963.[2] On the other hand, it created lines of discord between French West African countries and their Anglophone counterparts, even after the formation of ECOWAS in 1975.

At the dawn of independence, French interest in sustaining pre-existing colonial ties in Africa was pronounced, whereas Britain believed that Africa presented more challenges than opportunities that did not warrant serious engagement except where its material interests come under threat (Clapham, 1996). Thus, while the Cold War superpowers were engaged in South Africa and the Horn, France had free reins in other parts of Africa, including West Africa, where it saw an opportunity for some sort of cultural expansionism, or more specifically, an export destination for its "rich civilization" synonymized with *la Francophonie* (Schraeder, 2001; Thomson, 2010, p. 162).[3] Also, in the wake of African independence France was concerned with its global status in the Cold War order and the need to protect the interests of the Western alliance against communist threat (Charbonneau, 2008; Renou, 2002; Schraeder, 2001). This made sustaining the existing colonial relationship with French West African states an important component of its broader strategy to promote French power on the world stage.

The implication of French influence in West Africa was the line of discord it created between Anglophone and Francophone states, pitting Ghana and Nigeria against Senegal and Cote d'Ivoire. In addition to the strong personal ties President Leopold Sédar Senghor of Senegal and President Houphouet-Boigny of Cote d'Ivoire had with the leaders of France, their countries depended on French patronage for economic and military support and, as a result, were occasionally egged on by France to exacerbate rivalries with Nigeria and Ghana (Webber & Smith, 2002; Thomson, 2010).

On the one hand, these states were wary of Kwame Nkrumah's – first prime minister and president of Ghana – leadership ambitions in the continent, and his insistence on the formation of a continental union with supranational powers. At the time a rare area of convergence, between Francophone states and Nigeria, on the preference for a loose continental union supported by strong sub-regional groupings. On the other hand, they feared the dominance of Nigeria in an all-West African sub-regional organization due to its size and resources (Thompson, 2010). While "anti-Nkrumahist" sentiments would come to an end upon his ouster from power as Ghana's president, the rivalry between Nigeria and its Francophone neighbours will continue unabated, even strongly manifesting during the Nigerian civil war and the formative years of ECOWAS.

On the Anglophone side, Nigeria and Ghana were locked in a rivalry of their own, involving the nature and scope of the proposed African continental union. This ideological divergence played out in the form of a tussle for leadership, with Nkrumah going as far as withdrawing Ghana from the West African Currency Board and West African Airways (O. Ojo, 1980). As was the case with Francophone states whose rivalry with Ghana came to a halt upon the ouster of Nkrumah from power, Nigeria's rivalry with Ghana also cooled off. But this came after Nigeria banked on the support of Liberia as well as Francophone West African states to defeat the idea of a supranational continental union in favour of a loose union buttressed by strong sub-regional groupings.

The formation of ECOWAS, which Nigeria prioritized after the Nigerian civil war or Biafra war (1967–1970), further exposed the rivalry between the Anglophones and Francophones and the vague and fragile sense of interdependence that characterizes relations between them. The threat of French influence to Nigeria's internal stability and regional influence spurred its political elites to prioritize the creation of a conducive regional environment based on cordial relations with West African states. Thus, in 1972 Nigeria came up with a draft proposal for the creation of an all-West African regional organization (O. Ojo, 1980). Certainly, this was not the first attempt at integrating the sub-region to shore up cooperation. The *Communauté Financière Africaine* (CFA) franc, created in 1945 brought Francophone West African states under a common currency. Subsequently, in 1965, four West African states – Cote d'Ivoire, Liberia, Sierra Leone, and Guinea – signed an agreement initiated by William Tubman of Liberia to form an economic union for West Africa.

Pan-Africanism served as a unifying force for Anglophone West African states, as it emerged as the principal ideological tool for mobilizing regional solidarity and social cohesion based on a common racial identity (Adibe, 2001). While Anglophone states were unified by Pan-Africanism and the zeal to distance themselves from Britain, their Francophone counterparts were bounded by their association with *la Francophonie* under the aegis of *Afrique Occidental Française*, an association of all French-speaking states in West Africa – excluding Togo – unified by their commitment to the French Language and participation in the Franco-African summits (Schreader, 2001). Although these states were unified by the need for regional integration and the establishment of intra-regional trade links, they nonetheless disagreed on the imperative of reducing their dependence on France. Even more, states like Cote d'Ivoire, Burkina Faso, and Senegal whose leaders were strongly attached to France were against an all-West African economic grouping for fear of Nigeria's dominance (Adebajo, 2002).

With the strong support of President Gnassingbe Eyadema of Togo, Nigeria's diplomatic manoeuvres, discussed in Chapter 6, successfully led to the formation of ECOWAS. But, as Bach (1983) remarks, it appeared more like a synonym for West Africa and a symbol of African unity than an institutional framework for promoting collective self-reliance and cooperation. This was because, even with the formation of ECOWAS, Francophone West African states remained committed to *La Communauté Economique de L'Afrique de l'Ouest* (CEAO), which translates simply as West African Economic Community (WAEC), established in 1973 and the *Union Économique et Monétaire Ouest-Africaine* (UEMOA) as the cornerstone of their relationship and a counterbalance to Nigeria's idea of ECOWAS and influence (Schraeder, 2001; Adebajo, 2002).[4] With the death of Houphouet-Boigny – the staunchest opponent of cooperation with Nigeria – in 1993, ties between UEMOA and ECOWAS improved to the point that Nigeria attended the Franco-African summit held in 1996 at Burkina Faso (Schraeder, 2001).

This is not to suggest that the lines of discord between Anglophone and Francophone countries are completely erased, but ECOWAS brought to West African states a platform to not only negotiate the normative contours of West African foreign policies, but also deliberate and articulate common positions on sub-regional issues. In principle, West African states agreed to promote cooperation and integration on a range of issues including regional security, citizens' welfare, development, and economic stability (ECOWAS, 1993). Equally, they agreed on normative principles to guide the framework of security and political cooperation, such as the ECOWAS Declaration of Political Principles, which envisages a sub-region governed by respect for human rights, shared values, and democratic accountability (ECOWAS, 1991), and the Mechanism for Conflict Prevention, Management, Resolution, Peacekeeping, and Security of 1999, which allows for the proactive intervention in conflicts within the sub-region (ECOWAS, 1999).

These are in addition to the supplementary protocol on Democracy and Good Governance agreed in 2001, which emphasizes shared constitutional principles such as the separation of powers, commitment to democratic principles, the organization of free, fair, and transparent elections, freedom of the press, and association, decentralization of power and commitment to democratic principles, citizen participation in decision-making, freedom from religious, ethnic, racial, or regional discrimination, and, more importantly, zero tolerance for unconstitutional change of government. To demonstrate the seriousness of ECOWAS on these principles, the protocol authorizes sanctions against any state that violates these provisions (ECOWAS, 2001).

As Chapter 6 will discuss, it is this normative framework that guides Nigeria's relations with its neighbours. Even more, the extent of Nigeria's commitment to these principles is especially critical in estimating its attractiveness, given its leadership role in their conception and ratification.

Issues and Actors in West African Foreign Policies

The colonial legacy of state formation in West Africa engendered a political context where non-state actors are increasingly relevant, putting into contestation state-centric models of international relations. With issues in security, democratic consolidation, and trade forming the crux of deliberations between West African governments, new sets of international actors are shaping these discussions. Prominent of all are armed groups, who capitalize on limitations to state authority in African states to operate freely, building organized criminal and terrorist networks. On a positive note, non-state actors such as a growing diaspora, multinational corporations (MNCs), religious actors, and human rights advocacy groups, are becoming active participants in the foreign policies of West African states.

The issues confronting West African foreign policies have changed very little since the formation of ECOWAS, even as they manifest differently across the 15 states. Initially conceived as an economic community to drive trade and development, events in the sub-region transitioned ECOWAS from its singular economic orientation to cater to political and security concerns, necessitating the expansion of its scope and powers in 1993. A history of destabilizing civil wars in Nigeria, Liberia, Sierra Leone, and Guinea Bissau between the 1970s and late 1990s informed the formulation of mechanisms to ensure regional security, including the establishment of the ECOWAS Monitoring Group (ECOMOG), which was instrumental in ending civil wars in Liberia and Sierra Leone (Adebajo, 2002). In a way, these experiences emboldened West African governments to be more assertive in managing conflict in the region. This took the form of mediatory roles in political disputes and even civil wars in Guinea, Mali, Burkina Faso, Cote d'Ivoire, Niger, and, more recently, The Gambia (Khadiagala, 2018).

As the challenges confronting West African governments evolve, Guinea Bissau continues to contend with political instability, characterized by intermittent violent political upheavals, assassination, mutinies, coups, and counter-coups. As of the writing of this book, ECOWAS maintains an intervention force – ECOWAS Mission in Bissau (ECOMIB) – stationed in Bissau since 2012 (British Broadcasting Corporation (BBC) News, 2012; Khadiagala, 2018). This is as the rise of Islamic fundamentalism continues to be a major concern of West African foreign policies. In the words of the International Crisis Group (ICG), a global think tank researching and analysing global conflicts, "Jihadist movements are spreading like the desert, from north to south" (2019).

Nowhere is this more visible than in Nigeria, where fundamentalist groups such as AQIM, Islamic State West Africa Province, and Boko Haram are growing stronger, and strengthening their footprints in neighbouring states such as Niger, Chad, Mali, and Cameroun. Also in Burkina Faso, the rise of Jihadist groups such as the Group to Support Islam and Muslims is heightening security concerns in the coastal states of Ghana, Togo, Cote d'Ivoire, and Benin (ICG, 2019). The severity of this threat continues to haunt West African states, compelling ECOWAS to push for large-scale joint military operations that require intelligence sharing and joint border patrols. Whether West African states can pull together the resources required to stem this threat remains to be seen, but in the meantime, they are unable to come up with a unified response mechanism or cope with the number of people being displaced by counter-insurgency efforts in the Sahel where some of these groups operate (UNHCR, 2020a).

Further exacerbating the spectre of terrorism in the sub-region are issues such as narco-trafficking and the smuggling of SALWs (Mangan & Nowak, 2019). In 1998 West African governments adopted the Declaration of a Moratorium on the Import, Export, and Manufacture of SALWs, which was transformed in June 2006 into the ECOWAS Convention on SALWs. However, at no time is the illicit trade of SALWs direr than it is today, especially with political instability in Libya and the porous nature of West African borders (UN, 2020a). Also, the link between terrorism and the trafficking of drugs in West Africa is well established (Olukoshi, 2013). A study conducted by the UN Office of Drugs and Crime (UNODC) in 2013 noted rising concerns about AQIM's involvement in the trafficking of drugs from West Africa to Europe to the tune of $1.25 billion. In a similar vein, the UNODC highlighted the role of Boko Haram in facilitating the trafficking of heroin and cocaine across West Africa, proceeds from which are used to fund its operations in the Sahel (2017).

This brings to the fore issues of democratization and governance deficits, which West African states continue to contend with. Since independence, governments have struggled to implement measures designed to address challenges to state formation, institution building, and faltering economies. This is as decades of corruption, divisive politics, and economic mismanagement are causing disenchantment and eroding the ability of West African governments to impose their authority in the peripheral areas of the state, rendering them susceptible to the outbreak of violence and infiltration by organized criminal elements and terrorist groups. This is further exacerbated by the practice of mobilizing ethnic sentiments for political gains, which has in no small way broadened the lines of discord created by the arbitrary partitioning of the continent. This inextricable link between governance and security in the sub-region heightens the importance of constitutionalism, democratic governance, and human rights as linchpins of regional integration.

Barring the recent coup d'état in Mali, Guinea, Niger, and Burkina Faso, the constitutional change of government is one area where West Africa has gained tremendously. As noted previously, the last two decades witnessed improved levels of political inclusiveness and democratization in West African states, however, this is amidst poor infrastructure development, souring levels of corruption, and repressive and brutal tactics by state authorities – all of which raises questions about the commitment of governments to the ECOWAS supplementary protocol on Democracy and Good Governance.

Also worth mentioning is the lack of accountability, inclusiveness, and, more importantly, an enabling environment for participatory discourse, which erodes social trust and widens the gap in state–society relations (Doss, 2020). While these are domestic concerns, their propensity to lead to democratic disenchantment and challenges to juridical statehood, in a sub-region with contiguous boundaries and conflict spill-over, elevates them to regional-level issues. It is for this reason that ECOWAS encourages its member states to uphold the principles of democracy, good governance, and popular participation. And regional leaders like Nigeria have it as a staple of foreign policy to promote these normative principles.

With preferential trade agreements with erstwhile colonial powers still in force, especially in Francophone West Africa, the future of intra-regional trade looks bleak. West African governments acknowledge the need to reduce trade barriers to encourage intra-regional trade and economic development, and already 11 states have ratified the African Continental Free Trade Agreement (AfCFTA).[5] With trade and monetary barriers, as well as high transaction costs from currency conversion, impinging the flow of goods and services within the sub-region, West African governments are working towards the establishment of a common currency for all West African states known as the Eco. While the idea of the Eco started in 2000 with the five Anglophone ECOWAS states and Guinea (Conakry) under the West African Monetary Zone (WAMZ), it has since been expanded to include UEMOA states; however, the lines of discord separating Francophone West Africa from their Anglophone counterparts threaten to upend the process of creating an all-inclusive West African monetary union (Smith, 2020; Xuba, 2021).

The decision of UEMOA to proceed with the unilateral adoption of Eco, in what appears to be a simple renaming of the CFA franc in December 2019, blindsided WAMZ countries, whose preference is for a slower process that culminates in severing UEMOA's monetary ties to France (Smith, 2020; Ayeni, 2020). Of contention is the fact that Francophone West African states expect the Eco to be pegged at a fixed exchange rate against the Euro, as is the case with the CFA franc – a currency that symbolizes French influence over its former colonies. For WAMZ countries, Eco ought to be a new currency for all West African states and not a direct replacement of the CFA franc, as was agreed in principle when the leaders of ECOWAS member states met in June 2019. While it remains unclear if existing divergences undermining the implementation of a common currency can be bridged, its imperative to the facilitation of trade, especially with the AfCFTA coming into force, cannot be overemphasized.

From the problems of terrorism, organized crime, and democratic and governance deficits, to trade barriers, development deficits, and the need for a unified monetary policy, no one West African state can go it alone. This is why these issues are mostly coordinated within Regional Economic Communities (RECs) where coalitions can be mobilized. Even the AU recognizes this reality as it signed a memorandum of understanding (MOU) with RECs across the continent in January 2008 on the coordination of peace and security initiatives, essentially deferring major policies to RECs due to regional peculiarities associated with culture and politics (Khadiagala, 2018). In so far as the resolution of these issues requires the concerted effort of West African states within the institutional mechanism of ECOWAS, any workable solution will require multilevel engagement and collaboration. In this context, power moves from its traditional association with a zero-sum game to a positive-sum game, where "power *with* others" takes precedence over "power *over* others" (Nye, 2011, pp. xvi–xvii). This is where Nigeria's leadership comes to bear, as is the imperative of soft power as its strategic approach.

The expansion of foreign policy issues has engendered the emergence of new actors with growing importance in shaping the foreign policies of West African states. However, this does not erode the fact that the notion of "the big man of foreign policy" still holds in the sub-region, especially when the conduct of foreign policy remains the *domaine reservé* of central governments (Schraeder, 2001, p. 48). While the legacy of colonialism cannot be dismissed as a cause of this practice, the authoritarian legacy of West African governments sustained it into the 21st century. Nevertheless, the democratization of foreign policy that accompanied the adoption of democratic systems has given some operating room to other arms of government, specifically the legislature, to influence the conduct of foreign policy, albeit as rubber stamps (Schraeder, 2001). Within the executive, the changing nature of global politics has expanded the scope of foreign policies beyond economic and security issues, as foreign ministries draw on specialized agencies and other ministries of government to formulate and implement policies leveraging cultural resources to boost credibility and manage reputational security.

Also notable are the growing cross-border linkages between non-state actors that possess the ability to either disrupt or reinforce the role of the state in the conduct of foreign policy. While organized criminal groups are increasingly the subject of security interactions between West African governments, non-state actors such as religious leaders, MNCs, diaspora communities, and cultural actors are also active in the formulation and implementation of foreign policies (see Moderan, 2021). The emergence of resistance groups in the 1990s, especially in Liberia and Sierra Leone, is a case in point. Movements such as the National Patriotic Front of Liberia (NPFL) led by Charles Taylor not only defeated a national army but gained significant ground in the Liberian civil war to earn a seat at the table with state actors seeking ways to bring the war to an end (Adibe, 2001). The same was the case with the Revolutionary United Front (RUF) in Sierra Leone, which through the support of the NPFL destabilized successive Sierra Leonean governments between 1991 and 1996, before assuming power in 1997 (Adibe, 2001).

Beyond these disruptive forces are other non-state actors making positive contributions. Increasingly, West African citizens are taking advantage of the freedom of movement, as well as the right to residence and establishment that ECOWAS membership guarantees, engendering a flurry of mobility within the sub-region, with implications for foreign policy. While recent figures are unavailable, a study commissioned by the UNHCR in 2008 reveals that about 9 million West Africans are involved in cross-border mobility (Charrière & Frésia, 2008). A 2017 study commissioned by PricewaterhouseCoopers (PWC) reveals that 100,000 Nigerians emigrated to Niger, while Ghana and Benin saw an inflow of 70,000 and 50,000, respectively (Nevin & Omosomi, 2019, p. 5). It is also estimated that over 1 million Ghanaians currently reside in Nigeria (Mbewa, 2020).

The recent formation of the Nigerians in Diaspora Commission (NIDCOM) by Abuja to cater to its citizens operating outside the country illustrates the relevance of the diaspora in West African foreign policies. Long before now, Senegal changed the name of its foreign ministry to the Ministry of Foreign Affairs and of Senegalese Abroad in June 1993. These changes may not be unconnected with the fact that the diaspora fulfils the dual role of cultural ambassadors and economic actors. From an economic perspective, they drive foreign investment back to their home country, contribute to national economies through remittances, and may even leverage their relationships with host governments to influence policies in favour of their home country. They also carry with them aspects of culture that may be found alluring in host countries. The global popularity of Nigerian movies and music is by no small means due to the Nigerian and African diaspora who see in these cultural outputs aspects of their lived experiences.

This diffusion of power to non-state actors also applies to MNCs, which are becoming important actors in the foreign policies of West African states. Increasingly, West African corporations have assumed transnational dimensions, creating networks that span the sub-region. Nigeria's large market size gives its corporations an advantage, as they are more likely to establish branches across the sub-region. As will be further discussed in Chapter 5, banks such as Access, United Bank for Africa (UBA), Zenith, and Guarantee Trust Bank (GTB) have branches across the sub-region that are generating revenues, creating jobs for their host countries, and engaging in manpower development through philanthropic activities. While Nigerian companies, including Dangote Industries, feature prominently in the sub-region, MNCs like MTN of South Africa, Sonatel of Senegal, and Ecobank of Togo are increasingly prominent.

This trend in local companies investing in other West African states extends beyond Banks to include the construction sector where Dangote Industries has branches in West African states, including Senegal, Sierra Leone, and Ghana (African Business, 2020). An interview with a senior official in the Liberian ministry of foreign affairs revealed the extent to which his country's drive for FDI has been geared towards getting Dangote to set up a factory in Liberia, exposing the nature of interactions between governments and MNCs (S. Jackson, personal communication, January 27, 2020).

Also, worth noting is the role of religious actors in the foreign policies of West African states, especially in a sub-region where religion permeates every aspect of life, whether Christianity, Islam, or African Traditional Religions. In Senegal, marabouts, as Muslim religious leaders are called, are known to have assumed formal and informal roles in the conduct of foreign policy. Schreader (2001) notes the important diplomatic role these marabouts played in dousing tensions between Mauritania and Senegal during the 1989 war. In a formal capacity, Moustaffa Cisse, a religious leader, was appointed by President Diouf to the role of ambassador to Saudi Arabia and Egypt.

More recently, West African states are witnessing the expansion of charismatic Pentecostalism across the sub-region, creating cross-border networks of Christian movements with strong ties to state actors. President George Weah of Liberia and the former president of Ghana, John Atta Mills, were weekly visitors to the Synagogue Church of All Nations (SCOAN) in Nigeria, led by the late charismatic preacher, Prophet T. B. Joshua. While discussions in Chapter 6 suggest that Nigeria has been unable to leverage religious actors in the conduct of foreign policy, the cases of Senegal and Nigeria illustrate the potential role of religious actors in the foreign policies of West African states.

Nigeria's Relations with Ghana and Liberia

This section attempts to situate the relationship between Nigeria and Ghana, on the one hand, and Nigeria and Liberia, on the other, within the broader perspective of West African relational dynamics.

Nigeria–Ghana Relations

Characterized by common colonial experiences, linguistic similarities, geographical proximity, and a shared commitment to the unity of Africa, relations between Nigeria and Ghana have a chequered history – oscillating between friendship and rivalry. Save for the 1960s when these two giants of Africa's struggle for independence were in a tussle for continental leadership, relations have been mostly cordial. This is as occasional issues of economic protectionism and nationalism have often come up, creating lines of discord that are often resolved diplomatically.

It is worth recalling that being the first independent West African state in 1957 and possessing the leading economy in Africa, Kwame Nkrumah sought to position his country as the "Black Star" of Africa. As such, he championed Pan-Africanist ideals that moved for the creation of an all-African federation, with Ghana positioned as the nucleus and himself the leader (Adibe, 2001; Aluko, 1975). Without minimizing the influence of Nkrumah's ambitions on his country's foreign policy, Ghana was moved by the need to secure its independence, which hinged on the complete eradication of colonialism from the sub-region. While this aligned with the national interests of African states, Nkrumah's decision to advocate for the formation of a continental union with supranational powers pitted him against Liberia and notably Nigeria, who both preferred the formation of a loose continental union supported by strong sub-regional groupings sensitive to geographic peculiarities (Thompson, 1969; Adibe, 2001). This disagreement marked the beginning of a rivalrous post-independence relational dynamic between Nigeria and Ghana.

The ouster of Nkrumah from office in February 1966 came barely a month after the first bloody coup d'état in Nigeria's history had resulted in the assassination of its first and only prime minister, Abubakar Tafawa Balewa. This created a chain of events that rapidly degenerated into the Nigerian civil war. With Nkrumah and Balewa out of the picture, a period of normalization ensued in the relationship between both states, as successive Ghanaian leaders shelved Nkrumah's vision of a supranational continental union (Aluko, 1975). With this disagreement out of the way, a united Anglophone front was forged to counter Francophone interference in the Nigerian civil war, which negated the non-interference clause of the OAU. Beyond standing with Nigeria to challenge French interference, Ghana sought to prevent an all-out war by hosting leaders of Nigeria and Biafra in Aburi, although it sometimes faced accusations of being a biased umpire for demonstrating sympathy towards Biafra (Otoghile & Obakhedo, 2011). The Aburi Accords of January 1967 did fail to stop the civil war but marked a temporary departure from the conflictual relationship that characterized the era of Nkrumah.

The lowest point of this relationship came in the 1970s and 1980s. In late 1969, the economic downturn forced Ghanaian authorities to deport thousands of undocumented Nigerians under the Alien Compliance Order, a time when hundreds of thousands of Ghanaians were fleeing to Nigeria to seek better opportunities (see Peil, 1971; Aremu & Ajayi, 2014). When Nigeria's economic challenges started, the Shehu Shagari administration responded similarly by also expelling over 3 million undocumented West Africans, most of whom were Ghanaians, first in 1983 and again in 1985 (Adebajo, 2002; Wallis, 2010; Ayeni, 2020). While these actions strained relations between both countries, it was the bloody coup d'état carried out in Ghana by Flt. Lt. Jerry Rawlings in 1979 and his subsequent overthrow of the democratically elected government of Hilla Limann in December 1981 that drew Nigeria's steepest response. Nigeria halted the sale of oil at concessionary rates to Ghana after the first coup and the Shagari administration also refused to recognize Rawlings as the leader of Ghana.

The change in government in Nigeria that brought Ibrahim Babangida to power ushered in an important stretch in cooperative relations between Nigeria and Ghana that continued into the Obasanjo/Kufuor era. In 1988 both countries set up a joint commission to explore broad areas of bilateral cooperation, including the supply of petroleum products (Owusu, 1994). This dynamic continued into the elections of Olusegun Obasanjo and John Kufuor as presidents of Nigeria and Ghana, respectively, with the former donating police patrol vehicles to the latter to help tackle Ghana's internal security issues. Also, Obasanjo demonstrated his support for a stronger Ghanaian economy by selling oil at concessionary rates to the country.

The most significant event of this period was the Liberian civil war, as both countries invoked the 1981 ECOWAS Protocol on Mutual Assistance on Defence to justify their intervention. This was despite strong reservations from Francophone states, especially Cote d'Ivoire and Burkina Faso, who saw the intervention as support for Liberia's dictator, Samuel Doe, and an expansion of Nigeria's hegemonic ambitions. According to Adibe (2001, p. 29), "for Nigeria and Ghana, the NPFL had become an instrument both of Libya's suspicious intentions and of the Francophone bloc in West Africa." Thus, true to their commitment to seeing to the end of the civil war, Nigeria and Ghanaian officers dominated the command structure of ECOMOG, with both states also providing the bulk of resources to finance the process – a commitment, which they extended to Sierra Leone to combat the RUF insurgency.

Economically, President Kufuor capitalized on cordial relations with Obasanjo to shore up trade relations with Nigeria (Otoghile & Obakhedo, 2011). This period saw Nigerians racing to Ghana to pursue university degrees and also start businesses. Although mostly in the informal sector, trade relations between both countries skyrocketed to $528 million in 2008, and by 2010 it was estimated at $2.6 billion (Ghana Business News, 2008; Wallis, 2010). In addition, FDI from Nigerian companies soared considerably, with banks and insurance companies leading the pack (Wallis, 2010). Beyond the financial sector, other economic interactions between both countries were in the oil sector where the West Africa gas pipeline supplies oil from the Niger Delta to the Tema refinery in Ghana (Wallis, 2010). Equally, Ghana's discovery of oil in 2007 saw Nigerian companies flocking to the country to secure exploration licences. Even in tech, Nigerian companies are setting up shops in Ghana, capitalizing on stable power supply and security. For instance, Socketworks provides software to educational and government institutions in Ghana (Wallis, 2010). According to Ghana's High Commissioner to Nigeria, Rashid Bawa, the first half of 2021 witnessed Nigerian companies investing $7.07 million in the Ghanaian economy (Pulse Nigeria, 2021).

In recent years, relations appear to have been dampened by Nigeria's unilateral closure of its land borders with Benin, Niger, and Cameroun in August 2019 without forewarning authorities in Ghana. While Nigeria's objective was to stop the smuggling of goods, notably rice and petroleum products, in and out of the country, to Ghanaian traders, this was a slap on their faces given their dependence on Nigeria for supplies. The Ghana Union of Traders Association (GUTA) reacted to this decision by not only calling for a boycott of Nigerian products but also closing shops owned by Nigerians for violating the Ghana Investment Promotion Centre (GIPC) Act of 2013 (Vanguard News, 2019a; Ayeni, 2020). To Nigerian traders, the move by authorities to enforce the GIPC Act, just after the border closure, is specifically targeted at them. While such acts of protectionism are common in a sub-region where the imperatives of domestic politics compel leaders to protect local economic interests, it is unclear if these actions are specifically related to the border closure.

However, when a Ghanaian businessman demolished two buildings under construction within the premises of the Nigerian High Commission in Accra in June 2020, the Nigerian government accused its Ghanaian counterpart of hostility. Following strong condemnations from Abuja, the Ghanaian foreign ministry put out a statement promising to conduct an investigation (Ayeni, 2020). However, in no more than a month, Nigeria's Minister of Information and Culture, Lai Mohammed, put out a press release accusing Ghana of "acts of hostility" and "harassment of its citizens," citing amongst others irreciprocal acts such as the demolition incident at the high commission, which violates the Vienna Convention. Lai Mohammed also notes the deportation of Nigerians from Ghana, huge fees for resident permits, harassment of Nigerian traders, and recurrent association of Nigerians with crimes by the Ghanaian press (Premium Times, 2020).

In a statement refuting these accusations, Ghana's Minister of Information, Kojo Oppong Nkrumah, highlighted the "excellent relations" leaders of both countries share, suggesting that there is a firm commitment on both sides to maintain cordial relations (Ghana Business News, 2020).

Nigeria–Liberia Relations

Unlike the topsy-turvy dynamic that has come to characterize relations between Nigeria and Ghana, relations between Nigeria and Liberia have maintained a consistent pattern of cordiality and cooperation since the decolonization era. As discussed previously, debates surrounding the formation of a continental union, which pitted Nigeria against Ghana, placed Nigeria and Liberia in unison in terms of their shared preference for a loose intergovernmental organization. Similar to Balewa, President William Tubman saw the benefit of forging a united Africa, but was not only suspicious of Nkrumah's position but thought his idea to be rather "radical" and "impractical" (Adibe, 2001, p. 21). To counter Nkrumah's position, Tubman mobilized like-minded states, including Nigeria, to form the Monrovia group which would then go ahead to challenge critical aspects of Nkrumah's plan, including the idea of a united African military force.

Being a nation of black American settlers founded in 1847, Liberia's long-held independence allowed it to come to the aid of Nigerian nationalists who sought to evade the British by accommodating them in Liberia and giving them Liberian passports to travel outside the continent (G. Wallace, personal communication, January 22, 2020). Although the extent to which this relationship came to bear in the alliance patterns of the formative years of the OAU remains unclear, Nigeria and Liberia maintained strong bilateral ties so much so that President William Tolbert assumed a prominent role in trying to mediate the Nigerian civil war (Tarr, 1993). Thus, when Samuel Doe's bloody coup culminated in the murder of Tolbert in 1980, it was only normal that the Shehu Shagari administration join other West African states, including Cote d'Ivoire and Burkina Faso, to condemn the coup (Adebajo, 2002). Perhaps, being a democratically elected president averse to the uncon-stitutional change of government informed President Shagari's disapproving disposition towards Samuel Doe, given his similar disposition to the Jerry Rawlings coup in Ghana.

True to his disdain for Doe, which the Nigerian military hierarchy shared, Shagari not only shut down the Nigerian embassy in Monrovia, he joined Nigeria's traditional rivals – Cote d'Ivoire and Burkina Faso – who shared personal ties with William Tolbert, to adopt a deliberate policy of isolating Doe's regime (Tarr, 1993). Liberia's Foreign Minister, Baccus Matthews, was prevented from landing in Lagos to participate in the extraordinary OAU economic summit of April 1980. This was in addition to denying Liberia an invitation to attend the ECOWAS defence ministers meeting of May 1980, cancelling an AfDB meeting that was initially scheduled to hold in Monrovia, and excluding Liberia's delegation from participating in the May 1980 ECOWAS summit in Lomé (Adebajo, 2002). In reaction, Doe severed specific diplomatic relations with Nigeria, Cote d'Ivoire, and Burkina Faso, and his country's broader commitment to ECOWAS (Adebajo, 2002).

Similar to Nigeria's relations with Ghana, which improved significantly upon Gen. Babangida's ascension to power, Liberia's relationship with Nigeria equally took a positive turn, as Samuel Doe forged far-reaching political and economic ties with Nigeria, to the extent of even naming the University of Liberia's Graduate School of International Studies after Babangida, a ges-ture which he reciprocated by donating $1 million towards setting up the institution (Tarr, 1993; Adebajo, 2002). Under Babangida, Nigeria supplied Samuel Doe with machine guns and rifles to help quell the NPFL rebellion at its formative stages (Adebajo, 2002). In 1988, both countries signed a bilateral agreement on economic, scientific, and technical cooperation that has seen hundreds of Nigerians deployed to Liberia to teach and assist in the health sector (Adebajo, 2002). The following year, Nigeria helped Liberia reschedule its $30 million debt with the AfDB, invested $25 million in the Guinea–Liberia Mifergui iron ore project, and invested $4.5 million in Liberia's National Oil Corporation (Tarr, 1993; Aning, 1994; Adebajo, 2002). These are in addition to paying for the Liberian section of the Trans-African highway connecting the country with Sierra Leone, which was subse-quently named after Babangida.

While the highly personalized nature of West African politics lends its explanatory power to the decision to isolate Doe and the aversion of Francophone West African states towards the formation of ECOMOG, a debunked narrative is that it equally explains, not so much of Ghana's, but Nigeria's decision to intervene in the Liberian civil war (see Adebajo, 2002).

Certainly, with the end of the Cold War, Doe had lost his strategic value to the US, leaving him to the beck and call of Babangida. His trip to Abuja in May 1990 to seek Nigeria's intervention did propel Babangida to act. However, it will be simplistic to leave explanations for Nigeria's involvement in Liberia to Babangida and Doe's relationship. This is because, in addition to the fact that the NPFL held some Nigerians hostage and even attacked the Nigerian embassy, Abuja saw in Liberia an opportunity to bolster the country's influence, which is hinged on demonstrating credible leadership, especially in times of regional crisis (Adebajo, 2002). Regardless of one's estimation of Nigeria's motivations, this critical moment in Liberia's history marked an important turning point in its relationship with Nigeria, creating bonds of friendship that extend beyond state-to-state interaction to include cross-cultural dialogue between the people of both countries.[6]

This was evident in Nigeria's commitment to a negotiated settlement of the second Liberian civil war, which started in April 1999, just under two years after the end of the first. As part of the negotiated terms under the Accra Peace Agreement, two battalions of Nigerian soldiers deployed to Liberia as peacekeepers under the ECOWAS Mission in Liberia (ECOMIL), before being subsumed under the UN Mission in Liberia (UNMIL). Also, Charles Taylor was granted asylum in Nigeria as part of the peace agreement, before being handed over to Liberian authorities to stand trial for war crimes committed in Sierra Leone. Beyond these, Nigeria was at the helm of the rebuilding process after the election of President Ellen Sirleaf Johnson. This was mostly in the security sector where Nigerian military personnel featured in the security detail of the president and led the rebuilding process of the Armed Forces of Liberia (AFL). In July 2014, the Inaugural Session of the Nigeria–Liberia Joint Commission took place in Abuja where both countries signed agreements on cooperation in education, trade, culture, training of Liberia's foreign service officers, and mining (Ministry of Foreign Affairs, 2014).

While the signing of such joint agreements suggests the consolidation of existing relations, its emphasis on facilitating people-to-people contact through trade, technical cooperation, and capacity-building speaks to an emerging dynamic in the relationship between both countries where the scope of cooperation has expanded to also include non-state actors. For instance, the proliferation of Nigeria's cultural outputs – movies, music, churches – especially after the civil wars is creating cross-cultural dialogues between citizens of both countries that may be dubbed the "Nigerianization" of Liberia (see Chapter 7 for more on this).

As in the case of Ghana, economic interactions have seen the rise of cross-border economic activities, especially in the informal sector which is neither taxed nor monitored by the government. Within the formal sector, the last few years witnessed Nigerian banks set up branches in Liberia and Nigerian airlines plying the Monrovia–Abuja route daily. In an acknowledgement of this budding relationship, President George Weah awarded his Nigerian counterpart, President Buhari, Liberia's highest national honour: "The Grand

Cordon of the Knighthood of Venerable Order of the Pioneers" (Vanguard, 2019b).

Conclusion

This chapter set out to provide a background to the empirical section of this book, and in so doing assessed the relational dynamics of West African states and the more specific relationship between Nigeria and Ghana and Nigeria and Liberia. It reveals that except for Cape Verde, which sits off the coast of Senegal along the Pacific Ocean, all other states in the sub-region are geographically contiguous. This contiguity in geography, combined with the fact that the arbitrary partitioning of the continent placed people of similar cultures in different states, facilitates cross-cultural interactions between citizens of West African states that suggest a high level of cultural compatibility.

However, the negative effects of this colonial experiment cannot be minimized as West African states have struggled, or in some cases made no attempt, to build sustainable nations devoid of fragmentation along ethnic lines, leading to governance deficits. The implication is a security context that has evolved from the recurrent outbreak of civil wars to the worrisome situation of transnational security threats such as Islamic fundamentalist movements, narcotics trafficking, the proliferation of SALW, and maritime piracy. Addressing these security challenges requires a collaborative approach that heightens the utility of soft power, especially for regional leaders like Nigeria that, in most instances of regional crises, spearhead the mobilization of regional solutions.

This does not portend to be an arduous responsibility as a largely cooperative disposition permeates interactions between West African states, even if the Francophone–Anglophone rivalry that dominated the formative years of ECOWAS may not have completely dissipated. Certainly, Nigeria and Ghana are still locked in what can be best described as sibling rivalry, even if officials from both sides continue to maintain that relations are cordial and cooperative. While Nigerians and Liberians do not characterize their relationship in similar terms, cross-cultural contacts formed during Nigeria's intervention in the civil wars and high-level cooperation between the government of both countries suggest the existence of a cordial and cooperative relationship.

What these findings imply is that the use of soft power as a strategic approach is likely to be effective in the West African context. This is because there isn't any evidence, whether within the broader sub-region or the specific relationships between Nigeria, Ghana, and Liberia, that any rivalry exists that would warrant conscious efforts to prevent the flow of Nigeria's soft power activities into West African states. As such, it is important to interrogate the resources available to Nigeria that may likely cultivate attraction and how they have been applied towards its African policy. It is by making these determinations that we will be able to observe perceptions of Nigeria's qualities and attributes in Ghana and Liberia.

Notes

1 For more information on the operationalization of illegal trade in West Africa, see Benjamin et al. (2015).
2 Whereas Anglophone West Africa comprises Nigeria, Ghana, Sierra Leone, The Gambia, and Liberia, French West Africa comprises Cote d'Ivoire, Senegal, Mali, Niger, Guinea, Niger, Togo, and Burkina Faso.
3 La *Francophonie* symbolized the political and institutional framework of France's engagement with its former colonies, of which 23 are located in sub-Saharan Africa. Thus, in the same vein as its broader colonial goal of "civilizing" Africa, post-colonial relations were also guided by, or ingrained in, this idea (Schraeder, 2001, pp. 42 & 56).
4 The English translation for UEMOA is West African Economic and Monetary Union.
5 As of the writing of this book, Liberia, Cape Verde, Guinea Bissau, and Benin are the only West African states yet to deposit instruments of ratification (Trade Law Centre, 2021).
6 Beyond relations between both countries, this decision had far-reaching implications for West African foreign policies, as the non-intervention clause, which formed the basis of African unity, was set aside for collective security (Adibe, 2001).

References

Adebajo, A. (2002). *Liberia's civil war: Nigeria, ECOMOG and regional security in West Africa*. Lynne Rienner.

Adibe, C. E. (2001). Foreign policy decision making in Anglophone West Africa. In G. M. Khadiagala and T. Lyons (Eds.), *African foreign policies: Power and process* (pp. 15–40). Lynne Rienner Publishers.

African Business. (2020, May 16). *Africa's top 250 companies in 2020 by region*. Retrieved April 23, 2021, from https://african.business/2020/05/economy/africas-top-250-companies-in-2020-by-region/

African Development Bank. (2019). *Nigeria economic outlook*. Retrieved February 17, 2020, from www.afdb.org/en/countries-west-africa-nigeria/nigeria-economic-outlook

African Development Bank. (2020). *West Africa economic outlook 2019: Macroeconomic performance and prospects for regional integration and structural transformation in West Africa*. Retrieved December 28, 2020, from www.afdb.org/fileadmin/uploads/afdb/Documents/Publications/2019AEO/REO_2019_-_West_africa.pdf

Aluko, O. (1975). After Nkrumah: Continuity and change in Ghana's foreign policy. *Issue: A Journal of Opinion*, 5(1), 55–62.

Aning, E. K. (1994). *Managing regional security in West Africa: ECOWAS, ECOMOG, and Liberia*, Working Paper 94, Copenhagen: Centre for Development Research.

Aremu, J. O., & Ajayi, T. A. (2014). Expulsion of Nigerian immigrant community from Ghana in 1969: Causes and impact. *Developing Country Studies*, 4(10), 176–186.

Ayeni T. (2020, October 29). *Nigeria-Ghana trade tensions: Proof AfCFTA may not bring unity*. Retrieved December 28, 2020, from www.theafricareport.com/47795/nigeria-ghana-trade-tensions-proof-afcfta-may-not-bring-unity/

Bach, D. C. (1983). The politics of West African economic co-operation: CEAO and ECOWAS. *The Journal of Modern African Studies, 21*(4), 605–623.

BBC News. (2012, May 17). *Guinea-Bissau: First Ecowas peacekeeping troops arrive.* Retrieved April 20, 2021, from www.bbc.co.uk/news/world-africa-18110585

Benjamin, N., Golub, S., & Mbaye, A. A. (2015). Informality, trade policies, and smuggling in West Africa. *Journal of Borderlands Studies, 30*(3), 381–394.

Charbonneau, B. (2008). Dreams of empire: France, Europe, and the new interventionism in Africa. *Modern & Contemporary France, 16*(3), 279–295. https://doi.org/10.1080/09639480802201560

Charriere, F., & Fresia, M. (2008). West Africa as a migration and protection area. *In United Nations High Commissioner for Refugees.* Retrieved January 28, 2018, from www.refworld.org/pdfid/4a277db82.pdf

Chete, L. N., & Adewuyi, A. O.(2012). Dynamics of trade between Nigeria and other ECOWAS countries. *Accelerating growth through improved intra-African trade.* Washington DC: Brookings Africa Growth Institute .

Clapham, C. (1996). *Africa and the international system.* Cambridge University Press.

Collins, J. (2015). *Fela: Kalakuta Notes.* Wesleyan University Press.

Doss, A. (2020, September 29). *Safeguarding democracy in West Africa.* Africa Centre for Strategic Studies. Retrieved December 22, 2020, from https://africacenter.org/spotlight/safeguarding-democracy-in-west-africa/

Economic Community of West African States Declaration of Political Principles, July 6, 1991.

Economic Community of West African States Protocol on Democracy and Good Governance, December 21, 2001.

Economic Community of West African States Protocol Relating to the Mechanism for Conflict Prevention, Management, Resolution, Peacekeeping and Security, December 10, 1999.

Economic Community of West African States Revised Treaty, July 24, 1993.

Economist Intelligence Unit. (2020). *Democracy Index 2019. The Economist.* Retrieved February 22, 2020, from www.eiu.com/topic/democracy-index/

Ghana Business News. (2008). *Nigeria, Ghana record $525m trade volume.* Retrieved January 30, 2019, from www.ghanabusinessnews.com/2008/12/24/nigerianenterprises-oiling-ana%E2%80%99s-economy/

Ghana Business News. (2020, August 31). *Ghana's government refutes accusations of intimidation, mistreatment of Nigerians.* Retrieved April 29, 2021, from www.ghanabusinessnews.com/2020/08/31/ghana-government-refutes-accusations-of-intimidation-mistreatment-of-nigerians/

Golub, S. (2015). Informal cross-border trade and smuggling in Africa. In O. Morrissey, R.A. Lopez, & K. Sharma (Eds.), *Handbook on trade in development* (pp. 179–209). Cheltenham.

Hayden, C. (2012). *The rhetoric of soft power: Public diplomacy in global contexts.* Lexington Books.

International Crisis Group. (2019, December 19). *The risk of Jihadist contagion in West Africa*, Breifing No. 149. Retrieved June 13, 2020 from www.crisisgroup.org/africa/west-africa/cote-divoire-benin-burkina-faso/lafrique-de-louest-face-au-risque-de-contagion

Khadiagala, G. M. (2018, March 19). *Regional cooperation on democratization and conflict management in Africa.* Retrieved April 19, 2020, from https://carnegieendowment.org/2018/03/19/regional-cooperation-on-democratization-and-conflict-management-in-africa-pub-75769

Mangan, F., & Nowak, M. (2019). *The West Africa-Sahel connection: Mapping cross-border arms trafficking.* In Small Arms Survey. Retrieved March 28, 2020, from www.smallarmssurvey.org/fileadmin/docs/T-Briefing-Papers/SAS-BP-West-Africa-Sahel-Connection.pdf

Marc, A., Verjee, N., & Mogaka, S. (2015). *The challenge of stability and security in West Africa.* World Bank Publications.

Mbewa, D., O. (2020, August 28). *Nigeria accuses Ghana of acts of hostility, harassment of citizens.* Retrieved May 8, 2020, from https://africa.cgtn.com/2020/08/28/nigeria-accuses-ghana-of-acts-of-hostility-harassment-of-citizens/

Ministry of Foreign Affairs. (2014). *Liberia and Nigeria sign five cooperation agreements; Liberian diplomats to benefit scholarships.* Retrieved May 2, 2018, from www.mofa.gov.lr/public2/2press.php?news_id=1197&related=7&pg=sp

Mo Ibrahim Foundation. (2020). *2020 Ibrahim Index of African Governance (IIAG).* Retrieved October 8, 2020, from https://mo.ibrahim.foundation/iiag

Moderan, O. (2021, March 3). *Proliferation of armed non-state actors in the Sahel: Evidence of state failure?* Retrieved June 28, 2021, from www.ispionline.it/en/pubblicazione/proliferation-armed-non-state-actors-sahel-evidence-state

Nevin, A., & Omosomi, O. (2019). *Strength from abroad: The economic power of Nigeria's diaspora.* PWC. Retrieved March 6, 2020, from www.pwc.com/ng/en/publications/the-economic-power-of-nigerias-diaspora.html

Nye, J. S. (2004). *Soft power: A means to success in world politics.* PublicAffairs.

Nye, J. S. (2011). *The future of power.* Public Affairs Books.

Ojo, O. J. (1980). Nigeria and the formation of ECOWAS. *International Organization, 34*(4), 571–604. www.jstor.org/stable/2706513

Olukoshi, A. O. (2013, January 31). *Drug trafficking and its impact on governance in West Africa* [Paper presentation]. Centre on International Cooperation. WACD Background at the 1st meeting of the WACD in Accra, Ghana.

Otoghile, A., & Obakhedo, N. O. (2011). Nigeria-Ghana relations from 1960 to 2010: Roots of convergence and points of departure. *African Research Review, 5*(6), 131–145.

Owusu, M. (1994). *Ghana: A country study.* Library of Congress: Federal Research Division.

Palik, J., Rustad, S. Aas, & Methi, F. (2020). *Conflict trends in Africa, 1989–2019.* World Peace Research Institute Oslo (PRIO).

Peil, M. (1971). The expulsion of West African aliens. *The Journal of Modern African Studies, 9*(2), 205–229.

Premium Times. (2020, August 28). *Nigeria warns Ghana over harassment of nationals.* Retrieved April 28, 2021, from www.premiumtimesng.com/news/top-news/411290-nigeria-warns-ghana-over-harassment-of-nationals.html

Pulse Nigeria. (2021, November 10). *Ghana receives $7.07m FDI from Nigeria in 6 months.* Retrieved April 17, 2022, from www.pulse.ng/business/ghana-receives-dollar707m-fdi-from-nigeria-in-6-months/c9wmm0q

Renou, X. (2002). A new French policy for Africa? *Journal of Contemporary African Studies, 20*(1), 5–27. https://doi.org/10.1080/02589000120104035

Sangare, B. (2019). *Fulani people and Jihadism in Sahel and West African countries.* Foundation Pour La Recherche Strategique. Retrieved December 28, 2019, from www.frstrategie.org/en/programs/observatoire-du-monde-arabo-musulman-et-du-sahel/fulani-people-and-jihadism-sahel-and-west-african-countries-2019

Schraeder, P. J. (2001). *African politics and society: A mosaic in transformation.* Wadsworth Publishing Company.

Smith, E. (2020, September 29). *West Africa's new currency could now be delayed by five years.* Retrieved December 28, 2020, from www.cnbc.com/2020/09/29/west-africas-new-currency-could-now-be-delayed-by-five-years.html

Tarr, S. B. (1993). The ECOMOG initiative in Liberia: A Liberian perspective. *Issue: A Journal of Opinion, 21*(1/2), 74–83.

Thomson, A. (2010). *An introduction to African politics.* Routledge.

Thompson, B. V. (1969). *Africa and unity: The evolution of Pan-Africanism.* Longmans.

Torres, C., & Van Seters, J. (2016). *Overview of trade and barriers to trade in West Africa: Insights in political economy dynamics, with particular focus on agricultural and food trade* [Discussion Paper, No. 195]. European Centre for Development Policy Management.

Trade Law Centre. (2021, March 14). *Status of AfCFTA ratification.* Retrieved April 22, 2021, from www.tralac.org/resources/infographic/13795-status-of-afcfta-ratification.html

United Nations High Commissioner for Refugees. (2020a). *Nigeria emergency.* UNHCR. Retrieved December 4, 2020, from www.unhcr.org/uk/nigeria-emergency.html

United Nations Office on Drugs and Crime. (2013). *Transnational organized crime in West Africa: A threat assessment.* Vienna: UNODC.

United Nations Office on Drugs and Crime. (2017). *World drug report: The drug problem and organised crime, illicit financial flows, corruption, and terrorism.* Vienna: UNODC.

Vanguard News. (2019a, October 19). *Border closure: Ghana trade union votes to ban made-in-Nigeria products.* Retrieved April 29, 2021, from www.vanguardngr.com/2019/10/ghana-trade-union-votes-to-ban-made-in-nigeria-products-following-border-closure/

Vanguard News. (2019b, July 26). *Buhari receives Liberia's highest award.* Retrieved May 2, 2020, from www.vanguardngr.com/2019/07/photos-buhari-receives-liberias-highest-award/

Wallis, W. (2010). *Cautious trade between Ghana and Nigeria.* Financial Times. Retrieved November 4, 2020, from www.ft.com/content/59803f50-dbac-11df-a1df-00144feabdc0

Webber, M., & Smith, M. (2002). *Foreign policy in a transformed world.* Prentice-Hall.

World Bank. (2020a). *Population, total | Data.* https://data.worldbank.org/indicator/SP.POP.TOTL

World Bank. (2020b). *GDP per capita (current US$) - Sub-Saharan Africa | Data.* https://data.worldbank.org/indicator/NY.GDP.PCAP.CD?locations=ZG&most_recent_value_desc=true

World Data Lab. (2020). *World Poverty Clock.* Retrieved February 18, 2020, from https://worldpoverty.io/map

Xuba, M. (2021, January 14). *The Eco-currency: A new chapter for West Africa.* Future Africa Forum. Retrieved December 4, 2020, from https://futureafricaforum.org/the-eco-currency-a-new-chapter-for-west-africa/

5 Interrogating Nigeria's Soft Power Potential

Introduction

Contemplating Nigeria's soft power capabilities in West Africa begins with establishing what resources are available to it that may cause attraction. Soft power resources are the "vehicles that underlie power relationships" and stem from both domestic and international sources (Nye, 2011, p. 9). While some of these resources may be national possessions of material and symbolic character, others emerge from the values expressed in Nigeria's culture, the internal political practices it exemplifies, and the way it conducts itself externally. In a way, these resources are akin to deposits that must be tapped and converted by state actors into real power or capability (Fan, 2008).

As discussions in Chapter 4 suggest, West Africa presents a regional context that appears favourable to the exercise of soft power, given the largely cooperative relations between states in the sub-region and the nature of the challenges they confront. Also notable is that the heterogeneity of the populations of African states facilitates cross-cultural dialogues that enhance the compatibility of cultural variables. Against this backdrop, this chapter addresses the question of what potential sources of attraction exist within Nigeria that may be instrumental to the pursuit of its strategic objectives in the region. It assesses Nigeria's potential soft power resources across four analytical categories: economic, military, political, and cultural. It situates the examination of these power categories within the sub-regional and regional context, in a way that assesses their degree of excellence or importance vis-à-vis other West African states.

The chapter is divided into four sections. The first assesses the qualities and attributes of Nigeria's economy, as well as the economic activities that underlie its relations with West African states, while the second assesses Nigeria's military resources in terms of manpower, expenditure, combat proficiency, war-fighting inventory, defence policy, and military alliances. The third and fourth sections question the political and cultural dimensions of Nigeria's soft power potential, respectively.

DOI: 10.4324/9781003396628-5

Economic Potential

This section examines the qualities and attributes of Nigeria's economy, as well as the activities that underlie its economic relations with West African states. As such, it presents an overview of the Nigerian economy before exploring the nature of its economic interactions with West African states – trade, investment, and economic assistance. It also moves beyond the state to explore those transnational economic linkages that emerge from the activities of MNCs and diaspora entrepreneurs.

The Nigerian Economy at a Glance

Nigeria is a middle-income and emerging economy with a mixed blend of free market and state-interventionist policies. It is the largest economy in Africa and by far the largest in West Africa, given its GDP of $432 billion, which represents a quarter of the GDP of all sub-Saharan states put together and two-thirds of the total GDP of West African states (World Bank, 2020d). Its superior economic capability is even more glaring when one considers that the five smallest countries in the sub-region – Liberia, Sierra Leone, The Gambia, Cape Verde, and Guinea-Bissau – account for under 2% of West Africa's GDP.

Despite what may be considered an abundance of human and natural resources, Nigeria still runs an oil-dependent economy, with oil being the main source of foreign exchange earnings and government revenues, thus making the economy vulnerable to fluctuations in the world price of oil. As such, Nigeria's economy is beset by problems, including tepid growth rates, rising inflation levels, rising debt, and widespread poverty. Growth rates have declined steadily, reducing from an average of 7% between 2004 and 2014 to about 2% in the last five years (AfDB, 2019). Inflation levels have continued to rise, moving from about 8% in 2013 to 11.3% in 2019, causing the price of goods and services as well as unemployment levels to shoot up (AfDB, 2019). Poverty levels have continued to rise alarmingly, as unemployment is on the increase, moving from 14.2% in 2016 to 23.1% in 2018 (AfDB, 2019). These discomforting economic realities are in addition to a 43% decline in the flow of FDI into the country, reducing from $3.6 billion in 2017 to $1.9 billion in 2018 and dragging the regional average down by 15% (AfDB, 2019).

Consequently, the 2019 global competitiveness report released by the World Economic Forum (WEF) ranks Ghana (111th), Cape Verde (112th), and Senegal (114th) ahead of Nigeria (116th) in economic competitiveness (Schwab, 2019).[1] An in-depth look into the report suggests that apart from market size, labour market, innovative ability, and business dynamism, the majority of West African states considered in the report fare better than Nigeria. For instance, Ghana leads the region in creating an enabling business environment, whereas

Nigeria is among the worst performers (Schwab, 2019, pp. 242 & 141). While all the countries in the region perform poorly on human capital development, Cape Verde, Ghana, and the Gambia fare better than the rest. Overall, Nigeria fares badly when contrasted with Ghana, one of the fastest-growing economies in the continent, which has averaged a growth rate of 7% between 2017 and 2019. Compounding the issue of low growth is the lack of movement in other pillars of the economy such as economic stability and the strength of Nigeria's financial system. Also, Nigeria's health care system is in shambles, while other physical infrastructures such as roads and electricity remain poor with most businesses providing electricity for themselves.

Despite these, not all is as gloomy for Nigeria as the report suggests. The size of Nigeria's economy, buoyed by the size of its market, its entrepreneurial culture, and innovative capacity, especially in the realm of popular culture and tech, gives it a competitive edge over its regional neighbours, as will be elaborated below. Lagos – the financial hub of West Africa and the economic capital of Nigeria – epitomizes the country's success in this regard, accounting for more than a third of Nigeria's GDP (Pilling, 2018). Lagos is also home to the most important airport in the sub-region and its manufacturing and banking sectors lead similar sectors in other West African states. In addition, the city is known for its vibrant entrepreneurial and innovative culture that spurred the rise of Africa's largest arts, entertainment, and recreational industry, as well as one of the most advanced tech ecosystems in the continent (J. Miller, 2012, p. 6; Shapshak, 2019).

Capitalizing on deepening integration and cross-border economic linkages, Nigerian companies are making sizeable contributions to the growth and development of West African economies by creating jobs and reducing capital flights from the region. Also contributing to the growth of regional economies is the Nigerian diaspora, some of whom are students and business people capitalizing on favourable economic conditions other West African countries offer. These are salient variables that will be discussed subsequently. But first, it is important to explore the nature of economic interaction between Nigeria and other West African states.

State-Based Economic Potential

The contours of Nigeria's economic interactions with other West African states are assessed in this sub-section by discussing their trade relations and the extent to which Nigeria embodies such practices as promoting economic development, providing aid to lesser economies, and applying positive sanctions.

Trade Relations

The sheer size of Nigeria's market gives it an upper hand in the dynamics of trade within the sub-region, as it accounts for over 70% of total exports and 52% of imports (Torres & van Seters, 2016).[2] However, it operates a regional trade policy that is protectionist and marred with contradictions between trade and monetary policies. Nigeria's trade policies are geared towards protecting struggling industries, mostly in the agricultural sector, from import competition. As such, its overall trade disposition features excessive import barriers, an outright ban of select products, and poor trade facilitating measures (Golub et al., 2019; Orjinmo, 2019). For instance, agricultural products have tariffs exceeding the 35% threshold agreed upon under the framework of the ECOWAS common external tariff (CET).

This is a picture all too familiar across a sub-region where disparities in monetary, fiscal, and trade policies have shifted the dynamics of cross-border trade from formal to informal and/or illicit channels (Soulé, 2018). With protectionist policies in place, the cross-border trading of commodities has flourished through illegal channels, facilitated by the region's porous borders. As discussed previously, Nigeria's unilateral decision to close its land borders with Niger and Benin Republic to both import and export was also in a bid to curb the smuggling of banned goods into the country, particularly rice (Aljazeera, 2019).

While it remains legal for ECOWAS member states to place import restrictions on specific products, particularly agricultural, Nigeria's actions were not well-received in neighbouring states as the reaction of GUTA suggests. Benin was similarly averse to Nigeria's decision, as the border closure negatively impacted its informal sector. Informal cross-border trade along the Nigeria–Benin border makes up about 20% of the GDP of Benin and generates substantial employment, with the smuggling of gasoline alone employing over 40,000 people (Golub et al., 2019). Declaring his displeasure, President Patrice Talon of Benin criticized the border closure for bringing suffering to his people. On his part, Gaston Dossohoui, Benin's agricultural minister described the border closure as a "disaster" given its adverse effect on farmers who rely on exports to Nigeria (Onuah, 2019). On the contrary, Niger sought to mollify the Nigerian government by imposing restrictions on the export of rice to Nigeria.

In as much as the ban has been lifted, the Nigerian government is categorical on the need for the country to end the subsidization of the sub-region. Nigeria's decision to strong-arm its neighbours into curbing the illegal flow of goods into the country, although culminating in an agreement "to set up a [regional] joint border patrol force to tackle smuggling," remains indicative of Nigeria's overbearing economic influence in the region and the extent to which access to the country's huge market affects the dynamic of regional politics (Onuah, 2019). More importantly, it is indicative of the mercantilist nature of economic interactions at the sub-regional level.

Economic Aid and Technical Assistance

Driven by its leadership aspirations and the outcome of the civil war, Nigerian political elites saw regional integration not only as a pathway to growth and development but as a means to circumvent French influence in the sub-region. But to achieve this objective, it had to overcome France-backed opposition from Francophone West African states. This reality informed a foreign policy approach that emphasized the cultivation of cordial relations with other states in the region. Oil was key to this objective, as it proved a salient tool to build and nurture relations with West African states by providing the revenues to drive an ambitious policy of economic aid and technical assistance. This even took the form of selling oil to West African states at concessionary rates, especially in the face of the energy crisis of the 1970s. For instance, in 1975 Nigeria and Senegal entered an agreement to supply the latter with over 2 million tons of crude oil at concessionary rates (Aluko, 1976).

Also, economic assistance to less endowed African states through loans, financing of infrastructural projects, and development assistance became Nigeria's preferred tools of economic statecraft as the case of Liberia discussed in Chapter 4 already indicates. In 1972 an interest-free loan of $1.2 million repayable over 25 years was granted to the Republic of Benin (Tella, 2018). Nigeria also revamped the Porto-Novo highway for the sum of $1.7 million and assisted the Beninese government with $2.5 million to pay outstanding salaries of civil servants (Tella, 2018). Nigeria principally finances the ECOWAS Bank for Investment and Development, accounting for 60% of the bank's equity (Amuwo, 2014). In 1976, it established a "self-sustaining revolving fund" known as the Nigerian Trust Fund (NTF) domiciled with the AfDB – a fund that was worth $151million after its initial capital of $81 million was replenished with $71 million in 1981 (Ministry of Foreign Affairs (MFA), 2013, p. 4). This was specifically designed to "boost the development efforts of low-income regional member countries (RMCs) that require concessional financing to grow their economies and stabilize their social conditions" (MFA, 2013, p. 6).

With the end of the oil boom in the mid-1980s came domestic economic challenges that compelled Nigeria to modify its economic diplomacy strategy. Contrary to cash gifts which policymakers had come to see as wasteful, technical assistance was seen as a "more durable and visible form of aid" (Adebanwi, 2011, p. 23). Consequently, the NTAC was set up in 1987.[3] Thus far, over 6,000 volunteers, some of whom are medical doctors, journalists, teachers, engineers, and artisans have been deployed to over 40 countries in the global south, all at Nigeria's expense (Directorate of Technical Aid Corps (DTAC), personal communication, July 10, 2019).

Similarly affected by Nigeria's dwindling economic fortune was the NTF. Here also, Nigeria moved from providing low-interest loans to adopting a policy of technical cooperation. An agreement with the AfDB in 2014, dubbed the Technical Cooperation Agreement (TCA), allowed for the creation of a specialized technical assistance fund, known as the Nigerian Technical Cooperation Fund (NTCF).[4] As of May 2017, 93 projects were approved under the scheme, 22% of which are located in West African states (AfDB, 2017). Although Nigeria's foreign aid commitments have reduced significantly, it still provides financial support to West African governments as will be discussed further in Chapter 6.

Non-State-Based Economic Potential

This section highlights key potential soft power resources that fall within the purview of non-state actors – MNCs and diaspora entrepreneurs – given the transnational nature of their activities.

Nigerian MNCs

In a multi-actor regional context, Nigerian MNCs are active participants in the dynamic of economic relations. The last two decades witnessed the expansion of Nigerian companies across West Africa, some of them rising to rank amongst the most admired brands in the continent. For instance, Dangote Cement operates in nine African countries, including three in West Africa – Ghana, Sierra Leone, and Senegal (Dangote Cement, 2020). This is in addition to companies like Jumia (Ghana and Ivory Coast), Glo (Ghana), and Star Beer (Ghana and Sierra Leone) which operate in the sub-region (Adeoye, 2020; Gloworld, 2020; The Mail & Guardian, 2016). Within the banking sector, Nigerian banks also feature prominently in West African states. For instance, Access Bank has branches in Gambia, Sierra Leone, and Ghana, while the UBA has branches in Cote d'Ivoire, Ghana, Liberia, Senegal, and Guinea (Access Bank PLC, 2020; UBA, 2020a). The same is the case for GTB, Keystone, First Bank, and Zenith Bank.

These companies, mostly in the financial sector, operate in a network environment where contributions to the economic well-being and man-power development of host nations, engagement in humanitarian ventures, and adherence to ethical and social responsibilities facilitate economic, political, and cultural relations that influence the dynamics of regional politics (Melissen, 2005; Bell, 2016). By introducing new forms of financial products, expanding regional banking networks, and participating in joint supervision mechanisms, Nigerian banks deepen the banking sector of host nations and contribute to their economy. For instance, the UBA foundation champions the cause of improving literacy by building a culture of reading among African youths. In February 2019 it organized an essay competition in Senegal, which saw the best students win between $2,000 and $3,500 (UBA, 2020b). Similarly, the Aliko Dangote Foundation, the philanthropic arm of the Dangote Group, has expended over $100 million championing causes addressing issues such as pervasive poverty and malnutrition in children (Dangote Industries, 2020; Nsehe, 2019).

These practices tend to generate pull effects that progressively translate into influence. Already, Nigerian companies are some of the most admired brands on the continent. Based on "financial performance and consumer admiration," African Business Magazine ranks Nigerian conglomerate,

Dangote Industries, as the most admired brand in the continent (2019). Out of the seven West African brands in the top 25, four are Nigerian – Jumia, Star Beer, Glo, and Dangote – while Ghana's Kasapreko drinks, Ivory Coast's Sivop, and Benin Republic's Nanawax make up the remaining three (African Business, 2019). This recognition also extends to the banking sector where five Nigerian banks – GTB, UBA, Access Bank, Zenith Bank, and Fidelity Bank – feature in the top 25 most admired financial brands on the continent (African Business, 2019; Platt, 2019).

Diaspora Entrepreneurs

Unofficial estimates reveal that about 15 million Nigerians are in the diaspora, however, official estimates put this figure at 1.7 million (Nevin & Omosomi, 2019, p. 5). As cited previously, PwC reported in 2019 that of the top seven destinations of Nigerian emigrants in 2017, which include the US, UK, and Italy, there are three West African nations – Niger (100,000), Ghana (70,000), and Benin (50,000) (Nevin & Omosomi, 2019, p. 5). These individuals forge transnational networks, which facilitate not just economic but also cross-cultural dialogue. Their contributions to the development of Nigeria's economy through remittances have been addressed severally (see Lampert, 2014; Olatuyi et al., 2013), but the same cannot be said of their contributions to the economy of their host country and how these may translate into the kind of influence that may be instrumental to Nigeria's foreign policy objectives.

Although the Nigerian diaspora is spread across the sub-region, Ghana is particularly illustrative of the rising influence of Nigerian diaspora entrepreneurs. Akpah Prince, a columnist for the popular Ghanaian blog, Ghanaweb, was the first to point out that Nigerians occupy leading positions in most MNCs in Ghana (Ghanaweb, 2015). He notes that these individuals, including the likes of Eze (Dr) Chukwudi Jude Ihenet, Adeyemi Adetuwo, and Dele Momodu, "play a big part in the Ghanaian economy." Nigerians feature prominently in the informal sector as well, especially in retail and wholesale businesses.

Also contributing to the economy of West African states are affluent Nigerians who in an attempt to escape the flaws of Nigeria's educational system seek tertiary education in neighbouring countries and beyond. What is Nigeria's loss is a gain to neighbouring states that have seen tangible economic benefits from the inflow of Nigerian students. Figures from 2017 indicate that 9,172 Nigerian students are studying degree-awarding courses in Ghanaian tertiary institutions, making up over 70% of the foreign student population (Kamran et al., 2019). In 2014, Sanusi Lamido Sanusi, the former governor of Nigeria's Central Bank, reported that Nigerians expend an estimated $1 billion annually in tuition fees in Ghana, injecting much-needed funds into the Ghanaian economy and its educational system (Fatunde, 2014).

The extent to which these non-state actors have served the purpose of Nigeria's foreign policy will be addressed in Chapter 6, however, it is important to now turn to Nigeria's military to evaluate its attractive potential.

Military Potential

This section attempts an appraisal of Nigeria's military. It discusses the strength of Nigeria's military relative to other West African States by evaluating the quality and competence of the Armed Forces of Nigeria (AFN). It also assesses the combat proficiency of the AFN as well as the nature of security alliances Nigeria has with other West African states.

Relative Military Strength

In a sub-region where most states have modest economic resources to boost military spending, Nigeria has invested significant resources to improve its military capabilities, especially in the face of ongoing counter-insurgency operations in the northeast. Consequently, Nigeria's military resources are far superior to other West African states. Also, its specialized military training institutions attract officers from across the sub-region. However, its industrial base, like all other West African states, is heavily reliant on the West and China for weapons and non-lethal products.

The AFN, which emerged in 1956 from the Royal West African Frontier Force, ranks after Egypt, Algeria, and South Africa as the fourth most powerful military in the continent. This is predicated on a defence budget that almost equals the combined budgets of all other West African states. This is as Nigeria's military expenditure, as a percentage of GDP, has witnessed a downward trend since the 1980s, reducing from about 2% in 1980 to under 1% in 2019 (Stockholm International Peace Research Institute (SIPRI), 2020). Nonetheless, a defence budget of $1.9 billion in 2019 places it as the second-largest military spender in sub-Saharan Africa after South Africa, which expended $3.5 billion (SIPRI, 2020). From 2011 to 2019, it consistently led the West African sub-region in military spending, distancing regional rivals like Ghana and Cote d'Ivoire that operated a defence budget of $233 and $536 million, respectively, in 2019.

In consonance with its defence budget, Nigeria's 120,000 active personnel surpasses those of its West African counterparts, with countries like Cote d'Ivoire, Ghana, and Burkina Faso boasting 25,500, 15,500, and 11,200 active personnel, respectively (Global Firepower, 2020). The same is the case with its military equipment as the AFN is the most equipped and sophisticated military in West Africa, being able to field a spectrum of third- and fourth-generation land, air, and sea weapons. For instance, the Nigerian Air Force has an inventory of 200 to 250 aircraft of diverse use, including 16 Alpha Jet E trainer variants, 20 Alpha Jets, F-7NI (Chengdu J-7) light fighters, FT-7NI trainer variant, Chinese-manufactured CH3-UAVs, 3 C-130

Hercules, 13 Aero L-39, 10 Mi-24Vs as well as 20 Mi-35Ps and Mi-35Ms. Whereas Mali, Burkina Faso, and Niger only have 64, 34, and 33 aircraft, respectively, in their arsenal (Global Firepower, 2020; International Institute for Strategic Studies, 2020).

Beyond its superior manpower and warfighting inventory, Nigeria is also reputed for its prestigious tri-service military training institutions such as the Nigerian Defence Academy (NDA), the Armed Forces Command and Staff College (AFCSC), and the National Defence College (NDC). Whereas the NDA is known for its cadet or officer entry programmes, the AFCSC is a mid-level training college set up in 1976 to "produce operational-level military officers of the highest professional standard as well as to ensure standardization of staff duties" (AFCSC, n.d.). The NDC, which represents the highest military training institution in the country, is considered "a centre of excellence for peace support operations training at the strategic level in West Africa" (NDC, n.d.). As will be discussed in Chapter 6, these institutions have seen military officers from West African states enrol for various courses, including officers from the Ghanaian Armed forces (AFCSC, n.d., A. Yanet, personal communication, July 18, 2019).

Despite Nigeria's superior military capabilities, it is only a regional power because it cannot project force globally and possesses an operational ability limited to the defence of its territory and occasional interventions in peacekeeping. Notwithstanding its size and relative superiority, the AFN's combat proficiency is questioned by some observers who have noted that the AFN, reputed for championing the cause of regional security since the 1990s, is unable to deal with violent extremist groups upending the lives of people in northeast Nigeria and the Lake Chad Basin states of Niger, Chad, and Cameroun (see Omeni, 2015).

Nature of Military Alliances

Driven by the belief that an unstable and insecure region poses a national security threat, Nigeria has sought to maintain cordial military relations with West African states. As Festus Wasa, a deputy director at Nigeria's defence ministry points out, "your neighbour is your first line of defence," as such it is imperative to adopt a collaborative approach to address security challenges confronting the region (personal communication, July 3, 2019). Accordingly, he notes that Nigeria's relations with other West African states are characterized by "bilateral and multilateral cooperation in the areas of exchange of expertise, training, joint patrol, joint exercise and mutual understanding on sale and purchase of military equipment" (personal communication, July 3, 2019). This is in tandem with the Nigerian National Defence Policy (NNDP) of 2017, which lays down the principles undergirding Nigeria's security relations with West African states (Federal Republic of Nigeria (FRN, 2017).[5]

In addition to protecting the interests of the country, Nigeria's leadership aspiration in Africa is at the core of its national defence policy. Placing Africa at the centre of the country's external intervention, the NNDP emphasizes the need to strengthen the capacity of the AFN to participate "in complex political emergencies, including humanitarian assistance," which may be under the auspices of the UN, AU, ECOWAS, and other alliances (FRN, 2017). It also emphasizes the importance of intelligence sharing with other nations of the world, while reiterating the country's commitment to enhancing international peace and stability. Furthermore, it de-emphasizes the use of force, places human security concerns at the heart of its national security objectives, and mandates the AFN to participate in disaster relief operations, although this function is quite specific to the domestic environment and makes no mention of such disasters that may arise outside the shores of Nigeria.

Consequently, the AFN is involved in several bilateral and multilateral military alliances at the regional and sub-regional levels aimed at maintaining peace and stability. Under the framework of the Community of Sahel-Saharan States (CEN-SAD), which includes 13 West African states, the AFN collaborates with others to combat terrorist activities and intrastate conflicts in the Sahel. This security commitment was reinforced in the CEN-SAD defence ministers meeting held in Egypt in 2016 where the Sharm-el-Sheikh Declaration of 2009, designed to enhance "cooperation in the field of anti-terrorism and security," was adopted (UN Economic Commission for Africa, n.d.). In addition to CEN-SAD, Nigeria is an important member of the Multinational Joint Task Force (MNJTF), which includes Benin as well as the Lake Chad basin states – Cameroun, Chad, and Niger. Aimed at pooling resources from all member states to combat Jihadist groups, this alliance, which started in late 2014, has seen member states commit over 8,000 troops to the joint task force (ICG, 2020). Other military alliances featuring Nigeria, with regional security implications, are the ECOWAS Standby Force, African Union Standby Force, and the Islamic Military Counter Terrorism Coalition.

Finally, in furtherance of Nigeria's objective to promote peace, security, and stability in Africa, the AFN has participated in peacekeeping missions such as ECOMIB, AU/UN Hybrid Mission in Darfur, UNMIL, Multidimensional Integrated Stabilization Mission in Mali, and ECOWAS Mission in the Gambia (ECOMIG). As the next section will expatiate, these alliances are in tandem with an external disposition that prioritizes multilateral solutions to regional challenges.

Political Potential

This section seeks to unearth the soft power potential embedded in Nigeria's domestic and foreign policy. From an analytical standpoint, they are two sides of the same coin, in the sense that they are both located under the authority of the state. As states strive to maintain internal political order, they also have to look towards their external environment to fend off threats and forge partnerships.

Domestic Sources: Internal Political Values

Similar to the US, at least structurally, Nigeria operates a federal system of government where executive, legislative, and judicial powers are located at the federal and state levels. A local government system that operates autonomously, to a limited extent, and handles constitutionally enshrined responsibilities makes up the three levels of Nigeria's governmental structure. This system of political organization was adopted to mitigate the negative consequences of the amalgamation of the southern and northern protectorates that gave birth to the Nigerian state. Thus, federalism and, by implication, the federal character principle enshrined in the 1999 Constitution of the FRN were conceived to keep the country together, while mitigating tensions that may arise from sentiments of ethnic and religious marginalization.[6]

Operating in parallel with the federal character principle is the practice of power rotation, which functions as an unwritten agreement amongst the political elites within the "main" political parties. It is operationalized through the practice of "zoning," where political offices – elected or otherwise – are distributed along ethno-geographic lines across local, state, and federal levels to create a semblance of ethnic and religious inclusion. For what it is worth, these ordering principles have held the country together; however, federalism, as practised in Nigeria, remains a flawed exercise and, consequently, presents structural deficiencies that are today the bane of Nigeria's sociopolitical progress.

"Many of Nigeria's internal conflicts are manifestations of the structural and political flaws of its federalist framework" correctly notes the ICG in its report on Nigeria's federal experiment (ICG, 2006). Under the guise of upholding the federal character principle, Nigeria's political elites have gradually entrenched prebendalism into the fabric of sociopolitical practice (see Lewis, 1996; Demarest, 2020). Moreover, the need to ensure an equitable spread of political appointments invites the formation of extremely large and expensive government and the appointment of people whose only qualification for public office stems from their state of origin, a practice, which further enfeebles Nigeria's already weak institutions. By implication, Nigeria's democracy is at best dysfunctional and worst, moribund, both in terms of political practice and the model of governance it exhibits.

Nigeria has had a chequered political history characterized by an alternation between civil and military rule. The fourth republic that began in May 1999 brought an end to 29 years of intermittent military dictatorship and episodic democratic experiments – a move that signalled the embrace of such democratic values as the rule of law, political openness, and respect for civil liberties. Certainly, by way of political stability and international credibility, 21 years of sustained democratic consolidation have brought gains to Nigeria. The peaceful conduct of the 2015 presidential elections and the orderly transfer of power even led some to assert that the consolidation process may be nearing completion (Adogamhe, 2016). However, the 2019 general elections appear to have eroded these gains, as Nigeria returned to the old practices of militarizing elections, massive rigging, vote-buying, and violence – all of which raise questions about the country's ability to advance towards the path of good governance (Jannah, 2019).

While the conduct of elections and the peaceful transition that accompanies this process have enhanced Nigeria's credibility and legitimacy, the country remains a fledgling democracy where 21 years of constitutional democracy have done little to alter the authoritarian habits of the military era. Despite the regular organization of elections and the existence of a relatively safe space for free speech and association, adherence to democratic norms remains conditioned on political exigencies. Likewise, constitutionalizing consociationalism has engendered the politicization of ethnicity, thereby entrenching sectional loyalties to the detriment of citizen upliftment (Agwu, 2009; Bach, 2007).

Certainly, this domestic political context has negatively impacted governance, notably, the security environment where security challenges such as inter-communal violence, insurgency, and banditry are only worsening. While the country's Middle Belt region grapples with a decade-old conflict between nomadic herdsmen and farmers, the threat of Boko Haram persists in north-eastern Nigeria where 110 children were abducted from their school in Dapachi, Yobe State in February 2018 (Human Rights Watch (HRW, 2019). What emerged as a purely domestic security challenge has today grown to become Nigeria's main security and foreign policy preoccupation, resulting in joint military operations with neighbouring states. In fact, in June 2018, Boko Haram claimed responsibility for two suicide bombings in Adamawa state, costing the lives of 84 people. In 2018 alone, about 1,200 people were killed and 200,000 displaced as a result of the activities of Boko Haram and its affiliates (HRW, 2019).

With access to power virtually the same as access to the country's resources, corruption is endemic as a web of greedy politicians takes advantage of their position to exploit the state for personal aggrandizement. As the Corruption Perception Index released by Transparency International in 2019 reveals, Nigeria ranks amongst the most corrupt countries in the world placing 146 out of 180 countries, a decline from 2018 when it ranked 144th (Transparency International, 2020).

Even where the rule of law is concerned, the country's human rights profile calls into question its commitment. State and federal authorities are all too accustomed to use state security laws to arrest and persecute journalists and activists who appear critical of government policies and actions. Journalists such as Agba Jalingo, Jones Abiri, and Stephen Kefas were imprisoned at various times in 2019 at the behest of state governors (Committee to Protect Journalists 2019a, 2019b; Okonkwo, 2019). More recently, a string of campaigns by civil society organizations exposed the practice of arbitrary arrest, detention, and torture by security agencies such as the Police Special Anti-Robbery Squad and Department of State Services (DSS) (HRW, 2019). Nigeria's Vice President Yemi Osinbajo was even compelled to fire the Director-General of the DSS, Lawal Daura, for unlawfully invading and sealing the National Assembly, which was seen by most people as the culmination of a continuous practice of disregard for the rule of law.

It is against the backdrop of this unflattering domestic political profile that scholars have argued in favour of a national interest that prioritizes nation-building, nationalism, and domestic consolidation as against its outward orientation that prioritizes international politics (Agwu, 2009).

International Sources: Foreign Policy

Nigeria's foreign policy since independence has been consistent in its Afrocentric posture, despite the alternation between military and civilian administrations and the disproportionate influence these administrations exert on matters of foreign policy. The number of resident diplomatic missions Nigeria has in the continent compared to other regions in the world – 46 in Africa, as against 52 in other parts of the world – is a clear indication of the pre-eminence of the region in its external priorities. At the core of Afrocentrism is the advancement of the interest and well-being of African states and the entire black race over the national interests of individual states (Itugbu, 2017). These are in addition to the realist aspiration of projecting the country as a benign hegemon and an unbridled leader by demonstrating leadership, in what is widely referred to as "Pax Nigeriana" or "Nigerian peace" (Adebajo, 2002; Warner, 2016; Oshewolo, 2019a).

Pax Nigeriana has seen Nigeria take economic, military, and political actions to advance the interest of Africans in intra- and extra-continental affairs. In practical terms, this has taken the form of leading a unified African voice on global issues, acting as a spokesperson in sub-regional, regional, and international fora, participating in peace missions, providing economic assistance, and championing the cause for regional and sub-regional integration (Oshewolo, 2019b). All of these efforts are informed by the country's foreign policy objectives, which emphasize liberal political values such as cooperation, good neighbourliness, friendship, adherence to the rule of law, and social justice. However, as Warner (2016) rightly observes, the country continues to fail to live up to some of these values, especially in the domestic realm where it is lacking in relational authority. Equally notable is the country's commitment to multilateralism, a principle that Nigeria has embraced since early discussions in the late 1950s and early 1960s between the ideologically divided Monrovia and Casablanca groups on the framework of African integration (Oladimeji & Kirmanj, 2015).

Another exemplar of this commitment is the leadership role Nigeria played in the formation of the OAU and its transition to the AU. Not only were the final details on the structure and shape of the OAU ironed out in Lagos, the underlying principles of the organization reflected Nigeria's ideas, predilections, and imprimatur, in a move thought necessary by Prime Minister Tafawa Balewa to enhance the legitimacy of the country's foreign policy (Ogunbadejo, 1980). As Oshewolo (2019c) notes, the OAU offered Nigeria the podium to broaden its diplomatic reach and influence the outcomes of important events in the continent. The successful campaign against white minority rule in South Africa, the establishment of the AfDB, the New Partnership of African Development (NEPAD), and the African Peer Review Mechanism are some outcomes that have resulted from Nigeria's multilateralist disposition and leadership.

At the regional level, ECOWAS emerged from a Nigerian initiative conceived to advance its policy of good neighbourliness and friendship in West Africa. Nigeria saw ECOWAS as a means to circumvent the influence of France, which had supported the secessionist Biafra movement during the Nigerian civil war, while also deepening integration in the region to boost growth and development (Adogamhe, 2016). Beyond Nigeria's role in setting up the framework of this institution, Nigeria, on several occasions, assumed the leadership position of ECOWAS and hosted both regional and continental leaders at summits and meetings in the country.

Through these multilateral fora, Nigeria has been notably active in efforts to ensure peace and stability across the continent. When civil wars began to emerge in West African states, first in Liberia, Nigeria mobilized sub-regional support for the formation of ECOMOG and ECOMIL. Similar interventions in Guinea-Bissau (1998), Sierra Leone, and Cote d'Ivoire demonstrate Nigeria's commitment to regional peace and security. Adogamhe (2016) estimates that Nigeria expended about $12 billion on the peace process in Liberia and Sierra Leone alone, and as of 2014, was spending over $2 million supporting post-conflict African states. Beyond West Africa, Nigeria's intervention in the Chadian civil war, which took place from 1979 to 1981, is particularly notable. Although Nigeria's initial intervention was unilateral, it later joined other African states to maintain a peacekeeping force in Chad. Equally, it was part of the peacekeeping mission in Darfur and the AU observation mission to Rwanda. Under the auspices of the UN, Nigeria also participated in peace missions to Somalia, Western Sahara, Congo, and South Sudan (UN, 2019).

Despite its inherent internal democratic and governance deficits, Nigeria has not shied away from embracing its aspirational goals of promoting liberal democratic norms in the continent. Although duplicitous, this effort was upheld by the country's civilian as well as military administrations. In 2002, within the framework of NEPAD, Nigeria pushed for the adoption of the declaration on democracy and corporate governance, in a bid to enhance the standard of governance in the region and inspire confidence in foreign donors and investors (Adogamhe, 2016). Nigeria also provided monetary and logistical support to the democratic processes in countries like Guinea-Bissau,

Mali, and Burkina Faso; in a move that aligns with its commitment to promote democracy within the continent.

Cultural Potential

The partitioning of the African continent following the Berlin conference of 1884 created culturally diverse African societies, comprising different expressions of culture – folklore, arts, crafts, religion, movies, and music – that are transmissible from people to people and nations to nations, transcending space and time, and capable of affecting political outcomes if shared and compatible (Paek, 2004). With modern forms of communication in place and the accompanying increase in cultural contacts among African citizens, more people are increasingly aware of and exposed to the cultures of others. This section explores those expressions of Nigeria's culture that are likely to be attractive to West Africans.

Material Culture

With a population of over 200 million people cut across 250 ethnic groups and speaking 529 indigenous languages, Nigeria is one of the most culturally diverse nations in the world (World Bank, 2020). While the Hausa/Fulani, Yoruba, and Igbo represent the three major ethnic groups, relatively smaller groups such as the Ijaw, Tiv, and Ibibio exist amongst a large number of others. These diverse cultural groupings under a centralized federal authority have created a mosaic of cultural expressions and symbolic markers that distinguishes the Nigerian state from many others.

Scholars of social psychology have long explored the link between national symbols and intra-individual psychological responses (see Billig, 1995; Butz, 2009). Billig (1995) argues that national symbols can have two types of effects on individuals – conscious and unconscious – depending on their level of exposure to these symbols. Mostly serving the purpose of "symbolic reminders of nationhood," especially amongst people of similar nationality, national symbols are said to have the unconscious effects of increasing national identification and intra-group unity, however, the extent to which these symbols affect individuals from out-groups remains unclear (Butz, 2009, p. 800).

Like every country in the world, Nigeria has a repertoire of national symbols that were conceived at independence. These are the Nigerian national flag, coat of arms, national anthem, national pledge, and national flower (*Costus spectabilis*). They are symbols of national unity that symbolize the sovereignty and dignity of the country, as well as a spirit of oneness and patriotism amongst its diverse population. For instance, the green and white colours on the national flag allude to a resource-rich and peaceful country (Flagmakers, n.d.).

However, as the spate of ethnic conflicts and deep feelings of marginalization within the country suggests, these symbols have done little to inspire a feeling of oneness in the Nigerian people, at least domestically. Internationally, one may assume that they create familiarity with and some sense of knowledge of Nigeria, especially with the country's repeated appearances in regional and global sporting events such as the African Cup of Nations, FIFA World Cup, and the Olympics where these symbols are showcased. The playing of national anthems in global sporting events is not just rituals, they are also marks of identity like a brand does for a private company. Nigeria's consistent participation in sporting events has led to its national anthem featuring repeatedly on rankings of the best national anthems of participating countries (Telegraph Sport, 2018; Kerr-Dineen, 2016).

Colonialism introduced Nigerians to the English language and over a century later it remains the official language of the country and mode of instruction in all schools. Also, beyond official circles, it is the prevalent form of communication for most Nigerians. Given the predominance of the three main ethnic groups, there is no gainsaying that Hausa, Igbo, and Yoruba languages are also popular forms of communication, however, the English-based Nigerian pidgin is not only popular in Nigeria with over 75 million speakers but has assumed transnational dimensions (BBC News, 2017). As the BBC reports, it is widely spoken in Nigeria, Sierra Leone, Cameroun, Ghana, and Equatorial Guinea, making it one of the "most widely-spoken languages" in West Africa (BBC News, 2017).[7] Although different versions exist, they are largely mutually intelligible, granting the Nigerian variant a much wider appeal, given its dissemination through Nigerian music and movies.

Nigeria is also known for its beautiful lands, amazing landmarks, and well-developed arts and crafts. From tin and iron smelting, bronze, copper, and gold carvings to leather products, textiles, and fabrics, Nigerians have over the years developed a variety of crafts. These handicrafts, which are quite popular in rural and urban areas, are made through local raw materials and are to an extent specific to ethnic realities. For instance, the northern city of Kano is known as the centre of weaving due to its rich textile outputs, while pottery is often associated with the people of Ilorin and Ikot Ekpene.

The UN Educational, Scientific, and Cultural Organization's list of World Heritage sites features two Nigerian cultural landmarks: the Osun-Osogbo Grove and the Sukur Cultural Landscape (UNESCO, n.d). These are just two amongst others – the Lok Ikom Monoliths, the Ancient Kano City Walls, the Ogbunike Caves, and Oke Idanre Hills – that embody deep historical, cultural, and spiritual significance. The Osun-Osogbo grove, which is the sacred and mysterious home of the Yoruba goddess of fertility known as Osun reflects the essence of Yoruba culture (Adebowale, 2018). Its annual cultural ritual in Nigeria draws thousands of spectators from around the world.

While these material elements of culture will be revisited in Chapter 6, where I explore their utility in Nigeria's foreign policy, it is important to now turn to the popular aspects of Nigeria's culture.

Popular Culture

This sub-section assesses four elements of popular culture: Nollywood, music, iconic personalities, and the budding phenomenon that is charismatic Pentecostalism.

Nollywood: Nigeria's Movie Industry

Movies reflect the popular culture of a state and Nollywood, the second-largest movie industry in the world in terms of output, stands today as the biggest export medium for Nigeria's diverse culture (Dekie et al., 2015; Orewere, 1992). Described as the most dynamic form of visual media in post-colonial Africa, Nollywood provides narratives about the lived experiences of Nigerians and is deeply rooted in the cultural traditions and social texts of Nigeria's diverse ethnic groupings. In a similar vein, Nigerian movies tell tales of urban and rural community life using African costumes, idiomatic expressions, proverbs, cultural displays, and artefacts in ways that are appealing and relatable to diverse ethnic and religious African populations. As Serge Noukoué argues, African communities have long sought "for characters, tales, and stories that look like them," unlike the Western movies that dominated African screens from the pre-colonial era to the late 1990s (cited in Husseini, 2016).

Nollywood began in 1992 with the release of *Living in Bondage*, and since then it has transformed the media landscape across the region, emerging as one of the most dynamic forms of media in the history of Africa (Onuzulike, 2007). Mostly distributed through videocassettes, CDs, and, in recent times, cinemas, at least locally, innovations in digital technology in the form of satellite and online streaming platforms have facilitated its distribution to millions of Africans both within and outside the region. This is in addition to the regular organization of events like the Nollywood Week Festival and Roadshow Project, which are avenues used to project the best of the industry to global audiences and create transnational partnerships.[8]

It is estimated that over 2,000 Nigerian films are produced each year in three indigenous languages – Igbo, Hausa, and Yoruba – as well as in English (PwC, 2018; Haynes, 2005). Although Nollywood does not compare with Hollywood in terms of global appeal and reach, it still dominates movie content in the region and is the preferred choice of movies for a rich diaspora community who view Nollywood as a connection to their African heritage (J. Miller, 2012). As Larkin (2008) remarks, "the strength of this industry has turned Nigeria into one of the largest film producers in the world" (p. 174). While it does not compare to Hollywood and Bollywood in terms of value, the industry is worth an estimated $658 million (Akande & Brown, 2018). Although it remains unclear how much Nollywood generates in Africa and the full extent of its popularity due to the lack of scientific studies, in 2017 it generated $12 million in box office revenues just within Nigeria (PwC, 2018).

Beyond the sheer popularity and reach of the industry, it exposes the innovative skills of urban Africans in creating new forms of cultural production and dissemination that is evident in the emergence of online streaming platforms such as iRokotv and EbonyLife TV. Not only has Nollywood spurred the emergence of international partnerships amongst actors, producers, and marketers within the region, but it has also fostered relationships between industry practitioners and national governments. In what Yvonne Nelson, a Ghanaian actress, interprets as Nigeria's love and acceptance of foreigners, Ghanaians, over the last two decades, are active participants in Nollywood, collaborating in production and marketing (Akande & Brown, 2018). Ghanaian actors and actresses feature repeatedly in Nollywood movies, as do Nigerians in their movies, in what is suggestive of cultural compatibility, unity, and deepening integration.

One of the implications of the transnationalization of Nollywood is that Nigerian actors and actresses are now household names in the region, with enhanced access to national governments and prominent citizens. Genevieve Nnaji, Richard Mofe Damijo, and Desmond Elliot are among other popular artists that are today treated as cultural ambassadors. On two occasions, former President Yaya Jammeh of the Gambia invited notable Nollywood actors and actresses to The Gambia, in recognition of their contribution to propagating the ideals of Pan-Africanism (K. O. Kanayo, personal communication, July 30, 2019; F. Duru, personal communication, August 8, 2019). In the words of Jammeh, "Nollywood actors are Africa's Ambassadors" that should consider themselves Gambians (cited in CGTN Africa, 2015).

No doubt Nollywood has propagated positive aspects of Nigeria's societal norms and values that are in congruence with those of other African societies, shoring up the reputation of the country and providing a useful tool for the pursuit of the country's cultural, political, and economic objectives. However, not everyone is enamoured by the industry. As J. Miller (2012) notes, Nollywood's popularity "provokes complaints of oversaturation of local screens" in some African states, a point of view that this book corroborates in Chapter 7. As perceived continental ambassadors, the sight of Nollywood actors and actresses cosying up with former President Jammeh, an authoritarian leader, did irk some Gambians who wondered why they are associating with a known dictator (Okafor, 2016).

Nigerian Music: Afrobeats

Unlike Nollywood, the global appeal of the Nigerian music industry is a fairly recent development. Notwithstanding, its remarkable rise to global recognition, through talents such as Wizkid, Burna Boy, Davido, and Tiwa Savage, has engendered a "global craze for Afrobeats" (BBC News, 2019). Not only do these artists feature prominently in global radio playlists, and participate in music festivals, they are raking up awards within and outside the region to the extent that global music conglomerates such as Sony and Universal Music Group have set up offices in Lagos. More importantly, some of them have developed a cult following amongst foreign publics, giving them an outsized voice in influencing issues of transnational importance and adding a political component to the power of music.

Early Nigerian artists like Fela Anikulapo Kuti and his son Femi Kuti have long appealed to large crowds within and outside the region, specifically between the 1970s and 1990s. Since the turn of the century, Nigerians have begun to feature prominently on global music charts and awards at the same time. In 2012, Dbanj's *Oliver Twist* rose to number nine on the UK charts, bringing Afrobeats to the global limelight as the song was also nominated for the World's Best Song at the 2014 World Music Award. Nigeria's Wizkid featured in the "biggest track" of 2017, *One Dance* by Drake, reaching number one in 15 countries, including France, Canada, the UK, and the US. Just recently Burna Boy dislodged Wizkid as the first African artist to garner over 15 million streams on Spotify, beating the previous record set by Congolese artist Maitre Gims (Samanga, 2019; International Federation of the Phonographic Industry, 2018). In an unprecedented move, Beyoncé featured six Nigerians – Wizkid, Tiwa Savage, Teckno, Mr. Eazi, Yemi Alade, and P2J – in her album accompanying the release of the *Lion King*. These remarkable feats signify the growing popularity and ascension of Nigerian artists to international recognition.

Nigerian artists also feature prominently within the award circles, with Wizkid beating American superstars, Jay Z, Kendrick Lamar, and Drake to win the award for Best International Act in the 2017 MOBO Awards (MOBO, n.d.). The Best African Act award went to Davido for the track "If" which has thus far exceeded 110 million views on YouTube. Beyond the number of people who listen to their music, these artists also draw sell-out crowds to their shows within and outside the region. In 2018, Wizkid became the first African and only the second artist in the world after Beyoncé to sell out Minnesota's Skyway theatre, a remarkable feat that prompted Governor Mark Dayton to declare October 6 "Wizkid Day" (Agbo, 2018). In a similar vein, Wizkid is the first Nigerian artist to sell out the 15,000-capacity London O2 Arena in 2018, followed by Davido who achieved the same feat a year later.

In an interview with the BBC, DJ Rita Ray notes that "what makes Afrobeats so compelling is rhythm – Nigerians have always been hot on rhythms, it is the driving force of their music" (BBC News, 2019). While the rhythm resonates well beyond the region, these songs embrace their African descent and express Nigerian cultural values. In describing the extent of Davido's popularity in Africa, Norbrook (2020) rightly remarks, that if one "go[es] to far-flung villages in non-Anglophone countries [...] you will find many people who know his hits."

In the wake of xenophobic attacks on African immigrants in South Africa, in now-deleted tweets, Burna Boy, a Nigerian musical artist, took what can be described as a political stand by imploring black foreigners to defend themselves while promising to never set foot in South Africa until the government puts an end to attacks on black Africans (PM News, 2019). This statement drew the ire of South Africans, who protested Burna Boy's invitation to the African Unite concert – organized to harmonize Africans through music – that was to take place three months later in Cape Town and Pretoria. This reveals the extent to which digital media has further enhanced the voice of these celebrities beyond Nigeria and their ability to influence transnational issues, especially in a region where trust in political officeholders is very low and celebrities, including musicians, are increasingly influential in mobilizing public action (Gyimah-Boadi & Logan, 2020; Okalawon, 2020).

Through the instrumentality of their music, Nigerian artists promote the country's cultural values while incorporating music genres originating from neighbouring countries. Also, they influence music genres such as RnB and Grime, as well as other musicians in the region in a way that not only connects Africans but also connects them to the world. Empowerment programmes like *emPawa* launched by Mr. Eazi to boost African musical talents also enhance the ability of these artists to influence transnational audiences. As with Nollywood actors, these musicians have over the years built strong bond with foreign leaders that enhances their ability to influence. In the words of Davido, "I know eight presidents personally so you can imagine what I can do" (cited in Norbrook, 2020).

Iconic Personalities

In 2018, a reputation-management consultancy firm, Reputation Poll, released its inaugural list of the 100 most reputable Africans, featuring leading individuals in sectors as diverse as business, advocacy, entertainment, and government. While the list includes individuals from 33 countries, 21 Nigerians are featured on the list, including Vice President Yemi Osinbajo, the President of the AfDB, Akinwumi Adesina, and the present Deputy Secretary-General of the UN, Amina Mohammed (Akpah, 2019).

Nigeria also boasts of some of the world's most acclaimed writers, with the likes of Chinua Achebe, Wole Soyinka, and Ben Okri leading much younger and contemporary literary giants like Chimamanda Adichie, Chigozie Obioma, Chibundu Onuzo, Sefi Atta, and Helon Habila. As the BBC remarks, Nigerians are fantastic storytellers and they "love to be seen and heard," a character component that equally inspired the creation of a thriving multi-million-dollar entertainment industry as discussed previously (BBC News, 2019). As Nwaubani rightly asserts in an interview with the BBC "there are probably hundreds of Africans telling amazing stories all over the continent, but Nigerians are getting most of the attention because we are bold and loud" (BBC News, 2019).

Things Fall Apart, Achebe's debut novel published in 1958, is today a classic in post-colonial literature with translations in 57 languages and 20 million copies in global sales (BBC News, 2019). In 1986 Wole Soyinka became the first African to win the Nobel Prize for literature and five years after Ben Okiri's novel *The Famished Road* took home the much-coveted Man Booker Prize, formally known as Booker McConnell Prize (The Booker Prizes, 2019). Chimamanda Adichie, who speaks passionately about feminism, leads a pack of contemporary writers with over six awards including the prestigious Women's Prize for Fiction and the Anisfield-Wolf Book Award for Fiction for *Half of a Yellow Sun*.

Charismatic Pentecostalism

As Campbell and Page (2018) note in *Nigeria: What Everyone Needs to Know*, Nigerians are apt to describe themselves as very religious. Despite the secularity of the state, religion permeates both the public and private lives of most Nigerians. While it remains unclear the exact percentage of Christians and Muslims in the country, both world religions are fairly evenly represented, engendering a climate of contest for influence and supremacy, both at the social and political level, that has sometimes resulted in conflicts (Lugo & Cooperman, 2010). Beyond the intermittent outbreak of religious conflicts is the rising phenomenon of Christian Pentecostal movements with strong transnational linkages across the globe, creating possibilities for influence, especially in a sub-region where Christianity remains on the rise.

With parishes spread across the globe, strong cross-border links with regional and global Pentecostal movements, large followership among a huge diaspora community and foreign publics, and personal ties with both national and foreign leaders, Nigerian Pentecostal churches are major players in the dissemination and exchange of Christian ideals. What separates them from other denominations is their revivalist doctrine, charismatic character, prosperity gospel, and emphasis on the holy spirit and sanctification (Kalu, 2008; Anderson, 2010; Campbell & Page, 2018; Osinulu, 2017). Some are even known for propounding triumphalist narratives that emphasize the size of their congregation, a practice in line with their adherence to gospels that preach prosperity and place individual wealth as a sign of God's favour.

While the early emergence of the Pentecostal movement in West Africa has been traced to late-19th-century indigenous charismatic preachers such as William Wade Harris of Liberia and Garrick Sokari Braide of Nigeria, the 1930s and 1940s witnessed increased transnational interactions between American, British, and early African Pentecostals (Kalu, 2008; Osinulu, 2017). Being the country with the largest number of Christians in Africa, Nigerian Pentecostals were instrumental in propounding indigenous Christian gospels across West Africa by becoming missionaries in neighbouring countries

(Asamoah-Gyadu, 2005, p. 230). The 1970s and 1980s saw the emergence of a young generation of Nigerian Pentecostals particularly in college campuses such as the University College, Ibadan, with some of them evolving to lead independent churches of their own (M. Ojo, 2006).

Inspired by the works of American evangelists such as Kenneth Hagin and Franklin Hall, these Pentecostals were notable for ushering in a modern strand of indigenized Pentecostalism that draws heavily from the cultural and political heritage of Africans. This is evident in the emergence of independent churches with branches across borders that today facilitate the exchange of ideas and people across West Africa, in what Anderson (2001) calls the "African reformation." Notable among these churches are the Church of God Mission International founded by the late Benson A. Idahosa, the Redeemed Christian Church of God (RCCG) led by Pastor Enoch Adeboye, SCOAN, and Living Faith Church Worldwide (LFCW) Outreach led by Bishop David Oyedepo.

Consciously positioned as international organizations with a transnational appeal, these churches draw a sizeable following from all over the world. This is exemplified in RCCG's huge membership, which spans 197 countries including every African country, making it the largest Pentecostal church in Africa in terms of membership (RCCG, 2019). Also, figures from 2000 show that LFCW has footprints in 38 countries, including Ghana where it remains amongst the largest charismatic churches (Asamoah-Gyadu, 2005). While Nigeria's huge diaspora is notable for facilitating the expansion of these religious movements, the endearing personalities of these charismatic preachers have equally contributed.

In 2008, *Newsweek Magazine* named Pastor Adeboye among the 50 most powerful people in the world (L. Miller, 2008). In 2015, congressman Marcia L. Fudge of Ohio awarded Pastor Adebayo the certificate of congressional recognition for "being a compassionate leader, giving endlessly through community service, civic engagement and sincere altruism" (cited in Bolarinwa, 2017, p. 325; Ogunlami, 2015). Influential personalities in their own right, these charismatic individuals are adept at using the media, digital platforms, and books to disseminate their teachings. In addition, they regularly organize religious festivals, evangelistic outreaches, summits, annual conventions, and open-air crusades within and outside Nigeria. This creates opportunities for interacting and networking with local populations, not only as a means of boosting their membership but also to attract new converts. Beyond ministration, these men are also known for their humanitarian endeavours both at the local and international stages (see RCCG, 2018).

The political implications of this phenomenon can be found at two levels: domestic and international. At the domestic level, their strong ties to political elites afford them ample opportunity to influence the course of democracy and governance. For instance, RCCG boast of some of the most influential political personalities in Nigeria as members of its church, including the present vice-president of Nigeria. Political leaders and aspiring politicians are frequent visitors to these churches for blessings, counselling, and vote-courting. Former Nigerian presidents, Olusegun Obasanjo and Goodluck Jonathan, attended the Holy Ghost service, an event organized annually by the RCCG. Even President Muhammadu Buhari, a Muslim from Northern Nigeria, visited the church during the 2015 presidential campaign (Bolarinwa, 2017).

The foreign policy implication of this phenomenon is located in the relationship these leaders harbour with world leaders who seek spiritual guidance and recognize the need to tap into their large followership (Bolarinwa, 2017). Within the region, Pastor Adeboye shares close relations with national governments, sharing private moments with them on the sideline of his numerous religious programmes. Bishop Oyedepo, a regular visitor to Ghana, met with former President Kuffour during the Maximum Impact summit held in Accra in 2002. Both in the build-up to the 2017 presidential elections and after his victory, President George Weah of Liberia visited the late Prophet T. B. Joshua of the SCOAN for what may be assumed to be spiritual guidance.

Pastor Adeboye's active participation in UN-organized inter-faith prayer summits is indicative of the growing political influence of the charismatic movement. He collaborates actively with the Inter-Parliamentary Coalition for Global Ethics to mobilize political, academic, and religious leaders towards promoting a culture of peace. In 2016, Adeboye met with UN Secretary-General Ban Ki-Moon to seek ways in which the influence and goodwill of the RCCG could be instrumentalized to facilitate inter-faith harmony (Bolarinwa, 2017). There is no gainsaying that charismatic Pentecostalism has not only enhanced the reputation of the country but continues to attract religious tourists into the country, especially from neighbouring countries.

The Diaspora

As with other dimensions of Nigeria's culture, the spread of Nigerian charismatic churches in West Africa may be credited to the diaspora. This community, mostly made up of economic migrants in search of better opportunities outside Nigeria, is at the heart of regional networks established over time through trade, language, migration, and ethnicity. While the economic dimension of their potential utility in the pursuit of Nigeria's objectives in the region was discussed previously, here, their role as the physical embodiment of Nigerian culture and values is addressed. As more and more Nigerians build lives in foreign lands, they carry with them various aspects of Nigerian society, in the form of cuisine, fashion, and religious practices, which they most times reproduce through intermarriages and other forms of relationship. As stated elsewhere, these individuals forge transnational networks, which facilitate not just economic but also political and cultural interchange.

However, their engagement in illicit activities continues to be a drag on the country's image. In 2015, the MFA reported that 16,250 Nigerians convicted of various crimes are currently imprisoned across the globe, while about 420 of them are facing the death penalty (Ezeamalu, 2015).

Conclusion

This chapter assessed the diverse components of Nigeria's power resources by questioning what resources exist within Nigeria that may constitute an attractive source of influence. It reveals that Nigeria possesses the largest economy in Africa, although tepid growth rates, high indebtedness, worsening poverty, high inflation, and corruption continue to dent the country's economic competitiveness and by implication the appearance of a successful economy. The same can be said of its military, where possessing demonstrably superior military resources and participation in intra- and extra-regional peacekeeping efforts have not necessarily translated to combat proficiency, particularly in the domestic realm where the country continues to struggle with transnational violent extremist groups.

The inability of the military to handle Nigeria's domestic security challenges increasingly raises questions about its competence. As the analysis shows, some of these security challenges are connected with an internal political dynamic that continues to suffer from the flaws of a federalist framework or political organization that has entrenched a democratic system that is at best flawed, both in the practice of political contests and governance. While Nigeria's rich cultural diversity offers an array of potential soft power resources, politicians have sought to capitalize on this diversity to sow mistrust and divisions, thereby causing ethno-religious conflicts and a climate of political contest that is violent, corrupt, and to some extent authoritarian.

There exist, across these power categories, positive elements that may constitute an attractive source of influence. Economically, while intra-regional trade relations remain protectionist, the Nigerian government has repeatedly capitalized on its superior economic resources to aid the development of neighbouring states through debt relief, economic aid, and technical assistance. Beyond the purview of the government also lies transnational economic linkages centred around MNCs and Nigeria's diaspora community, which may constitute attractive sources of influence. Moreover, the size of Nigeria's market, its entrepreneurial culture, and its innovative capacity especially in the realm of popular culture and tech give it a competitive edge over its sub-regional counterparts.

The same can be said of Nigeria's military superiority, as security alliances within and beyond the sub-region have created a cooperative atmosphere that has seen Nigeria instrumentalize its military resources to come to the aid of such West African states like Liberia, Sierra Leone, and Mali. These security alliances are largely informed by a foreign policy posture that espouses such universal values as multilateralism, peaceful coexistence, the principle of good neighbourliness, and the promotion of democracy.

Equally, Nigeria's cultural diversity offers a wide array of cultural expressions – material and ideological – that are embedded in its budding entertainment industry comprising movies, music, comedy, and literature. Additionally, Nigeria's large Christian population has seen the emergence of a charismatic brand of Pentecostalism that currently attracts huge followership in the region. These different manifestations of cultural expressions are embodied in cultural actors who hold a lot of sway in the continent and possess the ability to instigate social change.

Notes

1 The WEF's global competitiveness index of 2019 defines competitiveness as "the attributes and qualities of an economy that allows for the more efficient use of factors of production" (Schwab, 2019). Accordingly, gains in the level of productivity of a nation's economy are understood to engender economic growth and speak to the well-being of the economy. For low-income countries, improved competitiveness may be construed as economic resilience and can be a source of pull.

2 In 2010, oil constituted the bulk of Nigeria's export to its regional neighbours, accounting for 90% of export revenues. Manufacturing accounted for about 5%, while agriculture, which was estimated at 3% in 2001, reduced to almost nothing in 2010 (Chete & Adewuyi, 2012).

3 Although the amount expended on TAC from the inception of the scheme is unclear, a summation of budgetary allocations to the programme between 2009 and 2018 amounts to N27 billion (Ogbonna & Ogunnubi, 2018).

4 The NTCF was conceived "as a special funding window from the NTF" with the objective of enhancing regional cooperation and integration by funding projects in different sectors such as health, education, agriculture, and governance in RMCs (AfDB, 2017).

5 The NNDP of 2017, although yet to be officially released by the Federal Ministry of Defence, is the latest iteration of the state's defence policy. It outlines the guiding principles of Nigeria's national security policy, as well at the nature of emerging threats confronting the state at four strategic levels: global, regional, sub-regional, and national.

6 The federal character principle mandates a system of political organization where all government revenues and appointments are apportioned equitably to reflect Nigeria's diverse ethno-religious composition.

7 According to Bilkisu Labaran, an editor with the BBC, "it is a language that really unites people and cuts across all sorts of barriers – ethnic, regional and socio-economic" (cited in BBC News, 2017).

8 The Nollywood Roadshow Project, an initiative by the Nigerian Export Promotion Council, was designed to promote and create distribution channels around the globe for Nollywood content. Thus far, Nollywood Roadshow has been organized in Kenya, South Africa, and London.

References

Access Bank PLC. (2020). *Country locations.* Retrieved February 5, 2020, from www.accessbankplc.com/

Adebajo, A. (2002). *Liberia's civil war: Nigeria, ECOMOG and regional security in West Africa.* Lynne Rienner.

Adebanwi, W. (2011). *Globally oriented citizenship and international voluntary service: Interrogating Nigeria's Technical Aid Corps Scheme* [Discussion paper 71]. Uppsala: Nordiska Afrikainstitutet.

Adebowale, O. (2018, July 29). *Check out these six UNESCO world heritage tourism sites in Nigeria. The Guardian.* Retrieved September 26, 2020, from https://guard ian.ng/life/check-out-these-six-unesco-world-heritage-tourism-sites-in-nigeria/

Adeoye, A. (2020, October 27). *Your package has arrived.* Rest of World. https://rest ofworld.org/2020/your-package-has-arrived/

Adogamhe, P. G. (2016). Nigeria's diplomacy: The challenges of regional power and leadership in a globalizing world. *Diplomatic strategies of nations in the global south* (pp. 213–238). Palgrave Macmillan.

African Business. (2019). *Africa's top 100 brands in 2019 – Global brands dominate Africa. African Business Magazine.* Retrieved February 16, 2020, from https://afri canbusinessmagazine.com/top-african-brands/global-brands-dominate-africa/

African Development Bank. (2017, May). *Nigerian Technical Cooperation Fund (NTCF): Integrating Africa Supporting Growth.*

African Development Bank. (2019). *Nigeria economic outlook.* Retrieved February 17, 2020, from www.afdb.org/en/countries-west-africa-nigeria/nigeria-economic-outlook

Agbo, N. (2018, October 8). *Minnesota governor declares October 6 'Wizkid Day'. The Guardian Nigeria News.* Retrieved November 16, 2019, from https://guard ian.ng/life/minnesota-governor-declares-oct-6-wizkid-day/

Agwu, F. A. (2009). *National interest, international law, and our shared destiny.* Spectrum Books Limited.

Akande, B., & Brown, D. (2018, October 2). *Moving Nigerian filmmaking beyond Nollywood.* CNN. Retrieved June 14, 2019, from https://amp.cnn.com/cnn/ 2018/10/02/africa/nigeria-nollywood-international/index.html?__twitter_impress ion=true

Akpah, P. (2019, September 20). *100 most reputable Africans 2018.* Reputation Poll. Retrieved December 29, 2019, from www.reputationpoll.com/africa100/

Aljazeera (2019). *Nigeria's land borders closed to all goods, official confirms.* Retrieved February 26, 2020, from www.aljazeera.com/ajimpact/nigeria-land-bord ers-closed-goods-official-confirms-191015191736317.html

Aluko, O. (1976). Oil at concessionary prices for Africa: A case-study in Nigerian decision-making. *African Affairs, 75*(301), 425–443.

Amuwo, K. (2014). *Nigeria's continental diplomatic thrusts: The limits of Africa's nominally biggest economy.* Policy Briefing 111. South African Institute of International Affairs (SAIIA), South African Foreign Policy Drivers Programme. South African Institute of International Affairs.

Anderson, A. (2001). *African reformation: African initiated Christianity in the 20th century.* Africa World Press.

Armed Forces Command and Staff College. (n.d.). *History.* Retrieved July 7, 2019, from www.afcsc.mil.ng/afcsc/acfmdispx.php?id=37

Asamoah-Gyadu, J. K. (2005). Half a century of touching lives: Nigerian charismatic personalities and African (Ghanaian) Christianity, 1953–2003. In C. J. Korieh & U. G. Nwokeji (Eds.), *Religion, history, and politics in Nigeria*: essays in honor of Ogbu U. Kalu (pp. 230–245). University Press of America.

Bach, D. C. (2007). Nigeria's' manifest destiny' in West Africa: Dominance without power. *Africa Spectrum, 42*(2), 301–321. www.jstor.org/stable/40175188

BBC News. (2017, August 21). *BBC Pidgin service launched in Nigeria*. Retrieved May 23, 2019, from www.bbc.co.uk/news/world-africa-40975399

BBC News. (2019, February 14). *Five things about Nigeria: The superpower with no power*. Retrieved May 18, 2020, from www.bbc.co.uk/news/world-africa-47217557

Bell, E. (2016). Soft power and corporate imperialism: Maintaining British influence. *Race & Class, 57*(4), 75–86.

Billig, M. (1995). *Banal nationalism*. Sage Publications.

Bolarinwa, J. (2017). The impact of Pastor Adeboye's Ministry on the society. In M. Omelewa, J. Odesola, O. Olubiyi, and A. Osuntokun (Eds.), *Pastor E. A. Adeboye: His life and calling* (pp. 319–329). Bookcraft Press.

Butz, D. A. (2009). National symbols as agents of psychological and social change. *Political Psychology, 30*(5), 779–804. https://doi.org/10.1111/j.1467-9221.2009.00725.x

Campbell, J., & Page, M. T. (2018). *Nigeria: What everyone needs to know*. Oxford University Press.

CGTN Africa. (2015, October 28). *Gambian President's land gift to Nollywood stars opposed by local filmmaker*. Retrieved May 24, 2020, from https://africa.cgtn.com/2015/10/28/gambians-president-land-gift-to-nollywood-stars-opposed-by-local-film-maker/

Chete, L. N., & Adewuyi, A. O.(2012). *Dynamics of trade between Nigeria and other ECOWAS countries. Accelerating growth through improved intra-African trade*: Brookings Africa Growth Institute, Washington DC.

Committee to Protect Journalists. (2019a, May 22). *Nigeria charges weekly source editor Jones Abiri under cybercrimes, terrorism acts*. Retrieved June 16, 2020, from https://cpj.org/2019/05/nigeria-charges-jones-abiri-weekly-source-terrorism/

Committee to Protect Journalists. (2019b, October 25). *Nigerian publisher Agba Jalingo charged with treason*. Retrieved June 16, 2020, from https://cpj.org/2019/09/nigerian-publisher-agba-jalingo-charged-with-treas/

Dangote Cement. (2020). *Pan-Africa operations – Welcome to Dangote Cement Plc*. Retrieved April 6, 2020, from www.dangotecement.com/pan-africa-operations/

Dangote Industries. (2020). *Foundation – Dangote Industries Limited*. Retrieved March 4, 2020, from https://dangote.com/foundation/

Dekie, A., Meers, P., Winkel, R. V., Bauwel, S. V., & Smets, K. (2015). Nollywood online: Between the individual consumption and communal reception of Nigerian films among African diaspora. *Journal of African Media Studies, 7*(3), 301–314.

Demarest, L. (2020). Men of the people? Democracy and prebendalism in Nigeria's Fourth Republic National Assembly. *Democratization, 28*(4), 684–702. https://doi.org/10.1080/13510347.2020.1856085

Ezeamalu, B. (2015). *How Nigerian govt. is abandoning its citizens on death row abroad. Premium Times Nigeria*. Retrieved June 27, 2015, from www.premiumtimesng.com/features-and-interviews/185721-how-nigerian-govt-is-abandoning-its-citizens-on-death-row-abroad.html

Fan, Y. (2008). Soft power: Power of attraction or confusion? *Place Branding and Public Diplomacy*, 4(2), 147–158.

Fatunde, T. (2014). *Focus on Ghana shows 75,000 Nigerians studying there. University World News*. Retrieved February 20, 2020, from www.universityworldn ews.com/post.php?story=20140529173131311

Federal Republic of Nigeria (2017). *Nigerian National Defence Policy*.

Flagmakers. (n.d.). *Flag of Nigeria – A brief history*. Retrieved November 4, 2020, from https://flagmakers.co.uk/media/wpdf2dwq/flag-of-nigeria-a-brief-history-download.pdf

Ghanaweb. (2015). *Top Nigerians ruling Ghana economically*. Retrieved March 7, 2020, from www.ghanaweb.com/GhanaHomePage/features/Top-Nigerians-Rul ing-Ghana-Economically-342119

Global Firepower. (2020). *2020 Nigeria military strength*. Retrieved April 14, 2021, from www.globalfirepower.com/country-military-strength-detail.php?country_id= nigeria

Gloworld. (2020). *About us*. Retrieved June 5, 2020, from www.gloworld.com/ng/about-us

Golub, S., Mbaye, A., & Golubski, C. (2019). *The effects of Nigeria's closed borders on informal trade with Benin*. Brookings. Retrieved February 26, 2020, from www.brookings.edu/blog/africa-in-focus/2019/10/29/the-effects-of-nigerias-closed-bord ers-on-informal-trade-with-benin

Gyimah-Boadi, E., & Logan, C. (2020, May 1). *Analysis | many Africans distrust their governments. how will that affect their coronavirus response? The Washington Post*. Retrieved April 27, 2022, from www.washingtonpost.com/politics/2020/05/01/many-africans-distrust-their-governments-how-will-that-affect-their-coronavi rus-response/

Haynes, J. (2005, June 9). *Nollywood: What is in a name? The Guardian*. Retrieved April 6, 2020, from https://tns.ng/nollywood-what-is-in-a-name/

Human Rights Watch. (2019, January 17). *World report 2019: Rights trends in Nigeria*. Retrieved January 28, 2020, from www.hrw.org/world-report/2019/coun try-chapters/nigeria

Husseini, S. (2016, January 24). *Serge Noukoue dreams big for Nollywoodweek in Paris. The Guardian Nigeria News*. Retrieved December 28, 2019, from https://guardian.ng/art/filmserge-noukoue-dreams-big-for-nollywoodweek-in-paris/

International Crisis Group. (2006). *Nigeria's faltering federal experiment*. African Report No 119.

International Crisis Group. (2020). *What role for the multinational Joint Task Force in fighting Boko Haram?* African Report No. 291.

International Federation of the Phonographic Industry. (2018). *Global music report 2018: Annual state of the industry*. Retrieved June 8, 2019, from www.ifpi.org/dl/ ?url=www.ifpi.org/downloads/GMR2018.pdf

International Institute for Strategic Studies. (2020, February). *The military balance: The annual assessment of global military capabilities and defence economics*.

Itugbu, S. (2017). *Foreign policy and leadership in Nigeria: Obasanjo and the challenge of African diplomacy (International Library of African Studies)*. I. B. Tauris.

Jannah, C. (2019, July 31). *Nigeria's 2019 election failed to meet standards for free, fair, credible polls – CSOs*. Retrieved June 17, 2020, from https://dailypost.ng/2019/07/31/nigerias-2019-election-failed-meet-standards-free-fair-credible-polls-csos/

Kalu, O. U. (2008). *African Pentecostalism: An introduction*. Oxford University Press.

Kamran, M., Liang, Y., & Trines, S. (2019). *Education in Ghana. WENR*. Retrieved April 24, 2020, from https://wenr.wes.org/2019/04/education-in-ghana

Kerr-Dineen, L. (2016, August 3). *Ranking the 15 best national anthems of the 2016 Olympics. FORTHEWIN*. Retrieved March 4, 2020, from https://ftw.usatoday.com/2016/08/ranking-the-15-best-national-anthems-of-the-2016-olympics

Lampert, B. (2014). Collective transnational power and its limits: London-based Nigerian organisations, development at 'home and the importance of local agency and the 'internal diaspora'. *Journal of Ethnic and Migration Studies*, 40(5), 829–846.

Larkin, B. (2008). *Signal and noise: Media, infrastructure, and urban culture in Nigeria*. Duke University Press.

Lewis, P. (1996). From Prebendalism to predation: The political economy of decline in Nigeria. *The Journal of Modern African Studies*, 34(1), 79–103. https://doi.org/10.1017/s0022278x0005521x

Lugo, L., & Cooperman, A. (2010). *Tolerance and tension: Islam and Christianity in sub-Saharan Africa*. Washington, DC: Pew Research Centre.

Melissen, J. (2005). *Wielding soft power: The new public diplomacy*. Netherlands Institute of International Relations.

Miller, J. (2012). Global Nollywood: The Nigerian movie industry and alternative global networks in production and distribution. *Global Media and Communication*, 8(2), 117–133.

Miller, L. (2008, December 19). *The NEWSWEEK 50: E. A. Adeboye. Newsweek*. Retrieved June 10, 2019, from www.newsweek.com/newsweek-50-e-adeboye-83039

Ministry of Foreign Affairs. (2013). *Directorate of Technical Cooperation in Africa (DTCA): Nigeria Technical Cooperation Fund*.

MOBO. (n.d.). *MOBO awards 2017*. MOBO Organisation. Retrieved April 27, 2022, from https://mobo.com/mobo-awards-2017#:~:text=The%20public%20voted%20for%20Dave,Marley%20won%20Best%20Reggae%20Act

National Defence College. (n.d.). *About the National Defence College – National Defence College Nigeria*. Retrieved September 6, 2019, from https://ndc.gov.ng/about/#1533026199621-94d7bc08-4b10

Nevin, A., & Omosomi, O. (2019). *Strength from abroad: The economic power of Nigeria's diaspora*. PwC. Retrieved March 6, 2020, from www.pwc.com/ng/en/publications/the-economic-power-of-nigerias-diaspora.html

Norbrook, N. (2020, January 6). *Nigeria's musical moment*. The Africa Report. Retrieved August 4, 2019, from www.theafricareport.com/21775/nigerias-musical-moment/

Nsehe, M. (2019). *The philanthropy of Africa's billionaires. Forbes*. Retrieved March 4, 2020, from www.forbes.com/sites/mfonobongnsehe/2019/01/09/the-philanthropy-of-africas-billionaires/

Nye, J. S. (2011). *The future of power*. Public Affairs Books.

Ogbonna, N. C., & Ogunnubi, O. (2018). Rethinking the role of Nigeria's technical aid corps as soft power: Rough diamond or fools' gold. *African Journal of Peace and Conflict Studies*, 7(2), 121–141.

Ogunbadejo, O. (1980). Nigeria's foreign policy under military rule 1966–1979. *International Journal: Canada's Journal of Global Policy Analysis*, 35(4), 748–765. https://doi.org/10.1177/002070208003500406

Ogunlami, Y. (2015). *General overseer receives certificate of congressional recognition in USA. Pulse Nigeria.* Retrieved May 2, 2020, from www.pulse.ng/communit ies/religion/pastor-e-a-adeboye-general-overseer-receives-certificate-of-congressio nal-recognition/4hpf1xp

Ojo, M. A. (2006). *The end-time army: Charismatic movements in modern Nigeria.* Africa World Press.

Okafor, B. (2016, November 18). *Followers blast actress Angela Okorie for supporting President Yaya Jammeh of Gambia. NigeriaFilms.Com.* Retrieved June 12, 2019, from www.nigeriafilms.com/movie-news/92-nollywood-diaspora/42403-followers-blast-actress-angela-okorie-for-supporting-president-yaya-jammeh-of-gambia

Okanlawon, T. (2020, November 1). *10 top celebrities who were at forefront of #endsars movement – P.M. news. PM News.* Retrieved April 27, 2022, from https:// pmnewsnigeria.com/2020/11/01/10-top-celebrities-who-were-at-forefront-of-ends ars-movement/

Okonkwo, R. O. (2019, December 9). *Nigeria has been quietly crushing press freedom – but now the world is watching.* Retrieved June 12, 2020, from https:// qz.com/africa/1764021/nigeria-under-buhari-has-been-crushing-press-freedom/

Oladimeji, T., & Kirmanj, S. (2015). Nigeria's multilateral policy and regional order of West Africa in the post-Cold War international system. *International Journal of Physical and Social Sciences, 5*(7), 682–698. http://dx.doi.org/10.2139/ ssrn.2653503

Olatuyi, A., Awoyinka, Y., & Adeniyi, A. (2013). *Nigerian diasporas in the South: Harnessing the potential for national development.* ACP Observatory on Migration, Research Report ACPOBS/2013/PUB06.

Omeni, A. E. (2015). *The Nigerian military contribution to counter-insurgency (COIN): A study of organizational culture, institution, doctrine and operations* [Doctoral dissertation, King's College London]. King's College London Repository.

Onuah, F. (2019). *Nigeria meets with West African neighbours on border closure.* U.S. Retrieved February 27, 2020, from www.reuters.com/article/us-nigeria-trade/ nigeria-meets-with-west-african-neighbors-on-border-closure-idUSKBN1Y12HX

Onuzulike, U. (2007). Nollywood: The influence of the Nigerian movie industry on African culture. *Human Communication, 10*(3), 231–242.

Orewere, B. (1992). Towards a film policy for Nigeria. In U. Ekuazi and Y. Nasisi (Eds.), *Films for development: Theory and practice at the crossroads* (pp. 308–319). Nigerian Film Corporation.

Orjinmo, N. (2019). *The border crisis fuelled by rice. BBC News.* Retrieved February 27, 2020, from www.bbc.co.uk/news/world-africa-50223045

Oshewolo, S. (2019a). A reconsideration of the Afrocentric principle in Nigeria's foreign policy framework. *GeoJournal, 86,* 1–8. https://doi.org/10.1007/s10 708-019-10114-1

Oshewolo, S. (2019b). Major contentions on Nigeria's Afrocentric policy. *India Quarterly, 75*(3), 1–15.

Oshewolo, S. (2019c, January 21). *Rhetoric and praxis: Nigeria's Africa diplomacy and the shaping of the African Union* [Paper presentation]. The Round Table. Retrieved December 28, 2020, from www.commonwealthroundtable.co.uk/ commonwealth/africa/nigeria/rhetoric-and-praxis-nigerias-africa-diplomacy-and-the-shaping-of-the-african-union/#

Osinulu, A. (2017). A transnational history of Pentecostalism in West Africa. *History Compass, 15*(6). https://doi.org/10.1111/hic3.12386

Paek, T. Y. (2004). The anatomy of cultural power: Elements and implications for global politics. *Pacific Focus, 19*(1), 137–168.

Pilling, D. (2018). *Nigerian economy: Why Lagos works. Financial Times.* Retrieved February 15, 2020, from www.ft.com/content/ff0595e4-26de-11e8-b27e-cc62a 39d57a0

Platt, G. (2019). *Best banks in Africa 2019: Innovating for profit. Global Finance.* Retrieved February 15, 2020, from www.gfmag.com/magazine/may-2019/best-banks-africa-2019

PM News. (2019, November 13). *Protest against Burna Boy in South Africa.* Retrieved March 18, 2020, from www.pmnewsnigeria.com/2019/11/13/protest-against-burna-boy-in-south-africa/

PricewaterCooperhouse. (2018, September). *Entertainment and media outlook: 2018– 2022: An African perspective* (9th annual edition). Retrieved March 28, 2019, from www.pwc.co.za/en/assets/pdf/entertainment-and-media-outlook-2018-2022.pdf

Redeemed Christian Church of God. (2018). RCCG is the Light Now in Europe that is Shining: Pastor Leke Sanusi. *Mission's Focus, 19*/1218. December 2018– February 2019.

Redeemed Christian Church of God. (2019). Examining missionary enterprise of the Redeemed Christian Church of God in Times and Trends of Events of the 21st century: Global and future trajectories. *Research and Development Unit Research Conference,* (May).

Samanga, R. (2019, December 6). *Wizkid is the first African to reach 8 million monthly listeners on Spotify. OkayAfrica.* Retrieved May 12, 2020, from www.oka yafrica.com/wizkid-first-african-to-reach-8-million-monthly-listeners-on-spotify/

Schwab, K. (2019). *The global competitiveness report 2019. World Economic Forum.* Retrieved July 28, 2020, from www3.weforum.org/docs/WEF_TheGlobalCompet itivenessReport2019.pdf

Shapshak, T. (2019). *Africa's booming tech hubs are "backbone of tech ecosystem" having grown 40% this year. Forbes.* Retrieved February 19, 2020, from www.for bes.com/sites/tobyshapshak/2019/07/11/africas-booming-tech-hubs-are-backbone-of-tech-ecosystem-having-grown-40-this-year/amp/

Soulé, B. (2018). *West African cross-border trade: Trends and opportunities.* International Centre for Trade and Sustainable Development. Retrieved February 28, 2020, from www.ictsd.org/bridges-news/bridges-africa/news/west-african-cross-border-trade-trends-and-opportunities

Stockholm International Peace Research Institute. (2020). *SIPRI Military Expenditure Data Base* [Table]. Retrieved March 18, 2020, from www.sipri.org/databases/milex

Telegraph Sport. (2018, June 28). *World Cup 2018: Every national anthem ranked – Can you guess the No 1? The Telegraph.* Retrieved from August 3, 2020, from www.telegraph.co.uk/world-cup/2018/06/28/world-cup-2018-every-national-ant hem-ranked/

Tella, O. (2018). Is Nigeria a soft power state? *Social Dynamics, 44*(2), 376–394. https://doi.org/10.1080/02533952.2018.1492833

The Booker Prizes. (2019, October 22). *A poem for The Booker Prize by Ben Okri* | The Booker Prizes. Retrieved February 12, 2020, from https://thebookerprizes. com/booker-prize/news/poem-booker-prize-ben-okri

The Mail & Guardian. (2016, May 11). *Exploring Africa's favourite beers.* Retrieved April 7, 2020, from https://mg.co.za/article/2016-05-11-exploring-africas-favour ite-beers-and-why-it-matters/

Torres, C., & Van Seters, J. (2016). *Overview of trade and barriers to trade in West Africa: Insights in political economy dynamics, with particular focus on agricultural and food trade* [Discussion Paper, No. 195]. European Centre for Development Policy Management.

Transparency International. (2020, January 10). *Corruptions Perceptions Index 2019 for Nigeria.* Retrieved June 12, 2020, from www.transparency.org/en/cpi/2019/results/nga#details

UNESCO World Heritage Centre. (n.d.). *Sukur Cultural Landscape.* Retrieved 8 August 2019, from https://whc.unesco.org/en/list/938

United Bank for Africa. (2020a). *About us.* Retrieved May 5, 2020, from www.ubagroup.com/about-uba/

United Bank for Africa. (2020b, August 20). *About UBA foundation.* UBA Group. Retrieved December 28, 2020, from www.ubagroup.com/uba-foundation/

United Nations. (2019). *Ranking of military and police contributions.* United Nations Peacekeeping. Retrieved December 9, 2019, from https://peacekeeping.un.org/en/ranking-of-military-and-police-contributions

United Nations Economic Commission for Africa. (n.d.). *CEN-SAD – Peace, Security, Stability, and Governance.* Retrieved January 9, 2019, from www.uneca.org/oria/pages/cen-sad-peace-security-stability-and-governance

Warner, J. (2016). Nigeria and "illusory hegemony" in foreign and security policy-making: Pax-Nigeriana and the challenges of Boko Haram. *Foreign Policy Analysis, 13*(3). https://doi.org/10.1093/fpa/orw051

World Bank. (2020). *Population, total – Nigeria | Data.* Retrieved March 5, 2021, from https://data.worldbank.org/indicator/SP.POP.TOTL?locations=NG

World Bank. (2020d). *GDP (current US$) – Nigeria | Data.* Retrieved January 28, 2020, from https://data.worldbank.org/indicator/NY.GDP.MKTP.CD?locations=NG

6 Nigeria's Foreign Policy Behaviour in West Africa

Introduction

Chapter 5 provided an exploratory account of Nigeria's soft power potential across economic, military, cultural, and political power categories by assessing their qualities and visibility. Amidst some grey areas, the discussion revealed strong cultural variables that may be attractive to West Africans. It also discussed Nigeria's superior military and economic resources, which inform a foreign policy disposition that prioritizes West Africa and contributes in various ways to the peace, stability, and development of the sub-region. In this chapter, I explore their deliberate translation from potential to capabilities in the conduct of Nigeria's foreign policy. This is instructive in understanding not just the nature of Nigeria's behaviour, but also the basis of prevailing attitudes and reactions towards Nigeria in Liberia and Ghana, which Chapter 7 addresses.

The 1999 constitution of the FRN places the conduct of foreign policy under the authority of the federal government, through the MFA and its specialized agencies. As with other aspects of public policy, the exercise of power through these institutions reflects a deliberate political choice that most likely stems from political argumentation. Thus, understanding the various expressions of Nigeria's power resources in its foreign policy requires an analytical approach that considers the goal of foreign policy, as stipulated in its constitution. Consequently, this chapter traces the evolution of Nigeria's African policy drawing from successive post-independence constitutions. Following this, it expatiates the different ways Nigeria's power resources have served the purpose of foreign policy, and to the extent to which they are specified, the targets of these policies.

It reveals a consistent African policy – driven by Nigeria's leadership aspirations – that successive governments have implemented differently using the country's economic, military, and human resources. Although Nigeria's national interest is securitarian, it is garbed under commitments to value objectives or normative principles such as good neighbourliness, racial equality, cooperation, regional democratic consolidation, and peaceful

DOI: 10.4324/9781003396628-6

coexistence. While there appears to be some coercive posturing in Nigeria's quest to meet its Afrocentric objectives, economic aid, technical assistance, cash gifts, development assistance, peacekeeping, and, to some extent, peace enforcement, targeted at governments and foreign publics alike, have characterized interactions with West African states.

These discussions will proceed in three sections. The first provides an overview of the constitutional evolution of Nigeria's foreign policy objectives. The second uses each specific objective as a framework to assess Nigeria's behaviour in Africa, with specific emphasis on the West African sub-region. Given the predominance of value objectives as guiding principles of Nigeria's external disposition, the third section assesses the extent of Nigeria's commitment to these values.

The Foreign Policy Objectives of Nigeria

This section assesses the evolution of Nigeria's African policy, starting with the transitional constitution of 1960 and culminating in the 1999 constitution, which provides the current framework of political organization.

The 1960 and 1963 Constitutions

Whereas the transition constitution of 1960 was completely silent on Nigeria's strategic objectives, the preamble of the republican constitution of 1963 listed the promotion of inter-African cooperation and solidarity, the assurance of world peace and international understanding, as well as "furthering the ends of liberty, equality, and justice" as Nigeria's founding principles. The only allusion to foreign policy in the 1960 constitution came in section 69, which authorized the federal government to enter into international agreements – a provision that was reiterated in section 79 of the 1963 constitution. Without clearly specified external objectives, Nigeria's African policy was shaped by the Cold War global context and the overbearing influence of colonial powers on newly independent African states. Nigeria's leadership aspiration in Africa, buoyed by its superior material capabilities, was also an influential factor in the country's external attitude.

Thus, in addition to the promotion of international cooperation, Nigeria's African policy embraced principles such as non-alignment, respect for the sovereign equality of all states, non-interference in the domestic affairs of others, and the complete eradication of colonial governments from the continent. Whereas respect for the sovereign equality of all states was emphasized to assuage fears of Nigeria's dominance, Nigeria also had concerns that regional adversaries may exploit its multi-ethnic composition to sow discord and slow the process of national integration (Okolo & Langley, 1973). What this implies is that concerns with self-preservation informed Nigeria's decision to make the non-interference clause a staple of its foreign policy, and part of the Charter of the OAU (Okeke, 1981). Also, Nigeria's recognition that all states, especially those in Africa, have a right to self-determination informed a foreign policy posture that frowned against colonialism.

The 1963 constitution was short-lived, as a military coup in 1966 resulted in its abrogation. However, this did not engender any notable alteration to the overall principles of Nigeria's external relations as the 1979 constitution, discussed subsequently, reveals.

The Presidential Constitution of 1979

The 1979 constitution, which brought an end to 13 years (1966–1979) of military rule, introduced an American-style presidential system of government. With a new system of government in place and a newly elected democratic administration headed by President Shehu Shagari came questions about who determines foreign policy and Nigeria's role in the committee of nations. Concerning the former, the constitution placed the conduct of foreign policy squarely with the executive arm of government or the presidency, which comprises the president, the National Security Council, and the National Economic Council. Regarding the latter, the 1979 constitution, specifically section 2 of chapter 19, provided the clearest statement on Nigeria's foreign policy since independence by noting:

> The [...] state shall promote African unity, as well as total political, economic, social, and cultural liberation of Africa and all other forms of international cooperation conducive to the consolidation of universal peace, mutual respect, and friendship among all peoples and states, and shall combat racial discrimination in all its manifestations.

While more specific and elaborate, the underlying objectives of the country's external relations did not deviate normatively from the 1963 constitution. However, it became clear that Africa was the centrepiece of Nigeria's foreign policy, a point reiterated in January 1980 by Shagari when he stated in his inaugural address that Nigeria "will extend [its] ... wholehearted cooperation to all African countries and organizations to bring about the unity of the African people and the rapid emancipation and development of all countries of Africa" (cited in Okeke, 1981, p. 210).

In a subsequent address to the National Assembly, President Shagari noted:

> In our foreign policy, Africa ... remains Nigeria's priority interest. We renew our pledge to support ECOWAS, the OAU, and the liberation movements in Africa. Let it be known that our commitment to the total liberation of our brothers in Zimbabwe, Namibia, and South Africa remains unshaken.
>
> (Cited in Okeke, 1981, p. 210)

As will be discussed subsequently, Nigeria's commitment to Africa did not waver, even when Shagari's administration was toppled and the 1979 constitution was suspended. It took 16 years of military dictatorship before a new constitution was promulgated.

The 1999 Constitution

In 1989 a new constitution was promulgated to usher in the third republic, but the transition process that would have led to its enforcement was interrupted by the Babangida regime. In 1999, a new constitution came into force – ushering in the fourth republic – that remains the guiding document for Nigeria's external engagement. Accordingly, section 19 lists Nigeria's foreign policy objectives as:

• The promotion and protection of the national interest.
• The promotion of African integration and support for African unity.
• The promotion of international cooperation for the consolidation of universal peace and mutual respect among all nations and the elimination of discrimination in all its manifestations.
• Respect for international law and treaty obligations as well as the seeking of settlement of international disputes by negotiation, mediation, conciliation, arbitration, and adjudication.
• Promotion of a just world economic order.

From the objectives above, it is evident that Nigeria's external objectives did not deviate substantially from earlier provisions except for the emphasis placed on the pursuit and protection of the national interest. What constitutes the national interest is a question that went conspicuously unanswered, in both policy and scholarly circles, until the Nigerian NNDP of 2006 and its latest iteration of 2017 provided clarifications.

Accordingly, the NNDP specifies that Nigeria's national interest is to be "derived from the shared values, goals and aspirations of its citizens, [which] could be broadly described as territorial, political, economic, scientific, and socio-cultural" (FRN, 2017, p. 17). The NNDP demarcates three categories of national interest: vital, strategic, and peripheral. Whereas the vital interests are internally oriented as they hinge on the survival of the nation, the strategic and peripheral interests, which are externally oriented may be easily construed to reflect the means through which the vital interests are secured (p. 19).

Nigeria's vital interests are realist in nature. They consist of protecting its citizens and national assets around the world, guaranteeing the sovereignty and territorial integrity of the nation, protecting Nigeria's economic resources wherever they may be, protecting democracy, and finally preserving the culture and well-being of Nigerians. Viewed as less vital, Nigeria's strategic interests emphasize regional security as well as the means of achieving the vital interests. While the regional security component specifically refers to combatting terrorism, insurgency, and other transnational crimes, Nigeria's peripheral interests emphasize a commitment to the international community by contributing to peace and security, providing humanitarian assistance, participating in environmental security operations, and promoting respect for human rights and international humanitarian law. To meet these interests, the NNDP emphasizes the use of diplomatic means, with force only necessary when the nation's essential trade and maritime routes are under threat.

What has been said so far reflects the objectives and principles guiding Nigeria's external interactions. As Nigeria gained in maturity and resources, in addition to the experience of a civil war, its core principles evolved to include an enlightened sense of the national interest, regional integration, multilateralism/interdependence, global equality, and democratic governance. Although the national interest emphasizes territorial and economic interests that are realist, the rest of the constitutional provisions do not deviate from previous constitutions in their liberalist and normative dispositions. What is also apparent is the centrality of African integration and unity, a move that has been interpreted as the recognition that Nigeria's global standing hinges on its credibility as a regional leader (T. Ojo, 2017; Agwu, 2009).

Nigeria's African Policy

This section evaluates Nigeria's behaviour in the implementation of its foreign policy objectives. While the objective of liberating the continent from colonialism has long been achieved, it is still worth considering given that Nigeria's role may still have a bearing on attitudes towards the country.

The Fight against White Minority Rule and Colonialism

Nigeria's tough stance against colonial and white minority rule in Africa is well documented in academic scholarship (see Gibson, 1972; Abegunrin, 2009; Agwu, 2013, p. 596). Diplomatically, Nigeria chaired the UN's Special Committee against Apartheid for 22 years – between 1972 and 1994. This is in addition to canvassing for economic sanctions against the apartheid regime (Tella, 2018, p. 11), moving for the exclusion of South Africa from the Commonwealth (Associated Press, 1986), and supporting boycott campaigns against it in such international sporting events as the Davis Cup of 1975 (New York Times, 1975), and the Montreal Olympics of 1976 (The Guardian, 1976). In what is suggestive of Nigeria's firm commitment to see the end of white minority rule in the continent, Campbell and Page (2018) attribute Nigeria's decision to nationalize British Petroleum's (BP) holdings in the oil and gas sector in 1979 to the need to "punish Thatcher's government for its policies towards then apartheid South Africa and white-ruled Rhodesia" (p. 149). This came after Thatcher's government permitted BP to export non-embargoed oil to South Africa (Itugbu, 2017, p. 10).

This foreign policy disposition was informed by Nigeria's own experience with colonialism and its Pan-Africanist aspiration of ridding the continent of Western imperialism. As such, Nigeria was an active participant in international efforts to free the former Portuguese colonies of Mozambique, Cape Verde, Guinea Bissau, Angola, and Sao Tome and Principe from the shackles of European imperialism by making financial contributions to decolonization movements (Saliu & Omotola, 2008; Tella, 2018). It is estimated that between 1960 and 1994 Nigeria expended close to $1 billion in the fight against white minority rule and colonization in Africa (Saliu & Omotola, 2008, p. 76). Under the first Obasanjo administration, Nigeria raised $37 million for the Southern African Relief Fund, which was set up in 1977 to provide education and welfare services to victims of apartheid (Tella, 2018, p. 11).[1] Frontline states like Botswana, Zimbabwe, and Zambia which suffered losses in their bid to accommodate members of the African National Congress (ANC) fleeing South Africa were supported by the Nigerian government with a donation of $10 million (Saliu & Omotola, 2008, p. 76).

Within the Portuguese territories, Nigeria was equally active, donating $20 million to the Movement for the Liberation of Angola (MPLA) and reportedly pledged another donation of $100 million (Tella, 2018, p. 12). Once Nigeria discovered that the US and the apartheid regime in South Africa were supporting the Union for the Total Independence of Angola, it donated arms to the MPLA (see Wilmot, 1989, p. 4). Following these, Nigeria and South Africa maintained strong conflictual relations owing to the former's support for the ANC and other decolonization movements in the continent. This even led to Pretoria joining France and Cote d'Ivoire to support Biafra's quest for independence during the Nigerian civil war (Agwu, 2013).

While the imperative of boosting its leadership aspirations cannot be minimized, Nigeria's role in the decolonization struggle typified its commitment to the continent. It also demonstrated its commitment to multilateralism and peaceful resolution of political disputes, as the country refrained from direct military confrontation over white minority rule and colonialism in the continent. To date, Nigeria's commitment to these ideals has not waned, as it remains committed to the independence of the Saharawi Democratic Republic from the Kingdom of Morocco. This partly informs Nigeria's refusal to support Morocco's ECOWAS membership bid.

Regional Integration as a Pathway to Enhanced Cooperation

Immediate post-independence Nigeria defined regional integration in mostly economic terms, a reflection of its stance during debates between the Casablanca and Monrovia groups. Nigeria held that a continental political union should be the end of a gradual process commencing with sub-regional economic integration, followed by "functional cooperation and coordination and leading towards, perhaps, a common market" (O. Ojo, 1980, p. 572). As discussed in Chapter 4, Nigeria's argument, at the time, was that sub-regional integration would reduce the dependence of Francophone West Africa on France and also increase the bargaining power of the sub-region, and by implication, Nigeria, against Europe. While the importance of opening Nigeria's large market to the sub-region cannot be minimized, the outbreak of the Nigerian civil war was equally influential in Nigeria's drive to contemplate regional initiatives aimed at eroding colonial influence in West Africa and improving its influence in Francophone West Africa (Bach, 2007).

To this end, the cultivation of cordial relations and trust among leaders in the region was prioritized by the Balewa administration and successive military regimes, notably that of General Yakubu Gowon. Nigeria's approach was transactional and persuasive in the sense that it mostly offered economic incentives to neighbouring states and, in some rare instances, protection. This was in the expectation that West African states would accede to its version of sub-regional integration. Thus, while certain expressions of Nigeria's foreign policy were meant to drive the integration process, others were conceived to maintain or sustain it within and beyond ECOWAS.

For analytical convenience, this section evaluates Nigeria's quest for regional integration by demarcating between pre- and post-ECOWAS strategies.

Nigeria's Integration Strategy – Pre-ECOWAS

Besides Cote d'Ivoire, Senegal, Mali, and Upper Volta (Burkina Faso), all other countries in the sub-region, to various extents, were open to the idea of an all-inclusive WAEC even if it took some diplomatic machinations on the part of Nigeria to get them on board. Nigeria was assured of the support of Anglophone West African states given their continuous commitment to the "principles of the Protocol of the abortive West African Regional Group."[2] Meanwhile, the Francophone quartet feared a potential Nigerian dominance, and as a result sought, with the support of Niger and Mauritania, the formation of a French alternative to WAEC, which, as discussed previously, was labelled CEAO, an objective, which came to fruition in 1973 (see O. Ojo, 1980, p. 597). The strategic disposition of these states towards WAEC came from the deep political and economic relations they shared not only between themselves but also with France.

This regional political context geared Nigeria's diplomatic offensive towards an unsuccessful attempt to circumvent the establishment of CEAO. Domestically, Nigeria overcame anti-integrationist sentiments with the help of the business community, under the aegis of the Nigerian Chamber of Commerce, Industry, Mines, and Agriculture (NCCIMA). Sub-regionally, NCCIMA was instrumental in mobilizing private sector support for integration in ten West African states. The government on its part toed the line of holding difficult negotiations with sub-regional leaders and building bilateral and multilateral coalitions. Buoyed by revenues from oil, Nigeria's approach mostly combined emotional and technical arguments about the benefits of regional integration, donation of cash gifts, and the financing of infrastructural projects.

Togo, Benin, and Guinea were the first Francophone countries to embrace the idea of WAEC. In April 1972, Togo formally joined Nigeria to set up a joint commission to explore wide areas of cooperation in trade, transport, monetary policies, and telecommunications (see O. Ojo, 1980). A history of cordial relations between both countries was particularly instrumental in convincing President Eyadema of the necessity of WEAC. With Togo's support, Benin was boxed in a corner but remained reluctant to work with Nigeria towards WAEC despite a history of cordial relations. In January 1971, Benin's Presidential Council requested an extension of bilateral economic ties to accommodate financial assistance and joint infrastructural projects such as revamping the highway between Idiroko and Port Novo and establishing direct telecommunication lines between Lagos and Cotonou. In Guinea, Nigeria's efforts were mostly facilitated by the animosity between Sekou Touré and President Senghor, which had resulted in Guinea's exclusion from the protocol agreement of CEAO in May 1970.

In April 1973, Mathieu Kerekou, as President of Benin, refused to sign the final treaty establishing CEAO. Rather, he affirmed Benin's commitment to its principal partners – Togo, Ghana, and Nigeria (O. Ojo, 1980). Before Kerekou's regime, Nigeria had, amongst other largesse, set up direct telecommunications between both capitals, revamped the Porto Novo highway for the sum of $1.7 million, and granted an interest-free loan of $1.2 million to Benin, all of which did not dissuade Benin from initialling the preliminary agreements of the CEAO in Mali (O. Ojo, 1980; Tella, 2018). With Guinea, Nigeria's approach was security-oriented, although it donated the sum of ₦50,000 to the *Jeunesse de la Revolution Democratique Africaine*. In a visit to Guinea in 1972, Gowon and his Guinean counterpart agreed to a defence and security pact.

Realizing the dual role the organized private sector could play in assuaging domestic anti-integrationist sentiments while also functioning across national frontiers, Professor Adedeji, Nigeria's Commissioner for Economic Development and Reconstruction, enlisted the support of NCCIMA. In his words, "the reality of the community rests largely in the hands of ... agents of socio-economic activity ... and their organized association like the chambers of commerce ... [which] must be induced to function across national frontiers" (cited in O. Ojo, 1980, p. 586). NCCIMA heeded the government's call and engaged its Anglophone and Francophone counterparts to form the Federation of African Chambers of Commerce, Industry, and Agriculture (FACCIA) in November 1972 – just some months after the Togo-Nigeria agreement. Like their Nigerian counterparts, the ten members of FACCIA envisaged greater opportunities arising from a common market, and as such lobbied their governments to support a common market. This was a significant breakthrough, as the FACCIA would become instrumental in getting West African governments to commit to ECOWAS.

Having secured Anglophone support, as well as the commitment of Togo, Guinea, and Benin, by 1973 Nigeria shifted its diplomatic offensive to the Francophone quartet. In July and August 1973, the Nigeria/Togo draft proposal was shuttled around West African capitals by the Professor Adedeji-led delegation. Considering CEAO countries may suffer potential losses in subvention from the European Economic Community (EEC) should WAEC be formed, Nigeria promised to offset this loss. With de Gaulle out of the way, Cote d'Ivoire's perception of Nigeria as a threat had begun to dissipate, with the former "believing in the possibility of a mutually rewarding all-West African economic community provided there was true friendship and mutual confidence" (Cited in O. Ojo, 1980, p. 596).

Although Nigeria had agreed in January 1972 to supply Niger with about 30,000 kilowatts of electricity amounting to ₦9.6 million, it wasn't until Lt. Col. Seyni Kountche became president in April 1974 that Niger committed to WEAC, but this was motivated by the need to secure Nigeria's oil and asphalt at concessionary rates (O. Ojo, 1980).

In February 1975 West African states took a decisive step towards the formation of ECOWAS with the adoption of the Lomé Convention by African, Caribbean, and Pacific (ACP) countries. This is because the ACP provided an institutional framework that allowed for the maintenance of extra-African economic relations, under a unified legal framework. This implied that membership of ECOWAS will no longer require Francophone states to sever ties with France. With Nigeria also acceding to the request of CEAO members that their association with ECOWAS would not require the renunciation of their membership of other regional or sub-regional groupings, including the CEAO, all was clear for the formation of ECOWAS in May, with its headquarters positioned in Abuja.

The Establishment of ECOWAS may be deemed a breakthrough, not the least because it institutionalized economic cooperation and integration at the sub-regional level, but also, Nigeria's vision for a continental union structured around strong sub-regional organizations prevailed. No doubt Nigeria's leadership and economic diplomatic schemes aided this effort, but other factors such as the ACP-EEC negotiations and concerted efforts by the business community were equally important.

Nigeria's Integration Strategy – Post-ECOWAS

With the establishment of ECOWAS, Nigeria's integration strategy shifted towards deepening and enhancing cooperation in the sub-region. The oil boom, which began in the 1970s, came to an end in the mid-1980s, engendering domestic economic challenges and increasing Nigeria's dependence on Western financial institutions. It is also worth mentioning that as more states in the continent and even West Africa began commercial production of oil, the strategic importance of Nigeria's oil as a tool of statecraft waned, as was Nigeria's ability to maintain its strategy of issuing out cash gifts (Campbell & Page, 2018). Consequently, the Nigerian government scaled back its political role within the continent and changed the nature of economic assistance it offered other African states. Technical assistance and cooperation became a staple of Nigeria's foreign policy.

The NTAC was set up in 1987 and legalized in January 1993 through Decree no. 27 in a move that signalled Nigeria's shift away from cash donations (Adebanwi, 2011). At the conception of the programme, General Babangida remarked that the scheme is designed to share Nigeria's technical expertise with "friends and neighbours" to foster a climate of mutual understanding and collective economic growth (cited in Ladan, 2006, p. 35). The objectives set out in Article 21 mirror this remark, as the DTAC was set up to establish meaningful contacts between the youths of Nigeria and those in recipient countries, as well as share Nigeria's technical expertise, as a form of assistance. It was designed to use the country's skilled manpower to engage the foreign public directly, improve the image and visibility of the country, and promote cooperation and mutual understanding amongst ACP countries.

Volunteers are experienced Nigerian professionals in various fields including education, engineering, medicine, and agriculture. They are presented as nominees by the Nigerian government at the request of beneficiary countries, which have the right to reject or accept any nominee. This transaction is predicated on an agreement between Nigeria and the recipient country on the one hand and between the volunteer and Nigeria on the other, spelling out the obligations of each party. Whereas Nigeria bears all financial burdens relating to the upkeep of volunteers for the duration of their deployment, recipient countries are to provide accommodation and free medical services, as well as guarantee exemption from local income tax.

Available data suggest that about 6,000 Nigerians have been deployed to over 40 countries around the globe since the inception of the programme (DTAC, personal communication, July 10, 2019). Notable amongst recipient countries are West African states such as Liberia, Sierra Leone, The Gambia, Ghana, Niger, Senegal, Benin, Burkina Faso, and Guinea Bissau. Although the amount expended on NTAC from the inception of the scheme remains unclear, a summation of budgetary allocation to the programme between 2009 and 2018 carried out by Ogbonna and Ogunnubi (2018, p. 134) amounted to a little under ₦27 billion, which when converted to US dollars without adjustment for inflation amounts to $75 million.

The fact that Nigeria deployed 50 volunteers to Liberia in July 2019 to help address challenges in the health and education sectors indicates Nigeria's belief in the efficacy of the programme (Agbakwuru, 2019). In April 2018, Nigeria's High Commissioner to Sierra Leone noted that over 500 TAC volunteers have been posted to his country since September 2009 (Premium Times Nigeria, 2018). No doubt African governments are appreciative of Nigeria's efforts in this regard. For instance, former Ethiopian Prime Minister, Meles Zenawi, notes the meaningful contributions Nigerian volunteers have made to the socio-economic development of the continent (Tella, 2018). Similarly, former Namibian president, Sam Nujoma, interpreted Nigeria's decision to send volunteers to his country as a sign of support for his government and the Namibian people (see Adebanwi, 2011). However, the question remains if the West African public feels the same way. As will be discussed in Chapter 8, not many of them are even aware that such a programme exists. The same is the case with Nigeria's technical cooperation initiatives.

As discussed in Chapter 5, the Nigerian government established the NTF to serve three purposes. First, to aid the development of RMCs through low-interest loans repayable over 25 years. Second, to contribute to the trust fund of heavily indebted poor countries in the region. Third, to fulfil its objective of contributing to the socio-economic development of Africa. However, the apparent fragility and fragmentation of African economies in an increasingly globalized world, combined with Nigeria's bid to align its economic diplomacy initiatives to its strategic interest, compelled the Obasanjo administration to reorient the NTF towards technical cooperation in 2001. This was designed to deepen integration and promote sustainable development.

Consequently, the Nigerian government established the Directorate of Technical Cooperation in Africa under the MFA to administer the programme. In April 2004 Nigeria signed a TCA with the AfDB to create a specialized technical assistance fund, known as the NTCF to be jointly administered with the AfDB. Conceived "as a special funding window from the NTF," the NTCF was designed to finance "technical and institutional support programs for the benefit of [RMCs], with a view of promoting greater intra-African technical cooperation through the mobilization of African expertise" (AfDB, 2017, p. 2). This mostly took the form of funding projects in different sectors such as health, education, agriculture, and governance in RMCs.

With the agreement entered in 2004, $25 million was moved from the NTF to the NTCF to fund institutional support and technical programmes (AfDB, 2017). One such programme is the Scientific and Technical Exchange Programme set up in 2006 to deploy Nigeria's technical and professional experts to African countries where they play the role of technical ambassadors and also serve the purpose of bridging the gap in technological knowledge between African states. In addition to this programme, the NTCF has also funded several projects, including the parliamentary capacity-strengthening programme for public finance management, accountability, and integrity in The Gambia, Ghana, Kenya, Malawi, and Sierra Leone. It equally provided post-graduate scholarships to African students from Liberia, Malawi, and Sierra Leone (AfDB, 2017). Between April 2004 and May 2017, the NTCF financed 93 projects across different sectors, with all 54 African countries benefiting in some form or another (AfDB, 2017). In terms of geographical spread, West Africa has had the highest number of interventions with 32% of projects focused on the sub-region (AfDB, 2017).

The Nigerian government has maintained its commitment to the initiative by renewing the existing agreement with the AfDB in 2018 for another ten years, that is, up until 2028 (S. Akintoye, personal communication, June 21, 2019). This demonstrates Nigeria's desire to contribute to the development of recipient countries, and its preference for enhanced cooperation and understanding as a means of minimizing threats to peace and stability, which remains an important component of its strategic objectives. What is particularly notable about Nigeria's technical assistance programme is its seeming altruistic character and the fact that it remains devoid of any known form of political conditionality.

Promotion of a Just Economic Order

As previously discussed, Nigeria's drive for sub-regional integration was based on the assumption that its large market would fare better with the creation of a common market with West African states. In a way, this suggests that Nigeria's prosperity was more or less tied to that of West African states. However, prevailing injustices in the global economic order appeared to be a stumbling block. As such, Nigeria believed that it had to forge a united front with developing countries to challenge injustices in the global economic order. This was an important feature of Nigeria's arguments during the formative years of ECOWAS, especially its emphasis on the need for collective self-reliance to help bridge the gap between the South and North. To President Obasanjo, the first democratically elected president of the fourth republic, there was an imperative for developing countries, laden with debt, to come together and seek a fair deal from the developed nations (Akinterinwa, 2004). In fact, President Obasanjo did not miss the opportunity to highlight the "immorality" of Africa's debt burden in every international forum (Itugbu, 2017, p. 13).

To Nigeria, a just economic order is fair trade relations between the global North and South, economic assistance and aid with reasonable and practical conditionalities, and increased investment in African economies. Nigerian leaders have always decried the apparent disparities in the world economic order where the liberalization of the global economy favours developed nations at the expense of developing nations. In the third D-8 summit held in Cairo, President Obasanjo emphasized these disparities by noting the unwillingness of industrialized nations to adopt measures within the World Trade Organization (WTO) that are beneficial to developing countries. His successor President Musa Yar'Ardua made similar calls in 2007 when he Championed "the emergence of a global economic system predicated on fairness, justice, and equity as the panacea to build a world of shared prosperity, peace and security" (cited in AllAfrica, 2007).

Described as an "activist president" given his commitment to secure a fair deal for Africa, Obasanjo's diplomatic strategy was geared towards mobilizing global opinion against the marginalization of African economies in the global distribution of wealth (Itugbu, 2017, p. 21). He decried the low levels of export from the region to developed countries and the failure of the latter to honour economic commitments to the continent. In addition, Obasanjo noted the declining share of Africa in the global trade for goods and services despite implementing wide-ranging economic reforms imposed by the International Monetary Fund and World Bank (Ubi & Akinkuotu, 2014). To the Nigerian government, a mutually beneficial partnership with the global north required fairer trade terms and the transformation of economic relations between Africa and Europe from dependence to interdependency. Obasanjo's speech to the Belgian parliament in July 2001 even called on Europe to help in the rehabilitation and industrialization of Africa, under a spirit of genuine partnership (see Ubi & Akinkuotu, 2014).

Through bilateral and multilateral arrangements, Nigeria sought to boost trade relations between Africa and the West, albeit unsuccessfully. Within the WTO, it sought to exploit the Generalized System of Preferences not just to benefit Nigeria but the region as a whole (Ubi & Akinkuotu, 2014). Regionally, Nigeria enshrined preferential trade clauses and concessions into the ECOWAS treaty and entered into economic partnerships with African states. Some of these partnerships include the African Growth and Opportunity Act, the Cotonou Agreement trade pact, NEPAD, and the creation of the AfDB. It also forgave debts owed by some African states, while also intensifying cooperative relations with developing countries across the globe.

In view of liberalizing trade for mutual and national development, President Obasanjo championed a "Fast Track" approach to integration in the early 2000s that sought the proclamation of West Africa as a free trade area and its transformation into a Customs Union. This endeavour led to the adoption of a CET that saw ECOWAS member states adopt a tariff structure that reduced weighted and unweighted average tariff rates from 25% to 17% and 29% to 18%, respectively (Ubi & Akinkuotu, 2014). The CET also saw Nigeria reduce its duty rates to 20% for finished goods, 10% for intermediate products, and 5% for raw materials. This is as duty rates for capital goods were completely removed (Ubi & Akinkuotu, 2014).

Promotion of Regional Security and Stability

Nigeria has been an active participant in the security dynamics of the sub-region since its independence. The country's efforts against colonialism and white minority rule may be construed as expressions of its goal of ensuring regional peace, security, and stability. With the end of the Cold War, the nature of conflicts in the region changed, as the fight against white minority rule gave way to civil wars where non-state actors featured prominently, in most instances as agitators for statehood and political inclusion. While civil wars have declined over the last decade, West African states, especially Nigeria, are dealing with new forms of security threats such as the rise of trans-border Islamic fundamentalist movements, smuggling in SALW, and banditry.

One way through which Nigeria sought to enhance regional security, especially at the height of ravaging civil wars, was by mandating the AFN and Nigerian Police Force to participate in peace support operations (PSOs). While this behaviour is suggestive of Nigeria's willingness and ability to contribute to international peace and security, it was also driven by the need to enhance its global profile and leadership credentials (FRN, 2017, p. 24). Nigeria's national interest was also at stake. The recurrent nature of intrastate conflicts in Africa, for the most part, engendered by the arbitrary partitioning of national boundaries and the accompanying nationalistic struggles and contest for juridical statehood, also informed a foreign policy posture that placed the mitigation of their contagious effects as a necessary condition for ensuring internal stability and regime security.[3] Put together, these factors place Nigeria's security engagement at the heart of the intersection between regional integration, peace, and development, on the one hand, and national stability and development, on the other.

Nigeria's foray into the practice of peacekeeping commenced in 1960 when the country deployed individual police officers (IPOs) to the UN operation in the Congo (ONUC). Since then, it has recorded over 20 participations in PSOs under the auspices of the UN, AU, and ECOWAS. This includes the deployment of military personnel, military staff officers, military observers, police advisers, IPOs, formed police units (FPUs), and civilian units.[4] Under the auspices of the UN and AU, Nigeria committed 1,500 troops to the AU Mission in Sudan (The New Humanitarian, 2004). The same applies to the AU Mission in Somalia (AMISOM), where Nigeria deployed 59 IPOs, 140 FPUs, and a senior leadership officer (AMISOM, n.d.).

In West Africa, Liberia and Sierra Leone illustrate Nigeria's commitment to regional peace and security. The spate of intrastate conflicts in West Africa compelled ECOWAS, whose mandate was purely economic, to include a peace and security component, culminating in the creation of ECOMOG. Nigeria bore most of the burden of ECOMOG as it committed both financial and human resources to stem the tide of conflicts in Liberia and Sierra Leone. In the former, it led regional efforts to oust Charles Taylor-led NPFL out of Monrovia in 1990. Although a peace agreement was signed in September 1996 between the warring factions, culminating in the organization of elections in July 1997 and the emergence of Charles Taylor as president, a second civil war broke out in 1999, just under a year after the withdrawal of ECOMOG.

While facing threats to his government from Cote d'Ivoire and Guinea-backed rebel groups – the Movement for Democracy in Liberia and the Liberian United for Reconciliation and Democracy – Charles Taylor was actively engaged in the civil war in neighbouring Sierra Leone by supporting the RUF. By late 2003, when both rebel groups had closed in on Monrovia, and Charles Taylor himself facing an indictment from the Sierra Leone Special War Crimes court, Nigeria led ECOMIL on another peace effort in Liberia. As part of the agreement brokered within a week of ECOMIL, Charles

Taylor resigned and was exiled to Nigeria where he was granted asylum until President Obasanjo handed him over to the war crimes commission.

In Sierra Leone, Nigeria similarly led ECOMOG to restore normalcy after Major Johnny Paul Koroma led a military coup that toppled the democratically elected government of Tejan Kabbah in May 1997. With the support of a 50-member UN Observer Mission in Sierra Leone, Nigerian troops joined ECOMOG forces already stationed in Freetown to dislodge Koromah's Armed Forces Ruling Council and the RUF. It also reinstated President Kabbah to his position as president in March 1998. Similar to Liberia, Nigeria was dominant in Sierra Leone, contributing 80% of troops and 90% of funds, which various scholars estimate to be in the excess of $10 billion (Obi, 2009; Adeniyi, 2018; Adebajo, 2004). It also suffered significant casualties, as over a thousand soldiers lost their lives in these missions (Tella, 2018).

What is clear is that Nigeria's legacy of peacekeeping in the sub-region leaves behind stable and democratic states in Sierra Leone and Liberia. Its global reputation has also gained tremendously from being an important contributor to international conflict resolution. This is also helped by the fact that Nigerians have at various times assumed strategic leadership positions in global peace operations. While Maj. Gen. Johnson Aguiyi-Ironsi served as force commander in ONUC, Maj. Gen. Chris Garuba, Lt. Gen. Isaac Obiokor, and Gen. Martin Agwai played strategic leadership roles in the UN Verification Mission in Angola, UNMIL, and UN Mission in Dafur, respectively (Adeninyi, 2018).

Over the last two decades, Nigeria's peace and conflict resolution strategy has gradually moved from a military interventionist to a mediatory and preventive orientation.[5] Nigeria has long been reputed for mediating regional conflicts as it wilfully combined such diplomatic practices with military interventions. In Liberia, following Samuel Doe's appeal for ECOWAS to help curtail the incursion of the NPFL, Gen. Babangida argued in favour of an ECOWAS mediatory role at the May 1990 ECOWAS meeting in The Gambia (Adibe, 1997; Obi, 2009). This plea led to the establishment of the Standing Mediation Committee, which included Togo, Ghana, Mali, Gambia, and Nigeria. As part of its mediatory role, a ceasefire was imposed and ECOMOG was formed.

Also, in Guinea-Bissau, after pleas from President Joao "Nino" Viera for ECOMOG intervention during the civil war, a committee made up of Nigeria, Ghana, Guinea, Burkina Faso, Cote d'Ivoire, Gambia, and Senegal was put in place to mediate the conflict. In concert with the Community of Portuguese-speaking countries, otherwise known as *Comunidade de Paises de Lingua Portuguesa*, ECOWAS got Viera and his erstwhile armed forces chief, Ansumane Mane, to sign a ceasefire agreement in August 1998. This agreement was short-lived, requiring a second mediation process that culminated in the signing of a second ceasefire agreement in November 1998 in Abuja.

As benign as its intent may appear, some of Nigeria's actions have not been devoid of criticism. In addition to allegations of grave human rights abuses by Nigerian soldiers in Liberia and Sierra Leone, Nigeria has some-times demonstrated a penchant for unilateral interventions to the chagrin of smaller and less powerful West African states (HRW, 1997; Obi, 2009). The HRW reported in 1997 that from the onset of Nigeria's intervention in Liberia, its soldiers were involved in grave human rights abuses. Also, Nigerian Alpha Jets carried out airstrikes on NPFL bases in the Port of Buchanan and Kataga that disproportionately targeted civilians, which falls contrary to international humanitarian law (HRW, 1994). These are in add-ition to charges that ECOMOG violated the medical neutrality clause by attacking hospitals and relief convoys (HRW, 1994).

West African states were also critical of Nigeria's high-handedness and, at times, unilateral disposition. For instance, to the chagrin of Ghana and Benin, Nigeria unilaterally replaced Arnold Quainoo, a Ghanaian, with Joshua Dogonyaro, a Nigerian, as ECOMOG force commander in Liberia (Amao & Maiangwa, 2017, p. 29). Also, West African states were particu-larly critical of Nigeria's hasty intervention in Sierra Leone, absent an official mandate from regional governments. According to Abass Bundu, the then Executive Secretary of ECOWAS, Nigeria's actions were "totally unwar-ranted and unjustified" (cited in HRW, 1997). As Blaise Campaore similarly remarked in an interview with Radio France International, "the agreements between the states of West Africa do not authorize military intervention to restore a regime or organize a counter-coup" (Cited in HRW, 1997).

With changing regional priorities and competing domestic pressures, including rising banditry across north-western Nigeria, the proliferation of SALWs, and the ongoing counter-insurgency in the north-east, Nigeria's for-eign policy preoccupation has been geared towards combatting Boko Haram and other domestic organized criminal activities. No doubt, these domestic security challenges are exacerbated by the proliferation of SALWs that began to manifest in the late 1960s during the Nigerian civil war. The fact that pres-ently an estimated 70% of SALWs in circulation within the sub-region may be found in Nigeria paints a picture of a regional and domestic security con-text characterized by the inextricable link between the country's variegated internal security challenges and trafficking in SALWs across West Africa.

Nigeria joined the Lake Chad Basin states and Benin to form the MNJTF. Authorized by the AU in March 2015 with a force level of 11,000 troops, the MNJTF is a combined multinational military set-up designed to police insurgent activities in the Lake Chad Basin (ICG, 2020). While this effort remains ongoing, questions persist about its effectiveness. Even efforts to curb access to illegal arms, as well as the broader arms trafficking trade across the sub-region through the adoption of the ECOWAS convention on SALWs, ammunition, and other related materials in June 2006 and the set-up of the Presidential Committee on SALWs, have also proven unsuccessful. While the complexities of these security challenges will continue to shape Nigeria's security engagement in the sub-region, it will also have to contend with questions wondering why a state reputed for bringing peace to Liberia and Sierra Leone is unable to deal with a home-grown insurgency for the better part of the last two decades.

Provision of Humanitarian Assistance

Nigeria's diplomatic engagement with African states includes a humanitarian component that is mandated by the constitution. Bolstered by its relatively superior economic resources, Nigeria often comes to the aid of African states in their moments of need. The cases of Sierra Leone and Liberia once against illustrate this point, as Nigeria's aid to these countries includes providing a haven for refugees and contributing to the post-war rebuilding efforts.

Nigeria played host to tens of thousands of refugees from Sierra Leone and Liberia at the Oru refugee camp in southwest Nigeria. In 2007, it granted 7,292 refugees – 5,619 Liberians and 1,673 Sierra Leoneans – who opted to remain in Nigeria access to education, work, and health care in an agreement that was signed between Nigeria, Liberia, Sierra Leone, ECOWAS, and the UNHCR (Reuters, 2007). Also, Babangida made donations to the Movement against Child Labour in Liberia, a group engaged in post-conflict reconstruction and peace-building efforts. It was involved with rehabilitating and reorienting orphans and kids without shelter. In November 1996, Nigeria's former First Lady, Maryam Abacha, equally donated $75,655 to the organization (Akinterinwa, 2006, p. 274).

Records of Nigeria coming to the aid of West African states date back to the great West African drought, which engulfed most of West Africa and the Sahel, including Mali, Niger, Senegal, and Chad, between 1972 and 1974 (Derrick, 1977). Despite confronting a similar challenge, Nigeria joined global agencies like the World Food Programme and EEC to support West African states by issuing the government of Mali a grant of ₦100,000 and coordinating the transportation of food from the southern Nigerian cities of Lagos and Port Harcourt to Niamey, the capital of Niger (Derrick, 1977). More recently in 2014, Nigeria came to the aid of the countries that were worst hit by the Ebola crisis: Liberia, Guinea, and Sierra Leone. Nigeria deployed 250 medical workers, including doctors, hygienists, and scientists as part of the AU's promise to mobilize 1,000 medical practitioners to Ebola-hit countries (BBC News, 2014).

Within the continent, Nigeria donated food items, clothing, and medications to countries suffering from drought and other natural disasters. This is exemplified by its donation of food items in March 2015 to drought-stricken Namibia. According to Reliefweb, a reputable source of information for humanitarian interventions in disasters and global crises, "Nigeria [...] donated three hundred tons of rice, seven hundred tons of maize, and three tons of fish fillets to Namibia [...] to help drought-stricken families" (2015). In response to Cyclone Idai which left over 1.6 million people homeless in the southern African countries of Zimbabwe, Mozambique, and Malawi,

Nigeria donated $500,000 each to the governments of these countries, in addition to 35 tons of relief materials and medical supplies (Frey, 2019).

These are practices Abuja has been accustomed to since the country's independence, but with Nigeria currently facing humanitarian challenges of its own, it is unclear if this foreign policy disposition can be sustained. The UN Office for the Coordination of Humanitarian Affairs (OCHA) reports that in Nigeria's north-east, where the Boko Haram insurgency festers, about 5.1 million people are at risk of food shortages due to famine and drought (OCHA, 2018). This is in addition to the displacement of over 2 million people, with about 200,000 Nigerian refugees spread across Cameroun, Niger, and Chad (UNHCR, 2020b).

Rebranding Nigeria

The need to create a positive image for Nigeria, although not articulated as a goal of foreign policy, became a national imperative at the beginning of Obasanjo's second stint as president. This was because Nigeria found itself in a precarious economic state due to negative economic policies and international sanctions (Ubi & Akinkuotu, 2014). The Abacha regime, widely held to be the most repressive in Nigeria's political history, had done much damage to Nigeria's reputation in the West, culminating in its suspension from the Commonwealth in 1995 (Commonwealth, 2013a) for the execution of Ken Saro-Wiwa and other Ogoni activists – an act, which in addition to others, violates the Harare Declaration (Commonwealth, 2013b).[6]

This came with some diplomatic implications, as the country was denied access to Commonwealth technical assistance as well as participation in Commonwealth meetings. It is unclear how Nigeria was perceived within Africa, as most African states were also governed by repressive regimes and displayed a heightened sense of commitment to African solidarity, but beyond the continent, Nigeria was completely ostracized. Confronting a burgeoning debt burden, as well as reduced FDI and development assistance, the Obasanjo administration tied the domestic economic imperative to an improved global image, one that the country's return to democratic rule was already bolstering.

Post-independence Nigeria has always contended with an image problem, at least in the eyes of the West, due to the violent nature of political contestations and the recurrent intervention of the military in politics. This began to take hold during the first republic, when the violent nature of electoral politics necessitated the first military coup of January 1966 followed by a counter-coup six months later, all of which culminated in the Nigerian civil war. Apart from the Murtala/Obasanjo military regime, which presided over the "golden era" of Nigeria's external engagement, and peacefully handed over power to a democratically elected president, all other administrations preceding Abacha's had image issues to contend with, ranging from excessive corruption, poor human rights record, to the repression of political oppositions.

During Babangida's regime, the country became seriously associated with the practice of advanced fee fraud, with some even suggesting that the government had a hand in it (Olukoshi & Agbu, 1995). As a consequence, Nigeria's technical assistance scheme was deliberately instilled with an image-laundering component, where NTAC volunteers were positioned as ambassadors to reflect a positive image of Nigeria in developing countries. This suggests that long before the fourth republic Nigerian leaders have been particular about the country's global reputation, although not at the level necessitated by the actions of the Abacha regime.

Early attempts to rebrand the country can be traced back to the late 1950s and early 1960s when the Nigeria government sponsored the production of movies, *Moral Disarmament* (1957) and *Bound for Lagos* (1962), which sought to portray "black as beautiful" and colonialist as "rapist" of Nigerian and African culture (Alawode & Sunday, 2013, p. 115). Nigeria launched the Voice of Nigeria (VON), its external radio broadcasting service, in 1961, to communicate Nigerian perspectives to West African audiences in English and French languages. In 1980 and 1991, its coverage area was expanded beyond the sub-region to include all of Africa and beyond. Although it targets mostly the Nigerian diaspora, Decree 15 of 1991, which established the independence of the corporation, emphasized such functions as expressing the country's culture, characteristics, and opinions in a way that enhances the country's image and its strategic objectives in foreign countries (B. A Shemang, personal communication, June 21, 2019; VON, 2012).

Benefiting from the goodwill that came with a peaceful transition from military to civilian rule and riding on his popularity at home and abroad, President Obasanjo personalized Nigeria's foreign policy process by embarking on what is now referred to as shuttle diplomacy to rebrand the country and regain the respect of the international community. In addition, the Obasanjo administration launched the "Heart of Africa Project" in 2004, designed to facilitate economic growth, address the eroders of the national brand, and promote Nigeria's brand assets that include locational and cultural assets, business brands, and important personalities (Alder Consulting, 2004). Despite costing Nigerian taxpayers a whopping ₦1.05 billion, the Heart of Africa Project was deemed a failure by the Yar'Adua administration and was replaced with another rebranding project dubbed "Nigeria: Good People, Good Nation" in 2009 (Folasade-Koyi, 2009).

"Nigeria: Good People, Good Nation" was predicated on the assumption that Nigeria's story is best told by its citizens. As such it was designed to boost tourism, invite foreign investment, and enhance Nigeria's global reputation by instrumentalizing the film industry and non-state actors with trans-border linkages (see Alawode & Sunday, 2013). Like its predecessor, it is widely adjudged to have failed for reasons bordering on lack of funds. Regardless of the paucity of funds, many Nigerians rightly scoffed at the idea of repairing the image of the country without confronting the inherent impediments of a rather favourable global imagery. These impediments reflect domestic challenges such as corruption, crime, insecurity, and infrastructural deficits (Economist, 2009). Yet again, another failed initiative was launched under the label "Fascinating Nigeria" in 2013. This time the government intended to promote Nigeria as a tourist destination country, touting the country's rich cultural resources.

In all these efforts, it is unclear who the government's intended targets are, but it is easily discernible that Nigeria has been more concerned with its image in the Western world – the source of FDI and development assistance to the country – than in Africa. Apart from NTAC, traces of image-laundering activities within Africa may be located in the "Nollywood Road Show Project," an initiative launched by NEPC and the MFA in October 2010 to promote Nigerian movies and explore opportunities for international artistic collaboration within the continent (Williams, 2011). Although the intent of its founders wasn't specifically geared towards improving the image of the country, there is no gainsaying that the potency of films to market and advertise suggests an image-laundering role for this initiative.

That these initiatives failed to have the desired effects for which they were conceived is indicative of the institutional deficiencies confronting Nigeria and its inability to effectively conceive and implement policies that are geared towards tackling the challenges denting the image of the country. In addition to some new trends, which manifested strongly during the administration of President Jonathan, such as the Boko Haram insurgency and cyber-crime, the country continues to grapple with such image-denting challenges as corruption, endemic poverty, insecurity, and violations of democratic norms. Some analysts even attribute Obama's decision to overlook Nigeria during his 2015 tour of Africa to the country's poor image (see Campbell & Page, 2018).

Nigeria's Commitment to Its Normative Principles

Undergirding Nigeria's strategic objectives is normative principles that are expected to inform, if not regulate, the country's external behaviour. As discussed earlier, these principles include a commitment to coexisting peacefully with other African states, promoting democracy, respect for international law and treaties entered with others, and finally the peaceful resolution of disputes. In this section, I assess Nigeria's role in promoting democracy across Africa and its level of commitment to peaceful coexistence and resolution of disputes.

Non-Aggression, Peaceful Coexistence, and Resolution of Disputes

In a demonstration of Nigeria's commitment to coexisting peacefully with African states, the NNDP emphasizes the formation of security alliances with friendly nations and respecting operational bilateral and multilateral defence agreements (FRN, 2017, p. 24). The NNDP stresses that these agreements may involve personnel exchanges, military educational assistance, information sharing, senior officers' visits, training exercises, and equipment and logistics supply. It also specifies that these practices must be geared towards enhancing international peace and security. Furthermore, the NNDP precludes the use of force in Nigeria's interaction with the international community except in situations where the country's trade and maritime routes are under threat, a situation that is yet to occur in Nigeria's post-independence history (FRN, 2017, pp. 12–13).

In Nigeria's post-colonial history, the country has been embroiled in two interstate conflicts: Chad in 1983 and Cameroun in the early 1990s. While the former, which stemmed from a border dispute, lasted between April and July 1983 and was characterized by occasional skirmishes resulting in the death of 75 Chadian and 9 Nigerian soldiers, the latter was a protracted dispute over the oil-rich Bakassi Peninsula lasting between 1996 and 2006. Regarding the border dispute, Nigeria peacefully ceded the disputed territory to Cameroun at the instance of the International Court of Justice ruling in 2002 (Uppsala Conflict Data Program, 2020).

Barring these rare instances of overt military confrontation, Nigeria's engagement with African states has been driven by its normative commitments. This is not just in terms of coexisting peacefully and resolving disputes, but also maintaining cordial military or security interactions with others, a disposition that suggests a certain level of commitment to binding agreements and treaties. As Wasa Festus, a deputy director in Nigeria's Defence Ministry, affirms, the country pursues "a peaceful foreign policy" and the AFN is authorized to act in furtherance of this objective (personal communication, July 3, 2019). Since independence, Nigeria has been altruistically disposed towards the pursuit of regional security by participating in bilateral and multilateral security agreements, as well as actively contributing to UN, AU, and ECOWAS-authorized peace support operations. This is in addition to the participation of the AFN in joint military exercises and personnel exchanges with African states, in a deliberate effort to boost cultural familiarity and enhance interoperability in the case of joint missions.

Nigeria's tri-service military institutions – the NDA, AFCSC, and NDC – are specifically reputed for facilitating military exchanges with countries well beyond the continent.[7] Aishatu Yanet, a research fellow at the NDC's Centre for Strategic Research and Studies, affirmed that 18 military officers from allied countries, including Liberia and Ghana, participated in the NDC's course 28 (personal communication, July 18, 2019). The Liberian Ambassador to Nigeria, Prof. Al-Hassan Conteh, also affirmed that several waves of his country's mid-level officers and military cadets have received training at the AFCSC and NDA, respectively (personal communication, September 10, 2019).

Nigeria is not alone in receiving personnel from other states, as the Ghana Armed Forces Command and Staff College (GAFCSC) and the Kofi Annan International Peacekeeping Training Centre have personnel from the AFN enrolled as part of efforts to enhance bilateral military cooperation (Graphic Online, 2020). A confidential interview with a senior military officer at the NDC revealed that Nigerian military personnel consistently participate in courses in Ghana. According to this interviewee, "I have done six [courses …] at different times" (personal communication, July 18, 2019). A minister at the Nigerian High Commission in Ghana, Shina Alege, also confirmed that some Nigerians are set to graduate from the GAFCSC (personal communication, September 3, 2019).

Nigeria has not coordinated any joint military exercise of its own but has joined other West African states to participate in US and France coordinated military exercises. Sequel to the Yaoundé Declaration signed in June 2013 on the Gulf of Guinea Security, Nigeria partook in US Africa Command (AFRICOM) sponsored joint maritime operations exercise, named "Obangame Express." This was conceived to enhance security cooperation as well as the collective capabilities of West African and Gulf of Guinea nations in areas of information sharing, tactical interdiction expertise, and maritime domain awareness (AFRICOM, n.d.). Similar exercises, dubbed "Grand African Nemo" – Navy Exercise for Maritime Operations – were conducted in 2018 and 2019 under the coordination of the French Navy on Nigerian waters.[8] In a demonstration of its superior naval capability in West Africa, Nigeria showcased its naval ships *Sagbama, Centenary*, and *Okpabana* during the 2019 exercise.

Spreading Democratic Values

As discussed in Chapter 5, Nigeria's experience with internal democracy is uninspiring in so many ways, nonetheless, the country has maintained a foreign policy posture that places the promotion of democracy across the continent as a strategic objective, whether under civilian or military regimes. In practice, some of Nigeria's behaviour appears to suggest a commitment to this objective, especially in situations where an unconstitutional change of power may have occurred. Nigeria rationalized its intervention in Liberia, Sierra Leone, and, more recently, The Gambia on the need to restore the will of the people. Apart from its willingness to sacrifice the blood of its citizens to restore "democratic governance" in African states, Nigeria has oftentimes made logistical contributions to the successful conduct of elections.

Although the Babangida regime recognized Samuel Doe in 1985, the administration of Shehu Shagari was particularly averse to the removal of William Tolbert, a democratically elected president in the 1980 coup. Several reasons have been adjudged for Nigeria's stance on Doe's regime, including promoting democracy. However, there was no doubt that Shagari was also concerned with the looming threat from his military, accustomed to intervening in domestic politics (Adebajo, 2002, p. 32). Regardless, Nigeria joined other African states to withhold diplomatic recognition for Doe's regime. As discussed previously, not only did Nigeria rupture diplomatic linkages by closing its embassy, but it also prevented Liberia's foreign minister from attending the extraordinary OAU economic summit of April 1980 in Lagos (Adebajo, 2002).

These actions illustrate the coercive dimensions of Nigeria's strategic engagement in the sub-region, as Abuja has not shied away from flexing its muscle to coerce erring regimes towards democratic practice, albeit hypocritical. For instance, a year before the Liberian case, Nigeria had reacted similarly to the Jerry Rawlings coup, as discussed in Chapter 4. More recent examples are Nigeria's intervention in Sao Tome and Principe in 2003 when the threat of force was instrumental in reinstating the ousted democratically elected president, Fradique de Menezes. The recent case of The Gambia is another instance where the country joined the likes of Senegal to launch a military invasion to remove President Jammeh after mediatory efforts had failed.

It also illustrates a contradictory and hypocritical component of Nigeria's drive for democracy in the continent. For instance, Sani Abacha – a brutal dictator – rationalized Nigeria's military involvement in Sierra Leone on the need to reinstate the democratically elected president, Tejan Kabbah. This remains the major documented reason for Nigeria's intervention in Freetown. Also, Babangida stood firmly behind Samuel Doe, even though he is a military dictator who ordered the execution of a democratically elected President, Robert Tolbert, and his son, Adolphus. This decision prompted Charles Taylor to label the Nigerian-led ECOMOG, a force made up of "undemocratic and self-perpetuating regimes" looking to "save the military dictatorship of Doe from collapse" (cited in Sesay, 1995).

Despite these apparent contradictions, Nigeria was instrumental in bringing the warring parties to a UN-supervised peace agreement in Abuja and was actively involved in the organization of presidential elections in July 1997 (Obi, 2009). Nigeria continues to maintain its commitment to democratic governance by supporting African states in the organization of elections as exemplified in its donation of 100 motorcycles and 15 Hilux vehicles to the Beninese electoral commission to facilitate the conduct of elections (Premium Times Nigeria, 2019). Also, during cash-strapped Guinea-Bissau's recently conducted legislative elections, President Buhari donated $500,000 to the government. This is in addition to 350 units of electoral kits, 2 light trucks, 5 Hilux vans, and 10 motorcycles to facilitate the conduct of elections (Omilana, 2019).

Conclusion

Nigerians are divided about perceptions of the country's external behaviour not just in West Africa, but globally. Although it remains unclear whether it is out of sheer patriotism or objective reasoning, a senior military officer who was a member of ECOMOG in Sierra Leone and also served as a military observer in Liberia is of the view that the Nigerian military is "perceived all over the world to be an instrument of stability ... [and] is looked upon as [a] credible force in the region." Referring to Africans, he subsequently notes that "they have confidence in us that when we get there, we are going to deliver" (Anonymous, personal communication, July 18, 2019). In his view, Nigeria's gallantry commands not just respect but also fear amongst West Africans, as the immediate capitulation of the military Junta in Sao Tome and Principe in the face of Obasanjo's threat suggests. Also, Aishatu Yanet maintains that "Nigeria has a very kind foreign face," a disposition which has informed its willingness to come to the aid of regional neighbours in times of conflict (personal communication, July 18, 2019).

Perhaps these views may be correct given that Nigeria's diplomatic initiatives appear mostly altruistic and rarely transactional with no immediate gain insight. They are akin to Arnold Wolfers' milieu goals, which are mostly conceived to enable powerful states, and in this context, regional leaders create an enabling environment to cultivate or sustain influence. In an apparent marginalization of those elements of structural and relational power that lie within the purview of non-state actors, particularly in the cultural domain, there appears to be an overbearing utility of economic and military resources in the actualization of Nigeria's strategic objectives in Africa.

As this chapter reveals, these resources have been particularly potent in the security domain where an evolving regional security context currently characterized by trans-border insurgency and organized criminal activities has required huge financial and military commitments from Nigeria. The formation of ECOWAS, which was achieved through convincing technical arguments, and the use of economic resources, including non-state economic actors, cash gifts, and development assistance, remains Nigeria's most prominent foreign policy accomplishment to date. This is so because it provided a forum where Nigeria mobilizes support for its strategic objectives. More importantly, it brought Nigeria closer to its objective of forging closer economic ties with West African states as the treaty's objectives were geared towards the elimination of customs duties, the establishment of a free trade zone, and provided a 15-year window for the establishment of a CET. In addition to these is the free movement of people and rights of residence for citizens of the community.

Since independence, Nigeria's ruling class believes that the country's geostrategic position and natural resources bestow upon Nigeria certain responsibilities amongst which is ensuring peace and stability in the continent. It is against the backdrop of this self-perception of regional leadership that the country has pursued its strategic and value objectives, albeit un-strategic, unsteady, and poorly implemented. While there appears to be some coercive posturing in Nigeria's quest to meet these objectives, which are mostly Afrocentric in scope, the country's strategic engagement in Africa has mostly taken the form of economic aid, technical assistance, cash gifts, development assistance, peacekeeping, and, to some extent, peace enforcement, targeted at governments and foreign publics alike, all in a bid to enhance its leadership credentials.

While some of these suggest behaviours that may resonate positively with elites in West Africa, in his article *Putting Nigeria First* Mailafia (2014) expresses doubt if these sacrifices have generated any "modicum of good-will" for Nigeria. Mailafia even contends that Nigeria is an "object of deri-sion" and that "Africans hate Nigerians" despite its efforts in the region, which contradicts the views of Aishatu Yanet and the senior military officer interviewed for this study. In Chapter 7, the study will subject this looming debate to scrutiny, by expatiating on Liberian and Ghanaian elite perceptions of Nigeria's foreign behaviour in West Africa and, by implication, the extent to which its resources and behaviour constitute an attractive source of influence.

Notes

1 Obasanjo is reported to have personally contributed $3,000 towards the fund, while senior members of his government contributed $1,500 each. These are in addition to federal civil servants who donated 10% of a month's salary towards the fund (Tella, 2018).

2 An illustration of this commitment can be deduced from the words of Ambassador Lafayette Diggs of Liberia, who expressed his country's wish "to work hand-in-hand most cooperatively with Nigeria [...] for the achievement of this most desir-able and worthy goal" of establishing a sub-regional economic community (Cited in O. Ojo, 1980, pp. 590 and 595)

3 This is evident in the statement released by the MFA during the Chadian civil war, when it noted that

these developments are as much threat to the stability of Chad as they are to the security of Nigeria for, another round of civil war in Chad which, from all indications, portends to be more ferocious than ever, would send thousands of Chadian refugees into Nigeria with serious economic, political and security consequences for this nation.

(cited in Akinterinwa, 1987, p. 1)

4 IPOs and FPUs are police officers seconded by their governments to serve in UN missions (UN, n.d.).

5 As figures from 2017 reveal, Nigeria presently ranks 14th in military and police contributions to UN operations, a position that is markedly down from 2001 when it ranked number one in the world (UN, 2019). Despite the apparent reduction in its involvement in peacekeeping mission, it nonetheless contributed 1,200 troops to the African-led International Support Mission in Mali in 2013 and provided air and sea support as well as 200 troops for ECOMIG, launched in January 2017.

6 The Abacha regime is reputed for overseeing Nigeria's most combative and defen-sive foreign policy owing to its brutal stance against domestic political opposition (Fawole, 2000; Zabadi, 2004). In addition to the execution of activists protesting the continuous degradation of Ogoni land by oil exploration activities, Abacha's

government was reputed for the wanton assassination of civil rights activists such as Kudirat Abiola, Alfred Rawane, and Bagauda Kaltho.

7　While the NDC provides training in peace support operations, the AFCSC is responsible for training operational-level military officers. The NDA is reputed for its officer entry programmes.

8　Operation "Grand African MEMO was designed to enhance tactical interaction between African navies, strengthen maritime security cooperation in the Gulf of Guinea, and build the capabilities of West African navies in countering illegal maritime activities" (Nigerian Navy, 2019).

References

Abegunrin, O. (2009). Nigeria and the struggle for the liberation of South Africa. *Africa in Global Politics in the Twenty-First Century*, 5–27. https://doi.org/10.1057/9780230623903_2

Adebajo, A. (2002). *Liberia's civil war: Nigeria, ECOMOG and regional security in West Africa*. Lynne Rienner Publishers.

Adebajo, A. (2004). Pax West Africana? Regional security mechanisms. In A. Adebajo and I. Rashid (Eds.), *West Africa's security challenges: Building peace in a troubled region*. Lynne Rienner Publishers.

Adebanwi, W. (2011). *Globally oriented citizenship and international Voluntary service: Interrogating Nigeria's Technical Aid Corps Scheme* [Discussion paper 71]. Uppsala: Nordiska Afrikainstitutet.

Adeniyi, A. (2018, April 24). *Peacekeeping contributor profile: Nigeria*. Providing for Peacekeeping. Retrieved September 26, 2020, from www.providingforpeacekeeping.org/2015/04/24/peacekeeping-contributor-profile-nigeria/

Adibe, C. E. (1997). The Liberian conflict and the ECOWAS-UN partnership. *Third World Quarterly*, *18*(3), 471–488.

African Development Bank. (2017, May). *Nigerian Technical Cooperation Fund (NTCF): Integrating Africa Supporting Growth*.

African Union Mission in Somalia. (n.d.). *Nigeria – Police*. AMISOM. Retrieved November 1, 2019, from https://amisom-au.org/nigeria-police/

Agbakwuru, J. (2019). *Nigeria to send 50 volunteers to Liberia. Vanguard News*. Retrieved December 3, 2020, from www.vanguardngr.com/2019/07/nigeria-to-send-50-volunteers-to-liberia/

Agwu, F. A. (2009). *National interest, international law, and our shared destiny*. Spectrum Books Limited.

Agwu, F. A. (2013). *Themes and perspectives on Africa's international relations*. University Press PLC.

Akinterinwa, A. B. (1987). Nigeria's peace policy in Chad. *Nigerian Forum*, *6*(5), 1–5.

Akinterinwa, A. B. (2004). Concentricism in Nigeria's foreign policy. In B. A. Akinterinwa (Ed.), *Nigeria's new foreign policy thrust: Essays in honour of Ambassador Oluyemi Adeniji* (pp. 428–460). Vantage Publishers Limited.

Akinterinwa, A. B. (2006). The role of Nigeria in the maintenance of international peace and security: ECOMOG as a case study. In M. Daura (Ed.), *Nigeria's technical aid corps: Issues and perspectives* (pp. 251–284). Dokun Publishing House.

Alawode, S. O., & Sunday, U. (2013). Home video as Nigerian image maker. *European Scientific Journal*, *9*(11), 110–128.

Alder Consulting. (2004). *The Heart of Africa Project*. Alderconsulting.com. Retrieved December 6, 2020, from https://alderconsulting.com/case_studies/the-heart-of-africa-project/

AllAfrica. (2007, November 12). *Nigeria: President Yar'Adua urges equitable global economic system*. AllAfrica.com. Retrieved August 7, 2018, from https://allafrica.com/stories/200711121415.html

Amao, O. B., & Maiangwa, B. (2017). Has the giant gone to sleep? Re-assessing Nigeria's response to the Liberian Civil War (1990–1997) and the Boko Haram insurgency (2009–2015). *African Studies*, 76(1), 22–43.

Associated Press. (1986, July 12). *Four African nations withdraw from Commonwealth Games. Associated Press News*. Retrieved April 4, 2022, from https://apnews.com/article/c6404c76554e02c16ae53c601636f5bc

Bach, D. C. (2007). Nigeria's 'manifest destiny' in West Africa: Dominance without power. *Africa Spectrum*, 42(2), 301–321. www.jstor.org/stable/40175188

BBC News. (2014). *Ebola crisis: Nigerian medics deploying to Sierra Leone*. Retrieved December 3, 2020, from www.bbc.co.uk/news/world-africa-30344311

Campbell, J., & Page, M. T. (2018). *Nigeria: What everyone needs to know*. Oxford University Press.

Commonwealth. (2013a). *Nigeria suspended from the Commonwealth*. Retrieved December 4, 2020, from https://thecommonwealth.org/history-of-the-commonwealth/nigeria-suspended-commonwealth

Commonwealth. (2013b). *Harare Commonwealth declaration*. Retrieved December 8, 2020, from https://thecommonwealth.org/history-of-the-commonwealth/harare-commonwealth-declaration

Derrick, J. (1977). The Great West African drought, 1972–1974. *African Affairs*, 76(305), 537–586.

Economist. (2009). *Good people, impossible mission*. Retrieved December 7, 2020, from www.economist.com/middle-east-and-africa/2009/04/30/good-people-impossible-mission

Fawole, A. (2000). Obasanjo's foreign policy under democratic rule: Nigeria's return to global reckoning? *Nigerian Journal of International Affairs*, 26(2), 20–40.

Federal Republic of Nigeria. (2017). *Nigerian National Defence Policy*.

Folasade-Koyi, A. (2009, March 13). *Nigeria: Heart of Africa Project was a failure – Akunyili*. AllAfrica.com. Retrieved December 28, 2019, from https://allafrica.com/stories/200903130573.html

Frey, A. (2019). *Nigeria donates $1.5m cash, relief materials to Zimbabwe, Malawi, Mozambique*. Club of Mozambique. Retrieved December 13, 2020, from https://clubofmozambique.com/news/nigeria-donates-1-5m-cash-relief-materials-to-zimbabwe-malawi-mozambique/

Gibson, R. (1972). *African liberation movement: Contemporary struggle against White minority rule*. Oxford University Press.

Graphic Online. (2020, June 26). *Junior Staff course 73 graduates from Ghana Armed Forces Command and Staff College*. Retrieved December 18, 2020, from www.graphic.com.gh/news/general-news/junior-staff-course-73-graduates-from-ghana-armed-forces-command-and-staff-college.html

Human Rights Watch. (1994, January 1). Human Rights Watch World Report 1994 – Liberia. Retrieved December 28, 2020, from www.refworld.org/docid/467fca7914.html

Human Rights Watch. (1997, November 9). *Nigeria's intervention in Sierra Leone.* Retrieved January 2, 2020, from www.hrw.org/reports/1997/nigeria/Nigeria-09.htm

International Crisis Group. (2020). *What role for the multinational Joint Task Force in fighting Boko Haram?* African Report No. 291.

Itugbu, S. (2017). *Foreign policy and leadership in Nigeria: Obasanjo and the challenge of African diplomacy (International Library of African Studies).* I. B. Tauris.

Ladan, M. A. (2006). The rights and obligations of a foreigner under international law. In M. Daura (Ed.), *Nigeria's technical aid corps: Issues and perspectives* (pp. 35–52). Dokun Publishing House.

Mailafia, O. (2014, February 10). *Putting Nigeria first. Business Day.* Retrieved October 20, 2020, from https://businessday.ng/columnist/article/putting-nigeria-first-2/

New York Times. (1975, July 4). *South Africa ban balked in Davis Cup.* Retrieved April 4, 2022, from www.nytimes.com/1975/07/04/archives/south-africa-ban-bal ked-in-davis-cup.html

Nigerian Navy. (2019). *Multinational Maritime exercise Grand African nemo begins in Nigerian waters.* Retrieved May 5, 2020, from www.navy.mil.ng/2019/10/30/ multinational-maritime-exercise-grand-african-nemo-begins-in-nigerian-waters/

Obi, C. I. (2009). Economic Community of West African States on the ground: Comparing peacekeeping in Liberia, Sierra Leone, Guinea Bissau, and Côte d'Ivoire. *African Security, 2*(2–3), 119–135.

Ogbonna, N. C., & Ogunnubi, O. (2018). Rethinking the role of Nigeria's technical aid corps as soft power: Rough diamond or fools' gold. *African Journal of Peace and Conflict Studies, 7*(2), 121–141.

Ojo, O. J. (1980). Nigeria and the formation of ECOWAS. *International Organization, 34*(4), 571–604. www.jstor.org/stable/2706513

Ojo, T. (2017). Nigeria, public diplomacy and soft power. In N. Chitty, L. Ji, G. D. Rawnsley, and C. Hayden (Eds.), *The Routledge handbook of soft power* (pp. 315–325). Routledge.

Okeke, C. N. (1981). Nigerian foreign policy under the constitution of the Federal Republic of Nigeria (1979). *Suffolk Transnational Law Journal, 5*(2), 201–212.

Okolo, J. E., & Langley, W. E. (1973). The changing Nigerian foreign policy. *World Affairs, 135*(4), 309–327.

Olukoshi, A. O, & Agbu, O. (1995, January 15–19). *The deepening crisis of Nigerian federalism and the future of the nation-state [Conference session].* Conference on 'Challenge for the Nation-State in Africa'. The Institute of Development Studies, University of Helsinki, Finland.

Omilana, T. (2019). *Buhari donates $500,000 to Guinea Bissau for election. The Guardian.* Retrieved March 3, 2020, from https://guardian.ng/news/buhari-dona tes-500000-to-guinea-bissau-for-election/

Premium Times Nigeria. (2018). *Nigeria deploys 500 technical aid corps volunteers in Sierra Leone.* Retrieved December 3, 2020, from www.premiumtimesng.com/ news/more-news/264012-nigeria-deploys-500-technical-aid-corps-volunteers-in-sierra-leone-envoy.html

Premium Times Nigeria. (2019). *Despite cash crunch, Nigeria donates vehicles, motorcycles to Benin Republic. Premium Times Nigeria.* Retrieved March 3, 2020,

from www.premiumtimesng.com/news/headlines/199219-despite-cash-crunch-nige
ria-donates-vehicles-motorcycles-benin-republic.html

Reliefweb. (2015). *Huge food donation from Nigeria ... for drought-stricken
Namibia. Reliefweb.* Retrieved December 4, 2020, from https://reliefweb.int/rep
ort/namibia/huge-food-donation-nigeria-drought-stricken-namibia

Reuters. (2007). *Liberian, S. Leonean refugees to settle in Nigeria.* Retrieved December
4, 2020, from https://uk.reuters.com/article/us-nigeria-refugees/liberian-s-leonean-
refugees-to-settle-in-nigeria-idUSL0759686620070807

Saliu, H., & Omotola, S. (2008) Can Nigeria get a UN Security Council seat?
South African Journal of International Affairs, 15(1), 71–85. doi:10.1080/
10220460802217975

Sesay, M. A. (1995). Collective security or collective disaster? Regional peace-keeping
in West Africa. *Security Dialogue, 26*(2), 205–222.

Tella, O. (2018). Is Nigeria a soft power state? *Social Dynamics, 44*(2), 376–394.
https://doi.org/10.1080/02533952.2018.1492833

The Guardian. (1976, July 19). *African nations boycott Montreal Olympics – archive.*
Retrieved April 4, 2021, from www.theguardian.com/sport/2021/jul/19/african-
nations-boycott-montreal-olympics-1976

The New Humanitarian. (2004, August 19). *Nigerian senate approves sending 1,500
peacekeepers to Darfur.* Retrieved January 28, 2020, from www.thenewhumanitar
ian.org/fr/node/218804

Ubi, E. N., & Akinkuotu, O. O. (2014). Nigerian foreign policy and economic development, 1999–2013. *International Area Studies Review, 17*(4), 414–433.

United Nations. (2019). *Ranking of military and police contributions.* United Nations
Peacekeeping. Retrieved December 9, 2019, from https://peacekeeping.un.org/en/
ranking-of-military-and-police-contributions

United Nations. (n.d.). *Individual Police Officers.* United Nations Police. Retrieved
May 18, 2019, from https://police.un.org/en/individual-police-officers

United Nations High Commissioner for Refugees. (2020b, April 17). *Across West
Africa dual challenge of conflict and coronavirus threatens millions of people.*
Retrieved April 21, 2020, from https://tinyurl.com/4h39jf78

United Nations Office for the Coordination of Humanitarian Affairs. (2018). *Nigeria.*
OCHA. Retrieved December 4, 2020, from www.unocha.org/nigeria

United States African Command. (n.d.). *Obangame Express.* Retrieved December 9,
2019, from www.africom.mil/what-we-do/exercises/obangame-express

Uppsala Conflict Data Program. (2020). UCDP. Retrieved December 13, 2020, from
https://ucdp.uu.se/statebased/858

Voice of Nigeria. (2012, March). *Brochures and Programme of Event for the
Commissioning of Voice of Nigeria Ultra Modern Transmitting Station.*

Williams, S. (2011). *Echoes from the Kenyan Nollywood roadshow. Daily Trust.*
Retrieved December 8, 2020, from https://dailytrust.com/echoes-from-the-kenyan-
nollywood-road-show

Wilmot, P. (1989). Nigeria's Southern Africa Policy 1960–1988. *The Scandinavian
Institute of African Studies, 8,* 2–15.

Zabadi, I. S. (2004). Nigeria's new multilateral diplomacy. In B. A. Akinterinwa (Ed.),
*Nigeria's new foreign policy thrust: Essays in honour of Ambassador Oluyemi
Adeniji* (pp. 343–358). Vantage Publishers Limited.

7 Elite Attitudes towards Nigeria in Liberia and Ghana

Introduction

In Chapter 4, I demonstrated a West African context characterized by patterns of interaction and issues amenable to the use of soft power. Subsequently, an exploration of Nigeria's soft power potential in Africa revealed the existence of potentially attractive resources, both in their latent and manifest forms, inherent in Nigeria's military, economic, cultural, and political power categories. Chapter 6 continued in this sequence of empirical analysis by exploring the utility of these resources in the pursuit of Nigeria's African policy. It revealed that Nigeria's economic, military, and human capital have served a national interest that prioritizes national security and the welfare of citizens. While there are visible expressions of coercive posturing in Nigeria's foreign policy behaviour, Abuja has mainly relied on the use of economic aid, technical assistance, cash gifts, development assistance, peacekeeping, and, to some extent, peace enforcement, targeted at governments and foreign public alike, to meet its strategic objectives and enhance its aspirational goal of sub-regional and continental leadership.

This chapter subjects these findings to the perceptive scrutiny of political and academic elites in Ghana and Liberia. It assumes that attraction lies in the perceptive disposition of those at the receiving end of Nigeria's policies, whether directly targeted at them or not. Insofar as attitudes towards Nigeria suggest favourable perceptions, the relationship between attraction and support for the country's objectives, as well as the effectiveness of soft power as a strategic approach may be explored.

As such, the aim of this chapter is to assess elite attitudes – negative and positive – towards Nigeria. It questions what elements of Nigeria's soft power potential, both in their inherent quality and instrumentalization by the state, constitute an attractive source of influence in West Africa and what factors drive this attraction. It also questions the challenges confronting Nigeria's projection of soft power by probing the unattractive elements of its power resources and the reasons for this. This is important because exploring attitudes towards Nigeria's resources and behaviour reveals its ability to

DOI: 10.4324/9781003396628-7

attract and persuade. To this end, the chapter presents analysed qualitative and quantitative data gathered from Ghana and Liberia.

The chapter is divided into four sections. The first section provides a detailed discussion of the data collection and analytical approaches used in deriving insights into elite attitudes towards Nigeria. The second section presents an overview of perceptions. The third section explains the attractive components of Nigeria's power resources and the reasons for their attractiveness, and the fourth discusses the unattractive components of Nigeria's power resources as well as the reasons behind this.

Data Collection and Analysis

Soft power affects actors differently, even within sovereign territories, making the impact of attraction on foreign policy outcomes heavily contingent on which actor finds the resources and behaviour of the agent attractive and the level of control they have over foreign policy decision-making (Fan, 2008). In most African states, issues of foreign policy are rarely determined by the yearnings or opinions of the masses, but by the personal preferences of leaders or, to minimal extents, an elite class of scholars, journalists, and government officials (Anderson, 2014).[1] As such, the study population in Ghana and Liberia was limited to what Pierre Bourdieu (1984) referred to as "symbolic elites."[2] These are people who make decisions on the allocation of resources. They are also individuals instrumental in defining problems and setting the agenda on issues of public or foreign policy. They shape public opinion on important issues, and as such, can provide pointers to the perception of the broader public (Page & Shapiro, 1983).[3]

Data Collection

Given the nature of the research problem, a mixed-method research approach was used to gather primary data from individuals in the cities of Accra and Monrovia. These were gathered through the use of semi-structured interviews and questionnaires. The sampling strategy devised to collect data in Ghana and Liberia was less concerned with drawing a representative sample, given that accurate information about the study population is not known, as the research prioritized individuals who have knowledge of Nigeria's African policy and the policies of their government towards Nigeria. This necessitated the use of a non-probability sampling method for the collection of qualitative and quantitative data, which required the minimization of randomness.

Put differently, it required the use of two sampling methods: purposive non-probability and snowball/chain-referral sampling. While it is important to recall that the choice of a mixed-method approach was informed by the need to account for the views of a broader audience of Ghanaians and Liberians towards Nigeria, and also provide an understanding of the reasons behind prevailing attitudes and perceptions to make inferences about the attractive and unattractive components of Nigeria's influence, this approach also helps to triangulate, increase credibility and also the likelihood of validity.

In Liberia and Ghana, political and/or state and academic elites were prioritized. While state actors were targeted based on positional criteria, to a large extent, non-state actors were selected based on reputation, especially those former diplomats with enough knowledge of Nigeria's African policy to have an informed opinion. Non-state actors such as journalists and academics were also targeted to observe opinions and attitudes towards Nigeria's soft power assets and behaviour in the sub-region. To facilitate the collection of data, through the conduct of interviews, questions were tailored to the official mandates and areas of responsibility of respondents. These respondents are officials of the foreign affairs ministry in Ghana and Liberia, past diplomatic officials with knowledge of their country's engagement with Nigeria, intellectuals or foreign policy experts, and journalists. Also, graduate students of political science and international relations in select universities in Liberia and Ghana were given questionnaires to fill out to broaden the scope of quantitative responses.

Drawing on Nye's prescription on the sources of soft power, the interview questions and questionnaire were designed to observe perceptions of Nigeria's qualities and behaviours across six categories: general favourability, people, military, economic, domestic and international politics, and culture. For instance, interviewees were asked about their perception of Nigeria's political values or economic competitiveness or its role in promoting regional integration and security. They were also asked about Nigeria's behaviour in the continent, their support for Nigeria's strategic objectives, and the imperative of heightened cooperation between their country and Nigeria. These are in addition to questions designed to test the familiarity of Liberians and Ghanaians with public diplomacy initiatives of the Nigerian government such as the NTAC and VON.

To ensure reliability, the questionnaires were modelled after the Anholt Ipsos Nation Brand Index (NBI) of 2019 and Holyk (2011), whose study made a compelling argument for the use of a subject-oriented approach to assess the soft power of states. This took the form of a comparative analysis of the soft power of China, the US, Japan, and South Korea in East Asia using a cross-national survey constructed around five indices: economic, diplomatic, political, cultural, and human capital.

Data Analysis

The qualitative data were subjected to thematic and content analyses using NVivo, in line with the works of Schreier (2012) and Gürsoy (2020) on *Qualitative Content Analysis in Practice* and "Reconsidering Britain's Soft Power: Lessons from the Perceptions of the Turkish Political Elite." The QCA is an approach to qualitative research and data interpretation involving the systematic description of meaning embedded in qualitative texts and their classification into coding frames by identifying themes (Hsieh & Shannon, 2005; Schreier, 2012). This positivist and interpretivist analytical approach, although mostly deductive, involves some level of inductivity since it is both variable and data-driven. While the main categories are determined by the theoretical underpinnings of the study, the sub-categories are in most instances informed by the data gathered.

A thematic criterion was used to select units of coding. This entails focusing on the relevant contents of the interview and selecting coded units based on topics discussed, meaning the change of a topic signals an end to one unit (Tesch, 1990; Schreier, 2012). With each transcript representing a unit of analysis, responses were coded into eight categories which include "positive model," "negative model," "more powerful, "not living up to its potential," "expression of support," "leadership," "sibling," and "rival." As Dey (1993) notes, coding is a conceptual process that is variable-driven, with each coding frame tantamount to a variable, and the sub-categories of each main category constituting the values of the variable. It is akin to what Coffey and Atkinson (1996) referred to as "reductive coding," in the sense that bits or pieces of data are categorized under labels or themes.

The evidence from these coding frames is presented in statistical form or in the form of percentages of coded references and buttressed with exemplars and descriptive evidence to boost trustworthiness. This is known as the quantitative analysis of qualitative data (Morgan, 1993). To further ensure the validity and reliability of the analytical process, the analysis strived to ensure "unidimensionality, mutual exclusiveness, exhaustiveness, and saturation" as suggested by Schreier (2012, p. 71). To ensure unidimensionality, which entails making sure that each category is unique and does not overlap with others, the coding process was repeated three times – two weeks apart from each process (Früh, 2007). This also helped in enhancing parsimony and concision. By striving for mutual exclusivity between categories, the analysis restricts a unit of coding to only one sub-category of a particular dimension. To ensure exhaustiveness, each unit of the coding material is assigned to at least a sub-category, while saturation is ensured by making sure no sub-category is left empty. Although saturation is not particularly necessary in a variable-driven approach, the fact that our analysis is also data-driven made it worth considering.

Overall, 800 paper questionnaires were distributed by hand in Liberia and Ghana, with 400 going to each country. Of these, about 94% of questionnaires were retrieved for analysis, amounting to 752. As Table 7.1 indicates, out of this number, 561 valid responses were analysed with 301 (53.7%) being Ghanaians and 260 (46.3%) Liberians. Given the objectives of the study, the quantitative data were not subjected to the analytical rigours of inferential statistics, rather they were subjected to descriptive analysis, given that their primary purpose is to triangulate the qualitative data. This

Table 7.1 Country Distribution of Respondents

		Frequency	Percent	Valid Percent	Cumulative Percent
Valid	Ghana	301	53.7	53.7	53.7
	Liberia	260	46.3	46.3	100.0
	Total	561	100.0	100.0	

analysis was centred around questions rather than problems or themes. As such, the presentation of data takes the form of percentages and frequency distribution.

Overview of Perceptions

Drawing from references to Nigeria's qualities and behaviour, eight main categories of perceptions were coded for analysis, as Figure 7.1 indicates. These exclude a neutral or residual category factored in to account for references that were not pertinent to the research objectives, and where interviewees did not provide clear responses.

As Table 7.2 indicates, the analysed portion of transcribed interviews assumed a coverage area of 55%, while 45% was labelled unclear and discarded. In total, 468 references were coded for analysis. Of these coded references 51% represented the views of Liberians, amounting to 239 references, while 49% represented the views of Ghanaians, amounting to 229 references.

As the "positive model" row suggests, most respondents in Ghana and Liberia referenced Nigeria in a positive light, amounting to 262 coded references or 55.9% of the overall coded references. This code applies where Nigeria's qualities and policies were referenced positively, suggesting that they reflect a good model or can be emulated. While in some instances interviewees were quite detailed in their assessment, in others, this was done in passing. With 52.7% and 47.3% of coded references, respectively, Table 7.2 equally reveals that Liberians and Ghanaians were not far apart in their positive perception of Nigeria.

The "negative model" category captures references where Nigeria was discussed in an undesirable manner or where Liberians and Ghanaians felt their country fared better and would not want to emulate Nigeria. In total, 102 references were coded in this category, amounting to 21.8% of total coded references. Negative sentiments about Nigeria were more pronounced in Ghana (62.7%) than in Liberia (37.3%). While this may not be unconnected with the subtle rivalry that exists between Nigeria and Ghana and the obvious developmental strides the latter continues to make, it also demonstrates disparities in how Nigeria is perceived even within its neighbourhood. In all, positive and negative sentiments towards Nigeria dominate

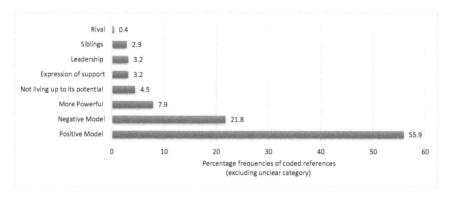

Figure 7.1 Overall Perceptions of Nigeria.

perceptions, as they combine to account for 77% of coded references and will form the crux of discussions in this chapter.

As Table 7.3 reveals, the findings of the QCA do not deviate substantially from the data gathered using questionnaires, as more Liberians equally have a favourable view of Nigeria than Ghanaians. Also, More Ghanaians have a less favourable view of Nigeria than Liberians. Overall, these findings appear to be in tandem with the QCA, as 67.7% of Ghanaians and Liberians find Nigeria attractive, while 20.9% find it unattractive.

The QCA reveals other positive sentiments towards Nigeria, that will form the basis of further discussions in Chapter 8, including perceptions of Nigeria as "more powerful" (7.9% of coded references), having "leadership" qualities (3.2% of coded references) and a "sibling" (2.9% of coded references). These are in addition to the willingness of respondents to support Nigeria's objectives and desire for more cooperation between both governments (3.2% of coded references). Together, these categories amounted to 17% of overall coded references even with, at times, generous interpretations. For instance, the category "more powerful" was used to capture references to Nigeria being a giant, big brother, and the most powerful state in the sub-region. Some of these references even alluded to Nigeria being the giant of Africa, a claim that is often repeated by political elites in Nigeria and informs their zeal to position the country as a leader in the continent.

The coding "sibling" was used to capture instances where Nigeria and Nigerians were referenced as brothers or sisters by Liberians and Ghanaians to describe the nature of their relationship. Contrary to the "more powerful" category that referenced more Liberian sentiments, this category was prominent amongst Ghanaians who perhaps see Nigeria as an equal partner, a feeling probably associated with their long-standing relationship of cooperativeness, although garbed under subtle rivalries. Liberians also perceive

Table 7.2 Breakdown of Perceptions by Country

Coded Categories	Overall		Liberia		Ghana	
	Number of Coded References	Percentage of Coded References (%)	Number of Coded References	Percentage of Coded References (%)	Number of Coded References	Percentage of Coded References (%)
Positive model	262	55.9	138	52.7	124	47.3
Negative model	102	21.8	38	37.3	64	62.7
More powerful	37	7.9	22	59.5	15	41.6
Not living up to its potential	21	4.5	14	66.7	7	33.3
Expression of support	15	3.2	9	60	6	40
Leadership	15	3.2	13	87	2	13
Sibling	14	2.9	5	35.7	9	64.2
Rival	2	0.4	0	0	2	100
TOTAL	468	99.8	239	51	229	49

Table 7.3 Overall Favourability of Nigeria

		Country		Total	Percent	Cumulative Percent
		Ghana	Liberia			
Opinion of Nigeria	Favourable	49	91	140	25.0	25.0
	Somewhat favourable	125	115	240	42.8	67.7
	Somewhat unfavourable	56	14	70	12.5	80.2
	Unfavourable	40	7	47	8.4	88.6
	No opinion	31	33	64	11.4	100.0
Total		301	260	561	100.0	

Nigeria as a brother or sister country, but they, more than Ghanaians, describe Nigeria as a big brother, which may be connected with the role Nigeria played during the civil wars or its largely superior capabilities.

References alluding to Nigeria's leadership credentials were categorized under "leadership" and were broadly interpreted to capture instances where the country is explicitly described as a leader for being at the helm of continental and sub-regional affairs, looking out for others, and living up to its responsibilities. For instance, in Liberia where Nigeria is widely acknowledged to have been responsible for the end of the civil war, it is held that the decision of the US to abandon Liberians during their time of need opened the door for Nigeria to demonstrate its leadership credentials, a responsibility which Nigeria fulfilled. This lends credence to assertions that it looks out for others. Rounding up positive sentiments towards Nigeria is the category "expression of support" which captures support for continuous cooperation with Nigeria or an alignment with it on regional issues. It also captures support for Nigeria to increase its influence, as this stands to benefit the broader sub-region.

While the categories "rival" and "not living up to its responsibilities" are not necessarily negative sentiments, they do not appear positive at face value either. As Figure 7.1 indicates, the category "rival" contained the least number of coded references and this is because only two references suggesting a competitive relationship with Nigeria were captured. Both came from Ghana and were specific to the existing rivalry between both countries when it comes to football. Surprisingly, there was no mention of cuisine, given the ongoing "Jollof rice" rivalry between both countries (see BBC News Pidgin, 2019). The category "not living up to its potential" captures references where Nigeria is seen to be unable to take advantage of its superior capabilities to assert its leadership in the continent and also unable to address its internal challenges such as insecurity, poverty, corruption, and a declining global image. For instance, some references allude to Nigeria as a "sleeping giant" who is unable to make the most of its resources and capabilities or even adequately assert its leadership in continental affairs.

As this sums up explanations of the main categories of perceptions of Nigeria, the next section discusses the attractive components of Nigeria's influence in Ghana and Liberia.

The Attractive Elements of Nigeria's Power Resources

To ascertain the attractive elements of Nigeria's power resources as well as what makes them attractive, references that fall under the "positive model" category were sub-categorized in Figure 7.2.

Culture represents Nigeria's most attractive source of influence, accounting for 46.6% of positive references followed by economic, foreign policy, politics/government, and military sources of influence, which account for 20%, 19.1%, 9.1%, and 4.9% of positive coded references, respectively. What this suggests is that there are attractive components across all categories of Nigeria's power resources, even within the domestic political realm. The ensuing discussions highlights these attractive elements.

Nigeria's Cultural Influence

The pre-eminence of culture, especially popular culture, as Nigeria's most potent soft power resource in West Africa is by no means surprising if we recall discussions in Chapter 5 about the array of cultural outputs that have emerged from Nigeria's religious and ethnic diversity. As Figure 7.3 suggests, Nigeria's cultural attraction is popular culture. Leading the pack in this category is Nollywood, which accounts for 24% of coded references. This is followed by the diaspora (19.7%), music (16.4%), charismatic Pentecostalism (13.1%), pidgin English (9%), fashion (5.7%), and literary icons (3.3%). A sub-category labelled "other" was created to accommodate

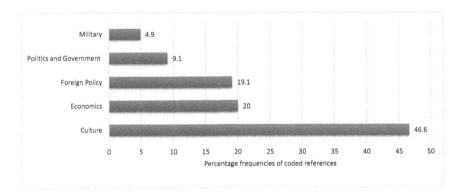

Figure 7.2 Co-Occurrence of Positive Model with Power Categories.

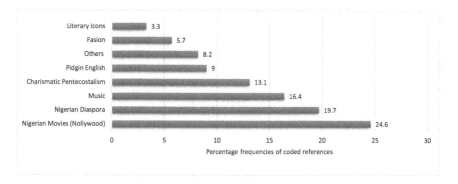

Figure 7.3 The Attractive Elements of Nigeria's Culture.

Table 7.4 The Influence of Nigeria's Culture

| | | Country | | Total | Percent | Cumulative Percent |
		Ghana	Liberia			
Nigeria's cultural influence in your country	A good thing	201	201	402	71.7	**71.7**
	A bad thing	100	59	159	28.3	**100.0**
Total		301	260	**561**	100.0	

other cultural variables that were referenced positively one to three times. These are comedy, education, festivals, cultural interactions between non-state actors, sporting prowess, and the Big Brother Naija television show. Together, they accounted for 8.2% of coded sub-categories.

These different elements of Nigeria's culture combine to make popular culture Nigeria's most potent source of attraction in Liberia and Ghana alike. Although this was widely acknowledged in the interviews conducted in both countries, it was further probed through the questionnaires to appreciate the reach of this sentiment. In Liberia and Ghana, respondents were asked the question "do you believe that Nigeria's cultural influence in your country is mainly a good thing or bad thing?" Table 7.4 reveals that a significant majority in both countries felt it was a good thing, although more Liberians than Ghanaians felt this way.

Nollywood

In Liberia where appreciation for Nollywood supersedes that of Ghana, the appeal of Nigerian movies is largely due to how the African culture is portrayed, especially the historical-cultural practices associated with the

African way of life. While Liberia is one of the oldest independent African states, the fact that it is originally a settlement of freed slaves from the US in many ways made the African culture somewhat "foreign." This led to what T. Jaye referred to as an identity crisis, with some Liberians, even to date, identifying as Americo-Liberians, which, in most instances, has the connotation of superior social status (personal communication, January 28, 2020).

Introduced to Liberians by Nigerian peacekeeping forces, in a demonstration of the interaction between culture, war, and the pursuit of peace, Nollywood revived the "Africanness" in Liberians. In the words of A. Sherif, a journalist in Monrovia, Nollywood "portrays the 'Africanness' we would love to emulate. It is redirecting Liberians to the African way of life" (personal communication, February 1, 2020). In as much as the movies reflect Nigerian culture, Sherif notes that "they are more African than others," referring to Bollywood and Hollywood movies.

Ghanaians have a vibrant movie industry – Gollywood – although not as big and appealing as Nigeria's. This may explain why Nollywood is not as popular in Ghana as it is in Liberia. To Ghanaians, the similarity in culture and, more importantly, the dexterity of the movie actors are the driving forces behind the appeal of the industry. S. Adjei attributes his attraction to Nigerian movies to "the professionalism attached to it [and] the naturality [with which] Nigerians conduct themselves" in the movies, a feat which he doubts his country's industry has been able to emulate despite strong collaboration between Ghanaian and Nigerian movie practitioners (personal communication, August 30, 2019). Beyond this is the cultural contribution these movies make to traditional and religious values. While H. Hanson-Hall notes that "it makes a cultural contribution in the sense that it tells us how to address elderly people" (personal communication, September 6, 2019), A. Tse-Tse highlights the religious dimensions of Nigerian movies, where the Christian faith is often promoted as supreme and God's power is ultimate (personal communication, September 7, 2019).

The Diaspora

That the diaspora follows Nollywood in Figure 7.3 may not be unconnected with the fact that this group of Nigerians possesses the inherent quality of being the biggest embodiment and transmitters of Nigeria's culture and values. This is evident in the role Nigerian peacekeepers played in introducing Liberians to Nollywood movies. However, this is not why Ghanaians and Liberians find them attractive. What is obvious from the QCA is that the personal qualities or character traits of Nigerians appear to resonate more positively in Ghana and Liberia than their cultural contribution. Words like ingenuity, transparent, work ethic, intelligence, honesty, straightforwardness, and daring were among other positive character traits associated with Nigerians. It is important to note that these sentiments are uniform in Liberia and Ghana and appear to be class-based, as all interviewees have had strong personal contacts with what can be described as their elite Nigerian counterparts.

What this implies is that favourable perceptions of Nigerians are mostly geared towards the "elite class", that is, those doing business, academics, or, broadly speaking, those operating in the formal sector. As B. Amakye-Boateng opines, there are a lot of good people amongst Nigerians, "especially their elites ... the Nigerian elite is more conscious, more gentle, more reasonable than the lower class," pointing to his Nigerian colleague at the University of Ghana to buttress his point (personal communication, August 29, 2019).

Nigerian Music – Afrobeats

Apart from its inherent quality, other reasons why Nigerian music sits among the top three sources of cultural attraction has to do with the fact that they are easily comprehensible, and in the word of R. Mensah, "relatable" (personal communication, September 2, 2019). In Ghana, a long history of collaboration between Nigerian and Ghanaian artists across different musical genres such as highlife, Juju music, and gospel music may explain strong positive sentiments towards Nigerian music. As Nigerian popular music reverberates across the continent, contemporary Nigerian and Ghanaian artists are continuing in the tradition of their forbearers by collaborating frequently, creating music that relays Nigerian and Ghanaian sociocultural experiences. This may explain why for the first time in this study more Ghanaians are endeared towards an aspect of Nigeria's culture than Liberians.

Liberians attest to the dominance or strong influence of Nigerian music in their country, but, beyond its quality, it remains unclear what other factors explain their attraction to it.

Charismatic Pentecostalism

To capture the broader sentiment of Liberians and Ghanaians on the influence of Nigerian Pentecostal churches, the questionnaire asked if respondents agree or disagree that Nigerian Pentecostal churches have developed religious traditions that are influential in their country. Table 7.5 shows that 68.5% of respondents, including 59% of Ghanaians and 79% of Liberians, attest to the strong influence of Nigerian Pentecostal churches, while only 6.4% disagree.

This will not come as a surprise to Liberians. According to A. Sherif, "Liberians have become [*sic*] the Nigerian way of life even in their worship and the way they conduct themselves even in their Christendom" (personal communication, February 1, 2020). Even in Ghana where the degree of influence appears to be lesser, likely because of the existence of equally influential charismatic churches, M. Nii-Dortey notes that "whether it is Winners, whether it is pastor Chris, and TB Joshua, [Nigerian charismatic pastors] are highly Idolized" (personal communication, August 30, 2019).

Table 7.5 Influence of Nigerian Churches

		Country		Total	Percent	Cumulative Percent
		Ghana	Liberia			
Nigerian	Strongly disagree	9	6	15	2.7	**2.7**
churches have	Disagree	12	9	21	3.7	**6.4**
developed	Neutral	101	40	141	25.1	**31.6**
traditions that	Agree	124	144	268	47.8	**79.3**
are influential	Strongly agree	55	61	116	20.7	**100.0**
Total		301	260	561	100.0	

To investigate the strength of this influence and the emerging phenomenon of religious tourism in Nigeria, the study further asked those who identify as Christians if they have travelled to Nigeria for a Christian religious programme. Overall, 83.7% of respondents identified as Christians, and a quarter of this number has travelled to Nigeria for religious programmes while three-quarters have not. This is expected, especially for M. Nii-Dortey who describes this phenomenon as a regular occurrence (personal communication, August 30, 2019). In Liberia, T. Jaye boasted of his knowledge of a personal friend who came from London to attend Late T. B. Joshua's church and another who repeatedly makes the trip to Nigeria by road to worship (personal communication, January 28, 2020).

What explains the adulation for Nigerian Charismatic churches? As the QCA reveals, the personality of the leaders is an important factor in the attractive force of this faith-based form of influence. While their philanthropic engagement was mentioned, one interviewee points to their teachings to explain his "love" for them (S. Adjei, personal communication, August 30, 2019). A. Conteh, who traced the history of these churches in his country to the end of the civil war, made a convincing submission by pointing to their size and grandiose style, in terms of the portrayal of wealth and success, as reasons why Liberians are attracted to them (personal communication, September 10, 2019). As will be discussed in the next section, this is also the reason why some find them unattractive, as their grandiose style tends to communicate that wealth comes from God rather than hard work.

Another reason observed for their attractiveness includes the moral contribution they make to Liberian and Ghanaian societies and the advisory role they play in governmental affairs, especially in Liberia where Late T. B. Joshua had strong ties with the political elites, including President George Weah.

Pidgin English

As discussed in Chapter 5, pidgin English is not unique to Nigeria but the Nigerian version appears to be the most popular in West Africa, a reality which in no small way may be attributed to Nollywood, Nigerian music, and the Nigerian diaspora. In describing the outsized influence of Nollywood in Liberian society, T. Jaye pointed to the extent to which Nigerian slang has become part of local parlance (personal communication, January 28, 2020). In Ghana, R. Mensah similarly points to the fact that "everybody is picking up" the Nigerian pidgin to convey his point about the resonance of Nigerian culture in Ghana (personal communication, September 2, 2019).

In the QCA, a deep appreciation for Nigerian pidgin came from Ghana, although the Ghanaian version is not too different and citizens of both countries can easily understand each other when this localized variant of the English language is spoken. To R. Mensah, it is the unique way that Nigerians speak the language that attracts, pointing to the use of the language by the BBC to buttress his point (personal communication, September 2, 2019). "It is a unique [and] convenient way of brushing away the Queens English and then just staying on the course that will not get anybody confused," he added (R. Mensah, personal communication, September 2, 2019). M. Nii-Dortey provided a deeper insight into the attractive force of pidgin English by highlighting the mixture of symbolism and local knowledge in the way Nigerians speak the language (personal communication, August 30, 2019). Referring to how pidgin English is used in Nollywood movies, Nii-Dortey noted the mixture of proverbs and axioms in a way that reflects the daily realities and lived experiences of Nigerians. This, he notes, makes the language attractive and worthy of emulation.

Fashion

Although in exploring Nigeria's soft power potential fashion was not considered a potential source of cultural attraction, it did emerge in the data as an attractive component of Nigeria's cultural output. As is the case with pidgin English, its popularity may also be attributed to Nollywood. However, the data suggest that its influence is only in Liberia, as Ghanaian respondents did not refer to it. This is not to suggest that Liberians do not have traditional dresses. They do. The Mandingo, Vai, Kissi, Kru, and Lorma tribes with cultural ties to Cote d'Ivoire, Guinea, and Sierra Leone are known for consistently dressing in traditional African attires. But, unlike Nigeria and Ghana where every ethnic group takes pride in dressing to their customs and tradition even on working days, this is not the case in Liberia, where being an Americo-Liberian and dressing in the "white man's" way is seen as a thing of pride and status.

As one respondent noted, this is no longer the case, thanks to cultural interactions between Liberians and Nigerians that began after the civil war (A. Sherif, personal communication, February 1, 2020). To quote A. Konneh, "culturally, whenever you find this diffusion of cultures, it is bound to show certain kind of similarities that you can attest to. So, the result is, there are many Liberians who dress like Nigerians" (personal communication, January 24, 2020). From Charles Taylor to Sirleaf Johnson and now George Weah, recent Liberian presidents are perceived to dress like Nigerians, at times to the distaste of their critics.

Literary Icons

Nigeria's literary icons, also discussed in Chapter 5 as a potential source of attraction, emerged in this study as one of the sources of Nigeria's cultural attraction. More so in Liberia than in Ghana, although in both countries some respondents acknowledge their contribution to African scholarship. In Liberia, notable Nigerian political scientists such as Claude Ake, Bala Usman, and Adebayo Adedeji are revered for their scholarly contributions to their academic discipline and for introducing an African perspective that is assumed to be lacking in contemporary academic scholarship. Adebayo Adedeji was particularly admired for his foresightedness and immense contribution to the Lagos Plan of Action and the Monrovia Declaration of 1979 (T. Jaye, personal communication, January 28, 2020).

Other literary icons such as Wole Soyinka and Chinua Achebe were also mentioned. As H. Hanson-Hall noted, the works of Chinua Achebe did positively impact relations between Nigeria and Ghana and played an important role in defining the physical structure of his country (personal communication, September 6, 2019). It remains unclear how Achebe's work may have done that, but there is no doubt that these African literary giants generate strong positive sentiments in Ghana and Liberia.

Other Attractive Elements

Other cultural elements that were referenced positively include education, Nigeria's sporting prowess, the Big Brother Naija reality television show, and comedy. The increased collaboration or cultural interaction between Nigerian and Ghanaian artists was also referenced in a positive light. The only allusion to Nigeria's material culture came in the form of positive references to cultural festivals organized in Nigeria such as the Osun Osogbo festival which B. Amakye-Boateng thought Ghana should emulate due to its economic benefit and contribution to tourism (personal communication, August 29, 2019).

References to Nigeria's sporting prowess, particularly amongst Ghanaians, entailed positive sentiments about the notable achievements of Nigerian footballers such as Segun Odegbami, Mikel Obi, and Nwankwo Kanu. Evoking sentiments of respect and admiration, there were acknowledgements that Nigeria fared better than Ghanaians in sports. In the words of M. Nii-Dortey, "in the areas of sports, particularly beyond football, you see that Nigeria does better in athletics and basketball" (personal communication, August 30, 2019). This sentiment mirrors the views of a majority of Liberians and Ghanaians who filled out the questionnaires as 64.4% agree that Nigerians excel in sports, while only 9.8% disagree.

Table 7.6 The Influence of Nigeria's Popular Culture

		Country		Total	Percent	Cumulative Percent
		Ghana	Liberia			
Level of influence of Nigeria's popular culture	No influence at all	4	3	7	1.2	**1.2**
	Slightly influential	13	5	18	3.2	**4.5**
	Somewhat influential	30	15	45	8.0	**12.5**
	Moderately influential	68	25	93	16.6	**29.1**
	Very influential	105	91	196	34.9	**64.0**
	Tremendous influence	81	121	202	36.0	**100.0**
Total		301	260	561	100.0	

The fact that Big Brother Naija, an annual reality television programme, and the emerging transnationalization of Nigerian comedy are referenced positively in Ghana and Liberia demonstrates the attractive force of popular culture as Nigeria's most potent soft power resource. To understand the consequence of this appeal in terms of influence, Ghanaians and Liberians who filled out the questionnaires were asked to rank the level of influence Nigeria's popular culture has on their country. Corroborating Figure 7.2, Table 7.6 shows that only 1.2% of respondents chose the option of no influence at all, whereas, 82.1% agree that it has some level of influence, including 36% who agree that Nigeria's popular culture has a tremendous influence on their society.

Nigeria's Economic Influence

As Figure 7.2 shows, Nigeria's economic power category follows culture as a source of attraction for Nigeria. In an indication that the ability of a people or country to foster enterprise and commerce can be a source of attractive influence, Figure 7.4 indicates that diaspora entrepreneurs are the most attractive component of Nigeria's economic influence (52.8% of coded references), followed by Nigerian companies and banks (18.9%). For the first time in this study, a state-based soft power currency emerged as an attractive source of influence with 15.1% of coded references alluding to the government's role in providing economic and development assistance to other states in the sub-region. This is followed by informal trade links between Nigerians and Ghanaians and the competitiveness of the Nigerian economy with 11.3% and 1.9% of coded references, respectively.

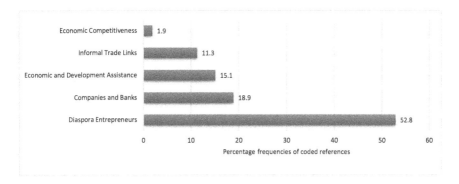

Figure 7.4 The Attractive Elements of Nigeria's Economic Power.

Diaspora Entrepreneurs

Although it remains unclear how many Nigerians are in Liberia, Ghana is amongst the foremost destination of Nigerians in the West African sub-region. The implication is that they constitute a strong source of cultural influence for Nigeria. From an economic perspective, their attractive force is again obvious, as their entrepreneurial ability is perceived favourably in Liberia and Ghana, making them Nigeria's most attractive source of economic influence.

Favourable perceptions of Nigeria's diaspora entrepreneurs mostly stem from their contribution to the development of their host country's economy, specifically the creation of jobs and payment of taxes. S. Kone even points to their role in motivating young Liberians to venture into the business world through partnerships (personal communication, January 27, 2020). Dominant in the vehicle spare parts business and the sale of household items, the business footprints of Nigerians vary considerably from construction, and real estate development, to the sale of vehicles, and electronics. In Liberia, some of these entrepreneurs are former soldiers, who established businesses after the war, while in Ghana they are mostly immigrants seeking to take advantage of the opportunities the Ghanaian economy affords.

Table 7.7 indicates that more Liberians (62%) than Ghanaians (35%) agree that Nigerians contribute positively to the growth of their economy, whereas, almost a similar number of Liberians (19.6%) and Ghanaians (21.2%) disagree. The reason for this disparity may be connected with the fact that while more Nigerians conduct business in Ghana, they tend to run afoul of local laws, which prohibit foreigners from engaging in retail businesses, a situation which has caused repeated clashes between Ghanaian and Nigerian traders in Kumasi and Accra. This may also be responsible for

Table 7.7 Contribution of Nigerians to the Host Country's Economy

| | | Country | | Total | Percent | Cumulative Percent |
		Ghana	Liberia			
Contribution to the national economy	Strongly disagree	10	18	28	5.0	5.0
	Disagree	54	33	87	15.5	20.5
	Neutral	130	46	176	31.4	51.9
	Agree	91	138	229	40.8	92.7
	Strongly disagree	16	25	41	7.3	100.0
Total		301	260	561	100.0	

Table 7.8 The Entrepreneurial Spirit of Nigerians

| | | Country | | Total | Percent | Cumulative Percent |
		Ghana	Liberia			
Nigerians have a great entrepreneurial spirit	Strongly disagree	16	9	25	4.5	4.5
	Disagree	10	17	27	4.8	9.3
	Neutral	47	23	70	12.5	21.7
	Agree	137	155	292	52.0	73.8
	Strongly agree	91	56	147	26.2	100.0
Total		301	260	561	100.0	

strong negative sentiments towards Nigerians, as will be discussed in subsequent sub-sections.

"If they come to trade and … they pay tax, it will definitely contribute," remarked B. Amakye-Boateng, but this is not all there is to his favourable disposition towards Nigerian entrepreneurs, as he is also enamoured by their entrepreneurial skills (personal communication, August 29, 2019). Comparing his countrymen to Nigerians, he notes that in business, "the Ghanaian is not as daring as the Nigerian, naturally." Mulling over the role colonialism may have played in this, he continued "our relationship with the colonial masters have probably affected our psyche in being risk-averse and being bold and venturing into things but Nigerians are not like that [...] Nigerians know how to outwit the Ghanaian."

In Liberia, S. Kone mentions how Liberians have gained from Nigerian entrepreneurs in terms of business management and organizational skills (personal communication, January 27, 2020). It is no coincidence that although Ghanaians are less positively disposed towards the contribution of Nigerians to their economy, 75% still agree that Nigerians have a great entrepreneurial spirit as Table 7.8 indicates, while 81% of Liberians share the same view. This indicates that the entrepreneurial drive of Nigerians outweighs their contribution to the national economy in the eyes of Liberians and Ghanaians.

Multinational Corporations

Similar to Nigeria's diaspora entrepreneurs, Nigerian MNCs are perceived favourably in Ghana and Liberia for their role in creating jobs and national economic development. These corporations, mostly in the financial or banking sector, are more prominent in Ghana than in Liberia, yet the QCA reveals that more Liberians (60%) are appreciative of their contribution than Ghanaians (40%). Table 7.9 corroborates this finding, as an overwhelming majority of respondents in Liberia and Ghana agree that Nigerian MNCs are making a positive contribution to the development of their economy.

In Ghana, 88% of respondents see Nigeria's contribution in a positive light, while only 12% perceive it negatively. Similarly, in Liberia, 94% perceive the contribution of these privately owned companies positively while only 6% have negative sentiments about their contribution. Taking into consideration the attractive components of Nigeria's cultural resources and the first two elements of the country's attractive economic influence, it is clear that, thus far, Nigeria's main sources of attraction are mostly in the purview of non-state actors.

Economic and Development Assistance

For the first time in this chapter, a state-to-state level interaction appears as a source of positive sentiment. This is predicated on Nigeria's development and economic assistance to both Ghana and Liberia, as well as its broader role in the African continent. In Ghana, positive sentiments were predicated on Nigeria's sale of oil at concessionary prices to the government of Jerry Rawlings (P. Aryene, personal communication, August 27, 2019). Also, M. Nii-Dortey referred positively to the donation of police vehicles to his

Table 7.9 Nigerian Companies and Economic Development

| | | Country | | Total | Percent | Cumulative Percent |
		Ghana	Liberia			
Contribution of Nigerian companies to host country's economy	Very positive	138	132	270	48.1	**48.1**
	Somewhat positive	127	113	240	42.8	**90.9**
	Somewhat negative	21	9	30	5.3	**96.3**
	Very negative	15	6	21	3.7	**100.0**
Total		301	260	561	100.0	

Table 7.10 Nigeria's Contribution to the Economies of West African States

		Country		Total	Percent	Cumulative Percent
		Ghana	Liberia			
Nigeria helps	Strongly disagree	5	9	14	2.5	**2.5**
West African	Disagree	45	37	82	14.6	**17.1**
states develop	Neutral	125	47	172	30.7	**47.8**
their economy	Agree	119	150	269	48.0	**95.7**
	Strongly agree	7	17	24	4.3	**100.0**
Total		**301**	**260**	**561**	**100.0**	

country by the Obasanjo administration in 2001 at a time of serious security crisis (personal communication, August 30, 2019). As discussed in Chapter 4, this was during the administration of President John Kufuor when the donation of vehicles to the Ghanaian police was leveraged by President Obasanjo to shore up relations between both countries (Modern Ghana, 2001). It is evident that these efforts resonate positively with Ghanaians.

As Table 7.10 indicates, this sentiment is widely held as more people in Ghana (41.8%) agree that Nigeria comes to the aid of West African states in developing their economy, while 16.6% disagree. The same is the case in Liberia as a sizeable majority (64%) attest to Nigeria's contribution to the development of their economy, while almost a similar number (17.6%) disagree.

In Liberia, President Babangida's financial contribution towards the establishment of the Ibrahim Babangida School of International Studies is highlighted as a contribution towards the country's development (D. Remongar, personal communication, January 22, 2020; G. Wallace, personal communication, January 22, 2020). While S. Kone (personal communication, January 27, 2020) notes Nigeria's role in the construction of the Liberian–Sierra Leonean section of the Trans-African highway, S. Jackson (personal communication, January 23, 2020) highlights Nigeria's helping hand in landing Liberia a financial commitment of $100 million from ECOWAS for the construction of roads as positive contributions to their country's economic development.

Informal Trade Relations

With 11.3% of coded references, informal trade links between Nigerians and their sub-regional counterparts are perceived as a positive occurrence in Ghana and Liberia. As discussed in Chapter 5, trade relations at the state-to-state level in West Africa are marred by protectionist policies and disparities in fiscal and monetary policies, leaving the bulk of trade to the informal sector. It is for this reason that when Nigeria opted to close its land borders in the summer of 2019, a channel through which informal trade flourishes, most of the outcry came from the informal sector. These are petty traders who rely heavily on informal trade links with their Nigerian counterparts for affordable goods.

For A. Konneh, who references this dimension of economic relations positively, this is a "significant" development that contributes to Liberia's economy (personal communication, January 24, 2020). A. Fofana attributes this budding relationship to the absence of industries in Liberia, but sees it playing a unifying role for both countries, as it encourages frequent interactions between the citizens of both countries (personal communication, January 29, 2020). In Ghana, the affordability of goods in Nigeria is a primary motivating factor in the informal trade between both countries. Goods like vehicle spare parts, a business dominated by Nigerians, are mostly sourced from Nigeria and sold at lower prices. This is in addition to other Ghanaians who frequently travel to Nigeria to buy these parts for their personal use. As J. Amuah notes, for over ten years "I have never bought any part for my car [in Ghana] including brand new tyres [...] because I will pay three times [above the market value] if I buy from here" (personal communication, September 3, 2019).

Economic Competitiveness

Rounding up the elements comprising the co-occurrence of positive sentiments with economic power is the competitiveness of the Nigerian economy. As discussed at the beginning of this section, only one coded reference fell into this category. While it is certainly not the only time the Nigerian economy was mentioned, it is the only time its competitiveness was suggested. Other instances where Nigeria's economy was referenced positively came when Liberians and Ghanaians described the country as an economic power or economically powerful given the relative differences in economic output between their country and Nigeria. That the competitiveness of the Nigerian economy did not feature prominently in the positive model category may not be unconnected with the reality of Nigeria's economic woes, including tepid growth rates, soaring inflation, rising poverty levels, and growing debts.

However, for the first time, the QCA contradicts the finding derived from the questionnaires as Table 7.11 indicates that a large majority of Liberians and Ghanaians find Nigeria's economy competitive; more so in the former than the latter.

The fact that just under 2% of respondents completely disagree with the assertion that Nigeria's economy is competitive puts into contestation the findings of the QCA, but this may be because the study categorized reference to "Nigeria as an economic power" in the powerful category, or maybe competitiveness is confounded with economic superiority.

Nigeria's Foreign Policy Behaviour

Despite an Afrocentric external posture, Nigeria's foreign policy ranks as the third source of attractive influence with 19.1% of co-occurrence between

Table 7.11 Nigeria's Economic Competitiveness

		Country		Total	Percent	Cumulative Percent
		Ghana	*Liberia*			
Economic competitiveness	Not at all	5	4	9	1.6	**1.6**
	Slightly competitive	15	9	24	4.3	**5.9**
	Somewhat competitive	55	19	74	13.2	**19.1**
	Competitive	104	50	154	27.5	**46.5**
	Very competitive	83	105	188	33.5	80.0
	Extremely competitive	39	73	112	20.0	**100.0**
Total		**301**	**260**	**561**	**100.0**	

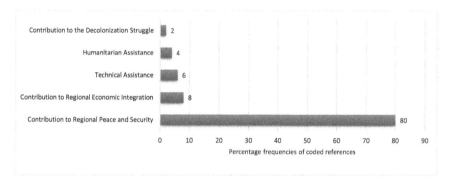

Figure 7.5 The Attractive Elements of Nigeria's Foreign Policy.

positive model and power categories. As Figure 7.5 reveals, this is predicated on Nigeria's role in promoting regional peace and security, championing regional economic integration, providing technical and humanitarian assistance, and contributing to Africa's decolonization struggle.

In a demonstration of the attractive force of Nigeria's security engagement in West Africa, its contribution to regional peace and security accounted for 80% of coded references in this category, while the other aforementioned coded categories amounted to only 20%.

Nigeria's Contribution to Regional Peace and Security

Nigeria's commitment to regional peace and security in Africa is quite pronounced. As such, it is no coincidence that Liberians and Ghanaians alike perceive this dimension of Nigeria's foreign policy behaviour favourably.

These sentiments are informed by Nigeria's interventions in the West African sub-region, specifically Liberia, Sierra Leone, Gambia, and Cote d'Ivoire.

With 27 coded references, a feeling of gratitude towards Nigeria's intervention during their country's civil wars dominate positive sentiments in Liberia. Liberians emphatically credit Nigeria for the peace and stability their country currently enjoys. "I've always maintained, and I teach this in my classes that had it not been for Nigeria, there would have been no Liberia today, given the fact that we went through a brutal civil war," noted A. Konneh (personal communication, January 24, 2020). This point was similarly echoed by G. Wallace when he remarked that "Nigeria's contribution to the peace process in this country cannot be denied [...] Nigeria committed to seeing this country return to peace, stability, and development," expending millions of dollars in the process (personal communication, January 22, 2020).

In Ghana, positive references towards Nigeria's contribution to regional peace and security amounted to 13 coded references. These sentiments extend beyond Nigeria's direct involvement in conflict resolution to include its multilateral approach to conflict resolution, specifically the cooperative relationship it maintained with Ghana in Liberia and Sierra Leone, and the fact that Nigeria showed up when an African country was in need. As one Ghanaian respondent noted, "when you talk of West Africa, you will mention Nigeria and then you will mention Ghana [...] I think Nigeria has played an important role" (anonymous, personal communication, September 6, 2019).

The disparity in perceptions of Nigeria's contributions to regional security is also evident in data derived from the questionnaires, as 80% of Liberian respondents are of the view that Nigeria's security role in the sub-region has increased stability, whereas, only 32% of Ghanaians feel the same way, with almost 45% holding that it has made no impact. While it remains unclear why this is the case, one can speculate that it may be connected to the fact that while Liberians are still consumed by gratitude, Ghanaians are confronted by a regional security context that is grappling with rising insecurity and the gradual penetration of violent extremist groups into the coastal states of West Africa, which include Ghana.

Nigeria's Regional Integration Efforts

As Figure 7.5 indicates, only 8% of coded references allude positively to Nigeria's effort in fostering regional integration in West Africa. These references were specifically geared towards the financial contributions Nigeria made towards the formation and maintenance of ECOWAS. Once again, positive references to Nigeria's ECOWAS contribution were mostly in Liberia as only one respondent in Ghana, emphatically noted that "Nigeria is virtually the one, in terms of finances, carrying ECOWAS" (anonymous, personal communication, August 27, 2019).

This is no different from prevailing sentiments in Liberia where T. Jaye noted Nigeria's financial contribution to ECOWAS and its hosting of the

Table 7.12 Nigeria's Role in Deepening Economic Integration

| | | Country | | Total | Percent | Cumulative Percent |
		Ghana	Liberia			
Contributes	Strongly disagree	7	9	16	2.9	2.9
to regional	Disagree	25	15	40	7.1	10.0
economic	Neutral	133	55	188	33.5	43.5
integration	Agree	114	148	262	46.7	90.2
	Strongly agree	22	33	55	9.8	100.0
Total		301	260	561	100.0	

headquarters, which he suggests allows Nigeria to exert its influence over sub-regional affairs (personal communication, January 28, 2020). On his part, S. Kone who was part of the group responsible for the name and design of the proposed single West African currency "Eco" tied Nigeria's role in this effort to its broader financial commitment to ECOWAS (personal communication, January 27, 2020). While A. Fofana contends that Nigeria has been unable to unify the region as a single political bloc, he nonetheless, gives Nigeria credit for playing a unifying role by facilitating the movement of people, goods, and services, and by implication, economic integration (personal communication, January 29, 2020).

Table 7.12 captures the broader sentiment of Liberians and Ghanaians in this regard as 56.5% agree that Nigeria's regional engagement has deepened integration, while only 9.9% disagree. This number is not in any way flattering and suggests a misappreciation for Nigeria's role, given that it bears most of the burden of ECOWAS since its formation.

Technical Assistance

Following positive perceptions of Nigeria's foreign policy of promoting regional integration is its technical assistance policy which Tables 8.6 and 8.7 in Chapter 8 suggest most Liberians and Ghanaians are unaware of. The fact that Liberians are one of the major beneficiaries of Nigeria's technical assistance programmes may explain why all coded references are from Liberian respondents.

As A. Conteh puts it, the brain drain in Liberia after the war was immense, combined with the challenge of a faulty educational system. This made Nigeria's technical assistance necessary and timely (personal communication, September 10, 2019). D. Remonger was more detailed in his assessment of the positive contribution Nigeria's technical assistance programme makes to the Liberian society, as he notes that it helps in manpower development and allows Liberia to save much-needed resources (personal communication, January 22, 2020). Even more important, he noted the contribution beneficiaries of the programme make to the development of Liberia, whether in terms of entrepreneurship or public service reforms.

Humanitarian Assistance

Positive perceptions of Nigeria's humanitarian endeavours are also solely in Liberia, where Nigeria's accommodation of refugees during the war is perceived as a positive occurrence. Of particular note is the way Nigeria catered for Liberian refugees by providing for their education in the country's foremost universities such as the University of Lagos and Obafemi Awolowo University. According to T. Jaye, Liberian refugees came back with good memories of their time in Nigeria, not just in terms of how the Nigerian government catered for them, but also in the friendly relationship they had with Nigerians (personal communication, January 28, 2020).

Nigeria's Role in the Decolonization Struggle

Summing up positive perceptions of Nigeria's external posture is the role it played in the decolonization struggle. It is unclear why most respondents did not discuss this aspect of Nigeria's foreign policy, despite being an important preoccupation of the continent in the 1960s and 1970s. However, the only positive allusion came in Ghana where Nigeria was commended for taking up the mantle of liberating the continent after the overthrow of former Ghanaian president, Kwame Nkrumah, who was at the forefront of this struggle.

Nigeria's Internal Politics and Government

At face value Nigeria's internal politics and government leave nothing to be desired, however, Figure 7.6, which records 9.2% of co-occurrences between positive sentiments and this power category, suggests that certain elements of Nigeria's internal political organization and practice appear to be attractive in Liberia and Ghana alike, albeit very little.

With 50% of coded references, Figure 7.6 suggests that the recurrent organization of multiparty elections in Nigeria since 1999 is the most attractive component of the politics and government power category. This practice, which has culminated in four successive peaceful democratic transitions, is perceived favourably in both Liberia and Ghana. While these sentiments do not appear to validate the overall practice of democracy in Nigeria, the fact that it reflects the absence of military coup d'état, suggesting the consolidation of democracy, and more importantly, projects a stack contrast from a history of military dictatorship may explain positive sentiments. Also important is the multiparty nature of Nigeria's elections, with two main political parties consistently jostling for power.

Although he makes clear that Ghana, one of the continent's most peaceful democracies, is way above Nigeria, one respondent remarks that "Nigeria

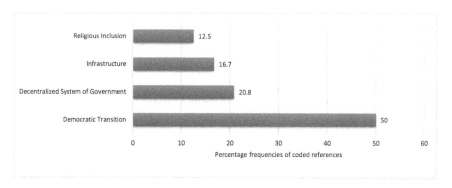

Figure 7.6 The Attractive Elements of Nigeria's Politics and Government.

[is] a little above some other [countries]. At least they seem to be practising democracy even though with intimidation" (anonymous, personal communication, September 6, 2019). The presidential election of 2015, which marks one of the best elections organized in Nigeria, and culminated in the rare occurrence of an incumbent president suffering defeat and peacefully accepting the outcome of the election, resonated positively amongst Ghanaians.

Following positive sentiments towards Nigeria's democratic transition is its decentralized system of government, which accounts for 20.8% of coded references. In Ghana and Liberia alike, Nigeria's structure of government generates positive sentiments as it decentralizes administration. Ghanaians are particularly attracted to this form of administrative and political organization because the administration of their country is mostly centralized in Accra. As B. Amakye-Boateng remarks, "if everybody is made to pay tax in [their] home town, I'm sure Accra will be decentralizing" (personal communication, August 29, 2019). To Nii-Dortey separating the administrative from the economic capital as it is done in Nigeria, where Abuja represents the administrative capital, and Lagos represents the economic capital, will help decongest Accra (personal communication, August 30, 2019).

Liberians are more attracted to Nigeria's local government system and had even sent representatives to study this third tier of Nigeria's governance structure during the administration of President Ellen Sirleaf Johnson. Describing the challenge confronting his country's administrative organization, S. Kone noted that

> we have this wild thing we call the counties but they have no authority. The power is still in the centre. It is still being controlled from here and because of that, there are a lot of things affecting those different regions.
>
> (personal communication, January 27, 2020)

From the collection of driver's licences to birth certificates, Liberians have to go to Monrovia, a reality that renders emulating the Nigerian system even more attractive.

Nigerians are quick to criticize the state of infrastructural development in their country, but the findings in this study appear to suggest that other Africans appreciate the level that it has attained in this regard, even if from a distance. With 16.7% of coded references, Ghanaians appreciate the level of development Lagos state has witnessed over the last decade. They particularly allude to the modernization of the transport sector, with the introduction of bus rapid transit in Lagos and the Chinese-financed railway projects taking place all over the country as worthy infrastructural developments to emulate.

With 12.5% of coded references, the practice of power rotation between Muslims and Christians sums up the positive aspects of Nigeria's internal political organization. To A. Tse-Tse, this unwritten rule where a Muslim president picks a Christian vice-president is a positive force in the maintenance of peace that internally diverse countries across the continent should look to emulate (personal communication, September 7, 2019).

Nigeria's Military

In a sign that military resources can also engender favourable perceptions, 13 coded references alluding to Nigeria's military co-occurred with the positive model category. Accordingly, Figure 7.7 indicates that of these coded references 53.8% are positive sentiments towards Nigeria's participation in military training exercises and personnel exchanges, while 23.1% are positive sentiments towards Nigeria's commitment to end the civil war in Liberia and the decisiveness of the military to meet this end. Equally, 23.1% of coded references capture sentiments positively referring to the strength or invincibility of the military.

Despite a history of military interactions with Ghana, positive references to personnel exchanges and training exercises were all from Liberia. It is unclear why this is the case, but possible explanations may be that respondents had no direct affiliation with the military, or because issues of this nature are not particularly of concern to Ghanaians and as a result are not topical, or because joint military exercises are purely a military process. What is clear is that Liberians are particularly appreciative of the role the Nigerian military played in revamping and restructuring the AFL after the civil war and providing them with training in its tri-military training institutes.

Also unique to Liberians are positive sentiments towards the decisive approach of the Nigerian military brass in bringing the war to an end, especially after the execution of Samuel Doe. In the words of T. Jaye, "they didn't come fooling around," referring to Nigerian soldiers, "if they say [...] they will go and bombard a territory, they will go and do it and [...] Liberians

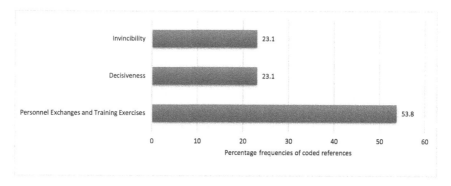

Figure 7.7 The Attractive Elements of Nigeria's Military.

Table 7.13 Nigeria's Military Strength

| | | Country | | Total | Percent | Cumulative Percent |
		Ghana	Liberia			
Nigeria's military strength	No strength at all	13	6	19	3.4	3.4
	Weak	26	8	34	6.1	9.4
	Somewhat weak	84	14	98	17.5	26.9
	Strong	105	40	145	25.8	52.8
	Very strong	51	80	131	23.4	76.1
	Extremely strong	22	112	134	23.9	100.00
Total		301	260	561	100.0	

loved them because of the no-nonsense approach" (personal communication, January 28, 2020). This point was also emphasized by S. Kone who notes that Liberians were yearning for peace and pleaded for Nigerian troops because "when they say this is it, that's it" (personal communication, January 27, 2020).

From the foregoing, it is no surprise that an equal number of coded references allude to Nigeria's military invincibility, a reputation built from the country's intervention in regional conflicts and successful restoration of peace in Liberia and Sierra Leone. The numerical strength of the military is an important factor behind these perceptive dispositions, but so also is its bravery in combat. As Table 7.13 indicates, perceptions of Nigeria's military invincibility appear to resonate widely, especially in Liberia where 43% perceive it as extremely strong, whereas only 7% of respondents in Ghana perceive it as such. This appears to validate the obvious lop-sidedness in the

QCA, where positive references to Nigeria's military power mostly persisted with Liberians.

However, these sentiments are increasingly called into question, with the Nigerian army mostly playing an internal security role, where it has been unable to deal with Boko Haram after almost a decade in active combat, as will be further discussed. Nonetheless, it will be heart-warming to Abuja that the Nigerian military is seen as a force for good by 61% of respondents in Liberia and Ghana, implying that a good majority finds its intentions benign and motivated by the need to ensure peace and security in the region.

In sum, discussions carried out in this section do suggest that Nigeria has attractive resources, more so in Liberia than in Ghana, with non-state actors accounting for most. As the next section will discuss, these attractive resources also have negative elements that if not addressed may erode some of this attraction and impact their utility in the conduct of Nigeria's foreign policy.

The Unattractive Elements of Nigeria's Influence

As Figure 7.1 indicates, coded references under the "negative model" main category amounted to 21.8% of the overall coded references. It is also worth recalling that these sentiments were more pronounced in Ghana where 62.7% expressed negative views across the different categories of Nigeria's power resources, as against 37.3% in Liberia (see Table 7.2). To ascertain the reasons behind these sentiments, these coded references are sub-categorized in Figure 7.8.

Figure 7.8 indicates that these issues fall under four power categories, with culture, once again, leading the pack with 58.8% of coded references. This is followed by politics and government (27.4%), Economics (7.8%), and finally the Nigerian military (5.9%). What is conspicuously obvious is the absence of Nigeria's foreign policy on this list, which implies that Nigeria's external

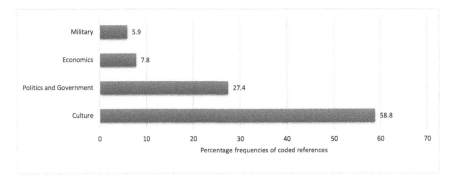

Figure 7.8 Co-Occurrence of Negative Model with Power Categories.

disposition in West Africa resonates positively, even if some Nigerians qualify it as un-strategic. This will be discussed in Chapter 8, but in subsequent sub-sections, the book discusses the negative sentiments underlying these different power categories.

Nigeria's Cultural Influence

As Figure 7.9 indicates, underlying negative perceptions of Nigeria's cultural resources are the Nigerian diaspora, Pentecostal churches, Nollywood movies, and finally the overbearing influence of Nigerian culture, otherwise referred to as cultural saturation. That these sentiments are uniform across Liberia and Ghana attests to the strong influence of Nigeria's cultural expressions and their ability to evoke both negative and positive sentiments. As the data and preceding analyses suggest, positive sentiments towards Nigeria do outweigh the negatives, nonetheless the latter can rise to outweigh the former if ignored. This makes understanding the reasons for negative sentiment even more important, especially for the purpose of foreign policy decision-making.

Despite their popular appeal, the diaspora constitutes the strongest challenge to Nigeria's soft power in Liberia and Ghana with 33 coded references capturing negative sentiments about the actions of some Nigerians. Contrary to previous discussions where positive sentiments were associated with Nigeria's "elite class," here the reverse is the case. In Ghana and Liberia alike, negative perceptions of Nigerians stem from the actions of individuals who are deemed to be part of the "lower class." To some of the respondents interviewed for this study, this group of Nigerians are only in their country "to only create problems." Words like aggressive, dishonest, fraudulent, and criminals were repeatedly used to describe the character traits of these Nigerians who they believe are responsible for such heinous crimes as rape, kidnapping, drug peddling, cyber fraud, armed robbery, and other antisocial activities. "Nigerians are bad in nature," a Ghanaian respondent contends (anonymous, personal communication, September 6, 2019).

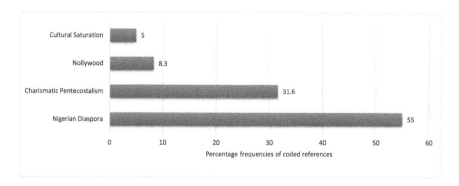

Figure 7.9 Unattractive Elements of Nigeria's Culture.

While these crimes are committed in collaboration with the locals, there is a palpable belief that Nigerians are the brains behind the operation, and only rely on locals for their knowledge of the terrain. "Ten people are arrested for serial killing, look at the names that come out, nine are Nigerians, and one Ghanaian who leads them to the place," notes B. Amakye-Boateng (personal communication, August 29, 2019). The image-denting implications of these activities can be deduced from the opinion of one Liberian respondent who opined that "when Nigeria is mentioned, drug is mentioned, crime is also mentioned" (A. Fofana, personal communication, January 29, 2020).

Tying the image of Nigeria to the activities of a few, especially where sentiments are negative, has implications for law-abiding citizens who are profiled and, in some instances, even stereotyped as criminals. This perceptive disposition is also not aided by another element of Nigeria's cultural exports – Pentecostal churches. Negative references to Nigerian Charismatic churches amounted to 31.6% of negative sentiments towards Nigeria's cultural influence. While the engagement of some of these churches in money laundering activities and drug-related crimes featured amongst issues driving negative perceptions, they are second to issues of doctrine, specifically the overemphasis on prosperity as opposed to salvation. To respondents in Ghana and Liberia, these churches are just money-making ventures or businesses that are inimical to growth and self-empowerment. With no probity of the source of financial contributions to the church, one respondent notes that "people can kill and bring money [to the church] and they see it as prosperity" (R. Mensah, personal communication, September 2, 2019).

Why are Nigerians to blame? one may ask, as they are not the only nationals with charismatic churches in these countries. The answer to this question lies in the widely held assumption that Nigerians introduced this brand of Pentecostalism where wealth and lavish lifestyles or the allure of success assume prominence over salvation. T. Jaye noted that they are "undermining the traditional churches," referring to the orthodox churches (personal communication, January 28, 2020), while a Ghanaian notes that "Nigerians have perfected religious slavery by exploiting Africans" (S. Adjei, personal communication, August 30, 2019). These sentiments are at times reinforced by the recurrent contestation that plays out in the open within these churches over management and money. Other causes of negative sentiments associated with Pentecostal churches include noise making and the constant promotion of the fear of the unknown, in the form of a possible attack from supernatural dark forces – a recurrent feature in Nollywood movies.

The constant images of these supernatural dark forces and sorcery, otherwise known as juju or witchcraft in some Nigerian movies is also one of the reasons driving negative sentiments towards Nollywood in Ghana and Liberia. With 8.3% of coded references, Nollywood follows charismatic Pentecostalism as one of the sources of negative sentiments towards Nigeria's cultural influence. As most respondents note, despite their inherent quality, Nigerian movies tend to portray an evil country where sacrifices such as the slaughtering of human beings and money rituals are common practices.

No doubt these kinds of images allow for the misconception of practices in Nigeria, with severe consequences to the overall image of the country. The fact that A. Fofana noted that some of his students enquired if these depictions of Nigeria are true, given that he studied in Nigeria during the civil war, speaks to the extent to which negative visual images can engender stereotypes and alter attitudes towards others in both positive and, in this instance, negative ways (personal communication, January 29, 2020). These negative sentiments are further reinforced when the involvement of some Nigerians in heinous crimes is taken into consideration.

Summing up negative sentiments towards Nigeria's cultural outputs is the overbearing influence these cultural forms appear to have in Liberia and Ghana. In the latter, the word "suppression" was used to capture the widespread appreciation for Nigerian music and movies at the expense of local outputs, culminating in fears that Nigeria's culture may take over. While this is unlikely to occur, these fears could potentially generate a competitive drive that may take a negative turn as the xenophobic attacks on Nigerians in South Africa may suggest. In Liberia, T. Jaye alluded to the domination of Liberia by Nigerian culture dating from the end of the civil war (personal communication, January 28, 2020). For now, appreciation for Nigeria's role in the civil war appears to trump these fears, but it is unclear how long this will last.

Democratic and Governance Deficits

In the previous section, this chapter discussed the attractive components of Nigeria's politics and government, which include the peaceful transfer of power from one democratically elected government to another, its decentralized governance system, developments in infrastructure, and power-sharing between Christians and Muslims. In a sign that may suggest the overall unattractiveness of Nigeria's democratic experiment, all of these elements accounted for 24 coded references, whereas 28 coded references expressed negative sentiments towards its politics and government.

It is true that very little can be made of this incidence, given the little gap between positive and negative references; however, when the issues informing negative sentiments are put in perspective, combined with the fact that most respondents were uncomfortable discussing Nigeria's internal affairs for fear that their responses may appear critical and ultimately negative, one may want to conclude that Nigeria's internal politics and government leave little to be desired. As Figure 7.10 indicates, 65.7% of negative sentiments in this category are geared towards the lack of democratic ethos in Nigeria's politics and government, while 39.3% are associated with failures of governance.

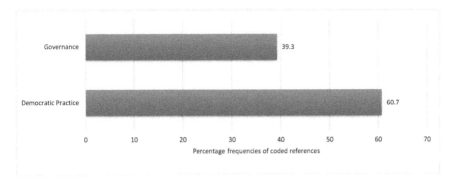

Figure 7.10 Unattractive Elements of Nigeria's Politics and Government.

Ghanaians and Liberians alike were emphatic in their assessment of Nigeria's internal politics when they noted that there is nothing to emulate in Nigeria. Apart from the transfer of power, which should naturally be a common occurrence in democratic societies, every other aspect of Nigeria's democratic practice appears negative. Prominent among issues informing these sentiments are the violent and hostile nature of elections and politics, the ethnicization of politics, a strategy that Nigerian politicians readily apply to mobilize voters, and the monetization of politics or what is normally referred to as vote-buying. Together, these issues inform negative sentiments towards Nigeria's democratic practice.

While Ghanaian respondents rightly believe that they are more advanced than Nigeria in the practice of democracy, Liberians argue the incompatibility of political systems with Nigeria for the lack of attraction. In a bid to appear less critical, while arguing towards the existence of a gap between the theory and practice of democracy in Nigeria, A. Fofana noted that "we took everything from America [...] we are using a political system in West Africa that is unique to Liberia" (personal communication, January 29, 2020). Contrarily, a Ghanaian respondent noted, "if you talk about political systems, I think Nigeria has to come [...] and learn from Ghana. There is nothing there at all" (S. Adjei, personal communication, August 30, 2019).

As Table 7.14 indicates, these views are widespread, especially in Ghana where only 20% agree that their country should emulate Nigeria in consolidating democracy. In contrast, this percentage was way higher in Liberia where 50% seems to find Nigeria worthy of emulation. This disparity may not be unconnected with the fact that compared to Ghana, Liberia's democratic practice suffers similar challenges to Nigeria, even if Nigeria has often played an important role in the conduct of elections there. However, the overall sentiments of the people of Liberia and Ghana appear to validate the sentiments captured in the QCA as only 33.7% deem Nigeria's internal democratic practice worthy of emulation.

Table 7.14 Democratic Consolidation in Nigeria

| | | Country | | Total | Percent | Cumulative Percent |
		Ghana	Liberia			
Your county should emulate Nigeria in consolidating democracy	Strongly disagree	36	19	55	9.8	9.8
	Disagree	78	32	110	19.6	29.4
	Neutral	127	80	207	36.9	66.3
	Agree	55	106	161	28.7	95.0
	Strongly agree	5	23	28	5.0	100.0
Total		301	260	561	100.0	

Table 7.15 Competency of Nigeria's Internal Governance System

| | | Country | | Total | Percent | Cumulative Percent |
		Ghana	Liberia			
Nigeria is competently governed	Strongly disagree	31	22	53	9.4	**9.4**
	Disagree	104	52	156	27.8	**37.3**
	Neutral	134	74	208	37.1	**74.3**
	Agree	27	99	126	22.5	**96.8**
	Strongly agree	5	13	18	3.2	100.0
Total		301	260	561	100.0	

Grand corruption, lack of respect for the rule of law, and insecurity featured among issues informing negative perceptions of Nigeria's internal governance system. One respondent even tied the failure of Nigeria to deal with corruption to the lack of advancement in its democratic practice, while another notes that if the country can deal with corruption, it will be one of the "best in the world, not only Africa" (R. Tomah, personal communication, January 22, 2020). These sentiments are also shared within Nigeria, prompting the Buhari administration to make the war on corruption a priority, at least rhetorically, as all indices and conventional wisdom point to rising corruption within government circles.

As Table 7.15 indicates, only 25.7% of Liberians and Ghanaians believe that Nigeria is competently governed. When broken down, this comprises 10% of Ghanaians and 43% of Liberians.

"Take the example of the rule of law, the way we approach the rule of law is very different from the way it is approached in Nigeria," noted A. Konneh (personal communication, January 24, 2020). When pressed to clarify, he noted that the Liberian national police director was held in contempt because he had refused to obey an order of the supreme court, whereas in Nigeria political officeholders flout decisions of the court without consequences. When put to Liberians and Ghanaian about the respect for human rights and the rule of law in Nigeria, only 36% agree that the Nigerian government respects the rule of law, while 24.2% disagree and 39.8% had no opinion.

Concluding issues of governance are perceptions of insecurity in Nigeria. This will not surprise anyone following events in Nigeria, as the security challenges bedevilling the country now extend beyond terrorism to include banditry, kidnapping of school children, and different forms of violent crimes. As Nii-Dortey notes, "these are terrible signals, very terrible signals" that do not bode well for the image of the country (personal communication, August 30, 2020).

Illicit Trade Practices and Trade Restrictions

As diaspora entrepreneurs are Nigeria's most attractive source of economic influence, so also do they constitute its strongest challenge, bearing credence to their influence within the West African sub-region. They, in addition to the government's protectionist policies, represent the unattractive components of Nigeria's economic power. As Figure 7.11 shows, 75% of coded references in this category captured negative sentiments of Ghanaians and Liberians towards illicit trade practices by Nigerians and their penchant for violating trade laws.

In Ghana where sentiments concerning the violation of trade laws are pronounced, Nigerian traders and their Ghanaian counterparts are often involved in squabbles leading to the intervention of state actors from both sides. These, at times, physical confrontations, which in some instances have dominated news headlines, have no doubt influenced negative sentiments towards a group of Nigerians that are also perceived to contribute to the growth of host economies.

In addition to this, the negative character traits associated with Nigerians also affect how their business dealings are perceived. Calling into question

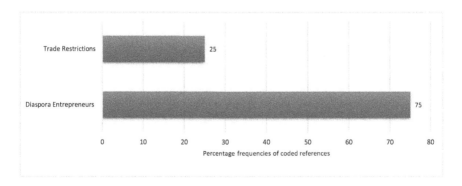

Figure 7.11 Unattractive Elements of Nigeria's Economic Power.

the fairness of Nigerians, a Ghanaian respondent notes that "Nigerians have a way of doing business that hijacks [...] they do not say they are doing monopoly but they have strategies [that exclude Ghanaians]" (B. Amakye-Boateng, personal communication, August 29, 2019). This sentiment was similarly echoed in Liberia where one respondent called into question the level of honesty and fairness with which Nigerians approach business dealings (A. Fofana, personal communication, January 29, 2020). These are in addition to sentiments that they sell fake products.

Summing up this category of negative sentiments is the issue of trade restrictions put in place by the Nigerian government. Despite being separated from Nigeria by Togo and Benin, Ghanaian traders were severely impacted by the border closure. As Nii-Dortey noted, "this policy hurt us a bit" (personal communication, August 30, 2019). This assertion is not far from those expressed by traders directly affected by the policy. For instance, Gabriel Nartey, a Ghanaian dealing in vehicle spare parts in Accra, whose business suffered because of the border closure, describes Nigeria's policy as "un-African" (Mwakideu, 2020).

Boko Haram and Breaches in UN Peacekeeping Norms

As discussed previously, the fact that most people in Liberia and Ghana see the AFN as relatively powerful, with a history of successful intervention in regional conflicts, in no small way raises concerns about its inability to deal with poorly trained and ill-equipped home-grown insurgent groups like Boko Haram. This is evident in Figure 7.12 as 50% of negative sentiments towards the AFN are associated with their inability to deal with Nigeria's internal security crisis. This is accompanied by negative sentiments towards the AFN for violating the UN non-fraternalization policy and arming different factions of the Liberian civil war. These issues account for 33% and 17% of coded references, respectively.

References to Boko Haram allude to reports that the group has infiltrated the AFN, thus making it difficult for it to contend with Nigeria's biggest

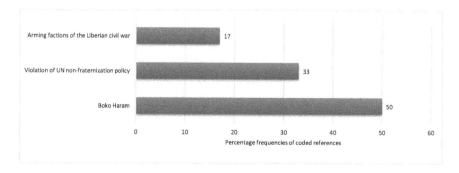

Figure 7.12 Unattractive Elements of Nigeria's Military Power.

security threat since the Nigerian civil war. While this calls into question the overall competence of the AFN, it is its seeming inability to deal with a home-grown security threat that has lasted over a decade and threatens the stability of the region that is baffling to respondents. This increasingly calls into question the invincibility of the AFN and may explain why only three coded references captured sentiments alluding to it as such. A respondent who expressed serious reservations about commenting on Nigeria's internal political issues simply noted, "I have problems with this Boko Haram stuff" (R. Tomah, personal communication, January 22, 2020). While this statement says little, a lot can also be made of it.

Other negative sentiments emanated from Liberia where Nigerian soldiers engaged in sexual relations with locals, a practice which runs contrary to the UN non-fraternization policies, setting out the parameters on the kind of relations peacekeepers can have with beneficiaries of security assistance. It is also held in some quarters that in as much as Nigeria was decisive in bringing the war to an end, it was responsible for arming some of the factions. An HRW report of June 1993 appears to corroborate these sentiments as it revealed some form of collaboration between anti-NPFL forces such as the United Liberation Movement for Democracy in Liberia and ECOMOG in Gbarnga (Human Rights Watch, 1993). These sentiments reveal the limits of waging war in the name of peace and how the conduct of peacekeepers can erode intangible benefits that accrue to states that engage in peacekeeping.

Conclusion

This chapter sought to assess elite attitudes in Ghana and Liberia towards Nigeria's power resources and foreign policy behaviour. This was specifically geared towards identifying what is attractive and unattractive about the "proverbial giant of Africa" and the reasons behind prevailing attitudes. The analyses reveal that the different categories of soft power potential, discussed in Chapter 5, contain attractive and unattractive elements, although the level of attraction varies between Ghanaians and Liberians, and overall perceptions suggest that attraction outweighs aversion. With culture leading the pack of attractive power resources, the chapter finds that Nigeria's soft power assets are mainly domiciled in the expressions, qualities, and actions of non-state actors. Nollywood, the Nigerian diaspora, and music emerged as the most important components of Nigeria's cultural soft power, which also includes Pentecostal churches, pidgin English, fashion, and literary icons. As a sign of their influence, cultural elements like the Nigerian diaspora, Nollywood, and Nigerian churches also evoke negative sentiments, although the positives outweigh the negatives.

These findings suggest that Nigeria's diaspora or, simply put, Nigerian citizens are the country's most attractive source of influence. Beyond their cultural influence, they also feature as Nigeria's strongest source of economic influence, leading other attractive economic variables such as MNCs, the government's economic assistance to African states, informal trade links, and the competitiveness of the economy. Nevertheless, prevailing attitudes in Ghana and Liberia suggest that their perceived involvement in illicit practices is a drag on their attractiveness. Other negative aspects of Nigeria's economic interactions with Ghanaians and Liberian stem from the government's protectionist policies.

Nigeria's external posture, which is purely within the purview of the government, emerged as the main source of attraction for state-centred interactions, as Nigeria's contribution to regional peace and security trumped other attractive components such as its contribution to integrating the sub-region, technical and humanitarian assistance, and contribution to the decolonization struggle. However, how it manages its internal affairs emerged unattractive to Ghanaians and Liberians alike. Apart from the structure of its political and administrative organization and the fact that elections are organized every four years, other aspects of Nigeria's politics and government were not worthy of emulation.

In a sign that what is traditionally seen as hard power resources can also generate soft power, the AFN emerged as an attractive source of influence due to the personnel exchanges and training exercises they engage in. Their decisiveness during the civil wars in Liberia and Sierra Leone and the perceived strength of the military was also appealing. However, their penchant for violating UN laws guiding the conduct of peacekeepers and their continuous struggle with the rising threat of Islamic fundamentalism in Nigeria are perceived unfavourably.

What these findings suggest is that Nigeria does have attractive power resources; however, the extent to which they have amounted to tangible foreign policy outcomes is still unknown. Thus, Chapter 8 evaluates the relationship between Nigeria's attractive power resources and tangible foreign policy outcomes. It also discusses the challenges Nigeria faces in projecting soft power, and how such challenges may be mitigated in light of changing regional and global political dynamics.

Notes

1 This does not in any way suggest that in specific instances the African public has not reflected on issues of international consequences. What it implies is that more times than not, they are preoccupied with domestic issues. Beyond this is another reality that the authoritarian tendencies of African leaders exclude their participation in foreign policy decision-making processes. Schmidt's (2012) work on African perceptions of the EU's soft power affirms this point. In the words of Schmidt, "international politics are too remote in countries where many people struggle for their daily survival" (p. 101).
2 Pierre Bourdieu (1984) describes them as people in the field of power, who dispose of important economic, cultural, social, and symbolic capital over others. According to Kotzé and Steyn (2003), elites are "societal agents through which

broader forces such as ethnicity, class, and religion are filtered to ordinary people" (p. 11).
3 This approach has been previously applied in studies observing attitudes or perceptions to make inferences on questions related to the foreign policies of states (see Schmidt, 2012; Kotzé & Steyn, 2003; Gürsoy, 2020).

References

Anderson, J. E. (2014). *Public policymaking*. Cengage Learning.

BBC News Pidgin. (2019, August 26). *Nigeria carry last for Jollof competition as Ghana win. BBC News*. Retrieved June 22, 2020, from www.bbc.com/pidgin/tori-49473890

Bourdieu, P. (1984). *Distinction: A social critique of the judgement of taste* (R. Nice, Trans.). Harvard University Press.

Coffey, A., & Atkinson, P. (1996). *Making sense of qualitative data*. Sage.

Dey, I. (1993). *Qualitative data analysis: A user-friendly guide for social scientists*. Routledge.

Fan, Y. (2008). Soft power: Power of attraction or confusion? *Place Branding and Public Diplomacy*, 4(2), 147–158.

Früh, Werner (2007). *Inhaltsanalyse* [Content Analysis] (6th ed.). Konstanz: UVK.

Gürsoy, Y. (2020). Reconsidering Britain's soft power: Lessons from the perceptions of the Turkish political elite. Cambridge Review of International Affairs. https://doi.org/10.1080/09557571.2020.1832959

Holyk, G. G. (2011). Paper Tiger? Chinese soft power in East Asia. *Political Science Quarterly*, 126(6), 223–254. https://doi.org/10.1002/j.1538-165X.2011.tb00700.x

Hsieh, H. F., & Shannon, S. E. (2005). Three approaches to qualitative content analysis. *Qualitative Health Research*, 15(9), 1277–1288. www.jstor.org/stable/1952796

Human Rights Watch. (1993). *Waging war to keep the peace: The ECOMOG intervention and human rights* (Vol. 5, No. 6), Human Rights Watch. www.hrw.org/reports/1993/liberia/

Ipsos Public Affairs. (2019). *Anholt Ipsos Nation Brands Index (NBI)*. Paris: Ipsos.

Kotźe, H., & Steyn, C. (2003). *African elite perspectives: AU and NEPAD. A comparative study across seven African countries*. Konrad-Adenauer-Stiftung.

Modern Ghana. (2001, October 2). *Nigerian car assembly plant donates to Police*. Retrieved November 9, 2019, from www.modernghana.com/news/17231/nigerian-car-assembly-plant-donates-to-police.html

Morgan, D. L. (1993). Qualitative content analysis: A guide to paths not taken. *Qualitative Health Research*, 3(1), 112–121.

Mwakideu, C. (2020, January 29). *Ghanaian traders livid at Nigeria border closure*. DW.com. Retrieved July 28, 2020, from www.dw.com/en/ghanaian-traders-livid-at-nigeria-border-closure/a-52189203

Page, B. I., & Shapiro, R. Y. (1983). Effects of public opinion on policy. *American Political Science Review*, 77(1), 175–190.

Schmidt, S. (2012). Soft power or neo-colonialist power: African perceptions of the EU. *Review of European Studies*, 4(3), 100–123.

Schreier, M. (2012). *Qualitative content analysis in practice*. Sage.

Tesch, R. (1990). *Qualitative research: Analysis type and software tools*. Falmer Press.

8 Foreign Policy Outcomes as a Measure of Soft Power Capability

Introduction

Even with peculiar challenges, evidence from Ghana and Liberia suggests that Nigeria does possess attractive sources of influence in West Africa, although most of these are within the purview of non-state actors where cultural and economic interactions between Nigerians and their sub-regional counterparts have given rise to cross-border activities and networks. From the rich African values portrayed in Nollywood films and the ingenuity and entrepreneurial skills of Nigerians to the quality and relatability of Nigerian music and the adulation of wealth and success in charismatic Pentecostalism, Nigeria's soft power currencies are diverse and in the firm grip of non-state actors. These are in addition to the uniqueness of the pidgin English, the developmental contributions of Nigerian banks, and informal trade relations between Nigerians and their sub-regional counterparts.

Despite strong positive sentiments in their favour, these soft power currencies feature sparingly as instruments of statecraft, resulting from a foreign policy approach by successive Nigerian leaders that rely mostly on money, guns, and manpower. In a sign that power resources traditionally reserved in the purview of hard or coercive behaviour can also be attractive, the instrumentality of these resources does evoke positive sentiments, specifically for their moral and benign application. Nigeria's legacy of economic and development aid, commitment to regional integration, technical and humanitarian assistance, and contribution to the decolonization struggle are central elements of its foreign policy that resonate positively in Liberia and Ghana. These are in addition to its security engagement, where the centrality of the AFN arouses positive sentiments for decisiveness, strength, and invincibility.

The question then arises, if soft power works. Specifically, to what extent have favourable perceptions of Nigeria's qualities, actions, and activities amounted to tangible foreign policy gains? Where attraction to Nigeria has not resulted in foreign policy gains, what are the challenges encumbering the effectiveness of Nigeria's African policy and how can these be mitigated? Leadership aspirations portend to be the most compelling explanation for

DOI: 10.4324/9781003396628-8

Nigeria's sparsely transactional and altruistic foreign policy posture. Nigeria's role in the formation of the OAU and its transition to the AU, its role in the struggle against colonialism and white minority rule, and spearheading the creation of ECOWAS are shreds of evidence of an external disposition that is geared towards the broader objective of shoring up its leadership credentials and creating an enabling environment for the exercise of its influence. To the extent that these goals are met, this chapter argues in favour of Nigeria's soft power in West Africa and the effectiveness of soft power as a tool of statecraft in intra-regional politics.

While conceding that power may not necessarily be effective, the study assumes that the true measure of effectiveness is when policy meets the expectations of reality. As such, two levels of effectiveness or outcomes – indirect and direct – are contemplated in this chapter. As such, it argues that whether in terms of indirect or direct effects, Nigeria may lay claim to a level of efficacy in its approach to foreign policy that is suggestive of a soft power behaviour. This is based on favourable perceptions of its leadership, influence, and the concomitant will for enhanced cooper- ation by elites in Ghana and Liberia. That the case for the effectiveness of soft power is made does not suggest an argument for the effectiveness of Nigeria's foreign policy approach, as the glaring gap between its diverse resources and foreign policy strategy exposes the inability of Abuja to come to terms with a changing international context where an attractive partner is one whose house is in order and the tools of statecraft extend beyond money, guns, and manpower, to also include intersubjective elem- ents disseminated through movies, music, and transnational cultural and economic networks.

The discussions in this chapter proceed in three sections. First, it addresses the question of effectiveness. Second, it highlights strategic issues or challenges affecting the projection of soft power in Nigeria's foreign policy. Third, it makes the case for addressing the domestic contradiction of Nigeria's for- eign policy and the imperative of a coherent framework that mobilizes the attractive elements of Nigeria's influence, including the implementation of a nation-branding strategy and a renewed approach to public diplomacy that capitalizes on a burgeoning digital space.

Between Attraction and Support for Nigeria's Objectives

This section questions the extent to which favourable perceptions of Nigeria's qualities and actions have altered the behaviour of West African states towards support for its foreign policy objectives. By focusing on two levels of outcomes – direct and indirect – this section attempts to ascertain the effectiveness of Nigeria's African policy and by implication its soft power capability and the efficacy of soft power as a deliberate approach to foreign policy.

Indirect Effects: Milieu Goals

Buoyed by its superior military and economic capabilities, and an aspiration for continental leadership, Nigeria projects the image of a big brother in Africa by pursuing such long-term goals as ensuring African integration, unity, and cooperation, eliminating all forms of discrimination, promoting respect for international law and treaty obligations, peacefully resolving international disputes, and promoting a just world economic order. These are in addition to ensuring regional security and upholding such value objectives as providing humanitarian assistance, promoting democracy, human rights, and international humanitarian law – all of which are equally enshrined in the mandates of ECOWAS and AU. As such, they reflect the shared interests of African states, rather than Nigeria's particularistic interest.

That these interests are shared is by no means a suggestion that they are widely practised, or Nigeria can secure the commitment of other states in the region. In other words, the permissive or non-obligatory nature of commitments to these shared values and interests limits what countries like Nigeria can hope to achieve, especially when it is also lacking in commitment. But, if we consider that some of these objectives are merely aspiratory while concrete steps are being taken to actualize others, it becomes worthwhile to juxtapose Nigeria's contributions with the current sub-regional reality to assess what progress has been made.

Indeed, Nigeria's role in promoting African integration and unity is well documented. It is the successful pursuit of this objective that culminated in the formation of the OAU and, later, AU. In July 2021, African states are expected to commence trading under the AfCFTA, gradually moving towards economic integration. While the free movement of people, goods, and services, as well as the elimination of protectionist policies across the continent, remains a distant reality, the ratification of the AfCFTA agreement by 31 states, including Nigeria, brings to the fore the spirit of the Lagos Plan of Action of 1980 and Nigeria's aspiration of a gradually evolving continental union that culminates with the establishment of a common market (Olagunju, 2021).

As discussions in Chapters 4 and 5 suggest, trade barriers remain the mainstay of West African trade relations where recurrent frictions between Nigeria and its regional counterparts continue to prevent the kind of economic cooperation anticipated upon the formation of ECOWAS. This is as the volume of intra-regional trade remains below 15% of overall trade (Torres & Van Seters, 2016). While trade relations between some countries in the sub-region are improving, take for instance Gambia and Senegal (Olagunju, 2021), French West Africa remains economically tied to France, and Nigeria still flexes its economic muscle, as the recent year-long shutdown of its land borders exemplifies. It is true that Nigeria is not the only country with protectionist trade policies in Africa, but its behaviour challenges its commitment to a just world economic order and raises questions about the ability of African states to implement the AfCFTA. Nonetheless, with the AfCFTA expected to gradually eliminate these barriers, lift over 30 million people out of poverty, and increase the income of over 60 million Africans living below $5.50 a day, Africa and West Africa appear to be on track to achieve the AU 2063 agenda (World Bank, 2020c).

The fact that Nigeria still carries the burden of ECOWAS demonstrates its commitment to an institution that is instrumental in the security dynamics of the sub-region. The present reality of the sub-region reflects a security context that has evolved from the mid-1970s to the late-1990s when Nigeria was actively involved in conflict resolution efforts. Civil wars have given way to new forms of security challenges – the proliferation of SALW, rising Islamic fundamentalism, maritime piracy, and narco-trafficking. While Nigeria is contending with these security challenges, as are other West African states, its contributions to the peace and stability of Liberia, Sierra Leone, and The Gambia has in no small way positioned West Africa as the home of some of the most stable states in the continent. As of 2015, West Africa suffered fewer conflicts and fatalities than any other region in the continent (Marc et al., 2015, pp. 1–9).

Even though Nigeria is struggling to deal with its internal security challenges, a fact that calls into question its military credentials, its role in the reassuring security profile of the sub-region ought not to be minimized. This is far from saying that Nigeria is solely responsible for these gains, as extra-continental actors are equally instrumental in resolving some of these conflicts. What is, however, apparent is that the fear of Nigeria's dominance, especially with Francophone West African states is gradually dissipating, probably because the country has failed to leave up to its potential or because Nigeria's military superiority has served the collective good of the region. Whichever way, security interactions between Nigeria and Francophone states, as "Operation Restore Democracy" exemplifies, suggest strong security cooperation amongst West African states. Another example is the MNJTF set up to coordinate the fight against insurgency in the Sahel.

With some of West Africa's conflict often the result of repressive and exclusive political and governance systems, Nigeria is at the forefront of promoting democracy, although, with a shaky record. In 2018, President Adama Barrow of The Gambia expressed appreciation for Nigeria's role in resolving the political impasse in his country arising from the disputed elections and Nigeria's overall disposition towards the promotion of democracy in the sub-region (Gambian Armed Forces, 2018). Even as it is important to avoid imposing Western understandings and interpretations of democracy on a sub-region that is ill-equipped, institutionally speaking, to handle both the constructive and disruptive dimensions of this idea of political organization, much of what is practised in West Africa is what Agwu (2013, p. 122) refers to as "ballot-box democracy." This captures a situation where the conduct of voting or elections, however imperfect, is tantamount to the practice of democracy, with other important constituent elements, including good governance, rule of law, equality, and human rights relegated to the back burner.

Through ECOWAS, Nigeria has been complicit in promoting this Western-backed practice both at home and abroad, under the guise of democratic consolidation and political stability, gradually eroding the gains recorded over the past two decades. As long as a winner emerges from this process, the loser is compelled to accept the outcome, sometimes forcefully, as in the case of Laurent Gbagbo of Cote d'Ivoire and Yahya Jammeh of The Gambia. The fact that not much is desired of Nigeria's democratic practice in Ghana and Liberia confirms its duplicitous approach to promoting democracy in the sub-region and exposes the hypocritical dimension of soft power that gives rise to question about its effectiveness as a foreign policy tool.

According to the 2019 Freedom in the World Report by Freedom House, Nigeria is amongst five West African states – Benin, Guinea, Mali, Nigeria, and Burkina Faso – that have suffered the most year-on-year decline in Freedom house index scores (Freedom House, 2019). Confirming the gradual regression of democracy in the sub-region, apart from Ghana and Cabo Verde who maintained their "Free" status from previous years, Senegal and Benin moved from "Free" to "Partly Free" (Freedom House, 2019). Although the era of military coup is behind the sub-region, save for Mali in 2020, the organization of flawed elections in Nigeria, restriction of political opposition in Benin and Senegal, restriction of political protests, and the heavy-handed approach by security operatives suggest a gradual regression. Attesting to this point, Temin and Linzer (2020) notes:

> For years [...] ECOWAS outpaced other regional organizations in Africa in its support for democratic norms, coming close at one point to institutionalizing a two-term limit for all West African heads of state. But such an initiative is hard to imagine now, especially given that Nigeria, the regional heavyweight with great influence over ECOWAS, is increasingly consumed by internal challenges.

With the coup in Mali, the recent reversal of earlier commitments to two-term limits by the presidents of Guinea and Cote d'Ivoire, the challenges confronting Burkina Faso with democratic transition, growing political instability in Nigeria, and the obvious reality in most of the region that democracy is anything but delivering on the promise of a brighter future, this system of government may be gradually losing steam, with military coups increasingly likely to occur (Doss, 2020). Mali may just be the beginning, not the end.

While the foregoing represents a simple illustration of the economic, political, and security context of West Africa vis-à-vis Nigeria's contributions, it nonetheless reveals that Nigeria's efforts have only made marginal gains. Notwithstanding, if Nigeria's sub-regional posture is deliberately designed to create an enabling environment to sustain its influence or boost its leadership credentials, ensure the continuation of cooperative relations and forge its image as a big brother, benign regional hegemon, partner, and friend – all of which may be captured as reputational security – Figure 7.1 indicates that its approach may be effective.

This is because the main category "more powerful," which captures references to Nigeria as a giant, big brother, and even economically and militarily powerful, appears to confirm that Nigeria's power status or influence is recognized. The fact that these references were more in Liberia (59.4%) than Ghana (41.6%), which has been at the receiving end of Nigeria's generosity in the security, political, and economic domains, attests to the point that coming to the aid of others can be a good way of boosting the influence and leadership credentials of regional powers. This, equally, validates Nye's thesis on the nature of behaviours that are likely to generate attraction. As A. Konneh notes, the first thing that comes to my mind when Nigeria is mentioned is "big power, big brother that we Liberians will always reflect in terms of the role they played in bringing stability to this country" (personal communication, January 24, 2020).

The fact that following the "more powerful" category in the hierarchy of perceptions is the category "not living up to its potential," which suggests that Nigeria has failed to take advantage of its immense resources whether at the domestic or regional levels all the more buttresses this point. This is because it reflects a tacit acknowledgement of Nigeria's superior power status. Perhaps, it may even suggest that long-held hopes of Nigeria one day shaping "the destiny of the continent by giving it a credible, dynamic and effective leadership" has not yet materialized (Oshewolo, 2019a, p. 6)

As Table 8.1 indicates, more people in Ghana and Liberia are of the view that Nigeria's influence in the sub-region has increased, followed by those who believe it has remained the same, demonstrating that its shortcomings have not completely eroded its influence. But for the lack of similar empirical accounts, it may have been insightful to juxtapose these findings with previous studies to determine if Nigeria is losing or gaining grounds within the sub-region.

Table 8.1 Perceptions of Nigeria's Influence

		Country		Total	Percent	Cumulative Percent
		Ghana	Liberia			
Influence of Nigeria	Increased	136	131	267	47.6	**47.6**
	Remains the same	100	84	184	32.8	**80.4**
	Reduced	65	45	110	19.6	**100.0**
Total		301	260	561	100.0	

Table 8.2 Perceptions of Nigeria's Leadership in International Institutions

		Country		Total	Percent	Cumulative Percent
		Ghana	*Liberia*			
Nigeria provides leadership in international institutions	Strongly disagree	10	0	10	1.8	**1.8**
	Disagree	29	10	39	7.0	**8.7**
	Neutral	126	13	139	24.8	**33.5**
	Agree	129	146	275	49.0	**82.5**
	Strongly agree	7	91	98	17.5	**100.0**
Total		**301**	**260**	**561**	**100.0**	

In terms of its leadership aspirations, the driving force of Nigeria's external posture, Figure 7.1 shows that Nigeria is perceived as a leader by more Liberians than Ghanaians. This finding corroborates Table 8.2, as 66.5% of Liberians and Ghanaians agree that Nigeria provides leadership in international institutions, a reflection of its leadership role in such multilateral fora as the AU, UN, and ECOWAS. That more Liberians than Ghanaians see Nigeria as a leader in the QCA could be because Ghana is gradually catching up with Nigeria – in economic terms and global credibility – and increasingly see Nigeria as a brother and partner than a leader *per se*.[1] And, this brings into contention the role of power asymmetry in shaping perceptions of less powerful states vis-à-vis their more powerful counterparts, especially on questions of leadership. Or perhaps, we may even allude to the indulgence of more powerful states by their less powerful counterparts for fear of being picked on.

If one of the goals of a soft power approach to foreign policy is to create an enabling environment for the exercise of influence, however contentious this may appear, it is clear that Nigeria may be close to that goal. This is due to the positive effects of its resources and actions on the attitudes of academic and political elites in Ghana and Liberia. As Table 8.3 reveals, 73.3% of Liberians and Ghanaians want their governments to cooperate more with Nigeria, which corroborates the findings of the QCA where just above 3% of coded references allude to more cooperation with Nigeria and support for its regional policies. But this should not obscure the fact that 42% of Ghanaians want their government to cooperate less with Nigeria. Perhaps, we may be underestimating the strength of the rivalry between both countries or even overplaying the strength of Nigeria's attraction in Ghana.

While the findings above do not prove causation, they are nonetheless compelling, suggesting that the overall attractiveness of Nigeria does have some role to play in these sentiments. That the impacts of the various components of Nigeria's attractive resources in shaping perceptions of its influence and leadership are not isolated in this study does not negate the fact they do have

Table 8.3 More Cooperation between Your Country and Nigeria

		Country		Total	Percent	Cumulative Percent
		Ghana	Liberia			
More or less	More	173	238	411	73.3	**73.3**
cooperation with Nigeria	Less	128	22	150	26.7	100.0
Total		**301**	**260**	**561**	**100.0**	

some role to play. What this implies is that Nigeria's soft power has created an enabling environment for the exercise of influence, whether the Nigerian state has been able to make the most of it or not. In sum, when the indirect effects of Nigeria's qualities and strategic disposition in West Africa on the subjectivities of Ghanaian and Liberian elites are scrutinized, especially in terms of perceptions of its influence and leadership, the claim can be made that Nigeria does have soft power.

However, the fact that long-term milieu goals associated with leadership and influence look promising for Nigeria does not imply that self-interested goals, where the indirect effects of attraction are expected to translate to direct effects or have direct policy impact, will also be achieved. For instance, while the EU successfully achieved its milieu goal of democratizing Central Europe after the Cold War, it was unable to get them to follow its lead on climate by matching its level of concession on carbon emission at the 2009 climate summit in Copenhagen (Nye, 2011). In the ensuing sub-section, the study extends the question of effectiveness to self-interested contexts where interests tend to collide and soft power's potency is mostly contested.

Voting Coincidence as a Measure of Direct Effects

In measures of foreign policy outcomes, UN voting practices often serve as indicators of a state's political influence or the effectiveness of its economic or political assistance to others (Singh & Macdonald, 2017; S. Rose, 2018). This is born out of the expectation that coming to the aid of others, indigent or otherwise, will likely attract their support in international fora. In some instances, states have even tied foreign assistance packages to UN votes as a way of extracting compliance with their foreign policy preferences. President Trump's threat to cut off financial assistance to countries who vote against the US's decision to recognize Jerusalem as the capital of Israel is a case in point that keeps with a practice dating back to the Reagan era (Landler, 2017; S. Rose, 2018).

In Nigeria, scholars and state actors alike often allude to the voting practices of West African states to argue the ineffectiveness of the country's diplomatic approach, even though Nigeria's external disposition was not conceived to frontally incentivize others (Oshewolo, 2019a; Akinterinwa, 2012; Ogbonna & Ogunnubi, 2018). The absence of voting records within ECOWAS indeed complicates the analysis of the voting coincidence of West African states with Nigeria. This is also the case with the voting records of West African states in global organizations. However, the number of times Nigeria has contested for leadership positions and emerged victoriously or suffered defeat may serve as a proxy because a region or continent-wide consensus, mobilized through the African Group, is central to the emergence of African representatives in global multilateral fora. On this note, to what extent have West African states supported Nigerian candidates in multilateral forums?

Nigeria has emerged more than any other country in Africa as a non-permanent member of the UNSC –1966–1967, 1978–1979, 1994–1995, 2010–2011, and 2014–2015 – in a boost to its bid for a permanent seat should the expansion of the UNSC happen (UNSC, 2021). Nigeria's Amina J. Mohammed is the current Deputy Secretary-General of the UN and Chair of the UN Sustainable Development Group. Even within the UNGA, Nigeria is only the third country in the world and the only one from Africa that has had two stints as President – Joseph Nanven Garba in 1989 and Tijjani Mohammad Bande in 2019 – thanks to the support of African states (UN, 2020b).

Beyond these two essential multilateral fora are other institutions where African states have demonstrated confidence in Nigerian leadership. Riding out the storm of the Trump administration's decision not to back her candidacy for the position of Secretary-General of the WTO in favour of South Korea's Yoo Myung-hee, Ngozi Okonjo-Iweala emerged as the first African and first woman elected to lead the apex trade institution, thanks to the endorsement of the Biden administration and the overwhelming support of other 163 members. In 2013, Olumuyiwa Bernard Aliu emerged as the first African to be elected as president of the International Civil Aviation Organization (ICAO) Council by a unanimous vote (ICAO, 2013a). While Burkina Faso and Cabo Verde were the only West African states in the ICAO's 36-states governing council saddled with the responsibility of electing the president of the council, other African states included South Africa, Cameroun, Tanzania, Kenya, and Congo (ICAO, 2013b). Also, Nigeria currently seats as one of Africa's representatives in the UN Economic and Social Council.

The foregoing serves an illustrative purpose and does not paint a full picture of African representations in global organizations. However, the fact that Nigeria has assumed relatively more leadership positions, certainly not without the support of the African Group, suggests its role in the continent influences or bears on the voting decision of African states, especially the African Group, which provides a forum to mobilize consensus on African representatives. To narrow the scope of this discussion to the African continent, the AfDB is currently led by Akinwumi Adesina since 2015. Despite efforts by the Trump administration to impede his re-election, based on unfounded allegations of favouritism, Adesina banked on the support of all the African member states to coast to re-election, perhaps in the spirit of African solidarity (African Courier, 2020).

Scholars of Nigerian foreign policy often contend that Nigeria has received far less in return for its contributions to Africa. While referring to Nigeria's monetary expenditure on the NTAC scheme, Ogbonna and Ogunnubi (2018) assert, "no evidence demonstrates that this huge investment has yielded any specific benefit in the advancement of Nigeria's position and interest" (p. 134). While it is unclear if they are alluding to interests beyond what is expatiated in this book, this conclusion is based on the electoral "setback" suffered by Nigeria in the 2017 Executive Council elections of the African Union Commission (AUC). While Fatima Mohammed, a Nigerian, lost to Smail Chergui of Algeria, Nigerian-backed Kenyan diplomat, Amina Mohammed, equally lost to Moussa Mahamet of Chad. These are in addition to the 2012 chairperson election where Nkosazana Dlamini-Zuma of South Africa defeated Nigerian-backed Jean Ping of Gabon (Ogbonna & Ogunnubi, 2018). The fact that these conclusions are drawn without recourse to the geopolitical dynamics and interests underlying these votes, especially in an organization where these factors trump ideological considerations as a criterion for electing officials, makes these assertions at best simplistic and at worst erroneous.

For some context, Dlamini-Zuma's emergence as the first female chairperson of the AUC at the summit of heads of state and government in Ethiopia happened in the absence of President Goodluck Jonathan who opted to remain in Abuja, and Prime Minister Meles Zenawi of Ethiopia who was thought to be seriously ill (Jobson, 2012). In addition to Ethiopia and Nigeria, Egypt strongly backed Jean Ping because, on the one hand, South Africa was breaking an unwritten rule which prevented the five largest financial contributors to the AU – Nigeria, Egypt, South Africa, Algeria, and Libya – from contesting for the office of the chairperson of the commission, and on the other, South Africa's victory may accord it an upper hand in the contest for a permanent seat in an expanded UNSC (Jobson, 2012). Thus, to make this defeat a question of Nigeria's influence is to ignore the strong influence of Egypt and Ethiopia in North and East Africa, respectively, or assume that Nigeria's influence supersedes theirs or even overestimate the reach of Nigeria's influence in Africa. Africa may be the centrepiece of Nigeria's foreign policy, but West Africa remains its sphere of influence.

While Jean Ping had narrowly won the first election but fell short of the two-thirds vote needed for victory, the absence of his main backers in the rerun, in a continent where personal diplomacy holds sway, combined with the historical significance of the possibility of the first female chairperson may have affected his chances. These are in addition to the fact that Dlamini-Zuma benefitted from the strong support of the Southern African Development Community. In a demonstration of Nigeria's influence and the importance of context in the assessment of power relationships, West African states were firmly behind Nigeria's support for Jean Ping but were weakened by the suspension of Guinea-Bissau and Mali from AU organs due to the unconstitutional change of government that had occurred in these countries some months before the vote (Affa'a-Mindzie, 2012).

Even more, in as much as Nigerians were not elected to the Executive Council in 2017, Ambassador Bankole Adeoye and Dr Aisha Abdullahi were elected in 2021 and 2013, respectively.[2] While the former is the present Commissioner for Political Affairs, Peace, and Security, the latter was the Commissioner, Political Affairs. There are indeed instances when Nigeria lost bids for non-permanent membership of the UNSC, even failing to gain the support of such West African states as Guinea, Liberia, and Sierra Leone in 2010 (Akinboye, 2013, p. 43). But, again, the underlying reasons for these votes are unclear, and these instances are not particularly sufficient to infer the erosion of Nigeria's influence or the ineffectiveness of its foreign policies, especially in West Africa.

An analysis by S. Rose (2018) on the link between US foreign aid and UN votes reveals that on important issues, with absence and abstention considered non-oppositional, recipients of US military and economic aid voted with the US "well over half the time," suggesting that giving out aid to states do not always amount to voting coincidence. It is important to note that the voting record used for this study was drawn from a US state department report of 2017 on voting practices in the UN, a year when the US ranked third on the global ranking of soft power (US Department of State, 2018; McClory, 2017). Similarly, in 2020 when Canada lost its bid for a seat in the UNSC to Ireland and Norway, it ranked 7th in the world in Brand Finance Global Soft Power Index, whereas Norway and Ireland ranked 17th and 24th, respectively (Brand Finance, 2020).[3] What this suggests is that voting coincidence may be an important indicator of soft power's effectiveness in determining foreign policy outcomes, but as scholars of power politics have noted power is not always effective, whether hard or soft. The fact that more times than not, West African states side with Nigeria suggests that the indirect effects of its attraction have some bearing in self-interested contexts.

Within West Africa, Morocco's stalled bid for ECOWAS membership, which began in January 2017, once again, illustrates Nigeria's soft power in the sub-region, but also the limitation of its applicability in self-interested contexts. Although Senegal is also in opposition, Nigeria's refusal to endorse Morocco's membership bid remains the main reason why it is currently stalled. This is even as Morocco maintains the support of two-thirds of the members of the ECOWAS parliament, and the majority of ECOWAS member states, including Cote d'Ivoire, Niger, Liberia, and Benin (Fabiani, 2018; Munshi, 2019). Luis Filipe Luis Tavares, Cabo Verde's double minister of defence and foreign affairs, emphatically remarked in 2018 that Morocco's bid depends on the support of Nigeria and called on Rabat to focus its "excellent and dynamic diplomacy [...] on convincing Nigeria on the benefits of [its] membership" (Koundouno, 2018).

Regardless of Nigeria's recognition of the independence of Western Sahara, in recent years Morocco and Nigeria have maintained cordial relations. In addition to their agreement to construct a 5,660-km gas pipeline connecting both countries, Morocco's phosphate giant, OCP investment, is constructing a fertilizer plant in Nigeria and both countries maintain strong trade relations that put Nigeria above other African states as a destination for Morocco's exports (Munshi, 2019).

While what is of interest here are not the reasons for Nigeria's misgivings towards Morocco's bid, it is instructive to note that sub-regional power dynamics play an important role. It is not far-fetched to speculate that Nigeria worries about its influence, given Morocco's superior capabilities and strong economic ties with most West African states, worth over a billion dollars in investments and trade. Rather, what is of note is that despite strong favourable sentiments towards Nigeria, Liberia maintains strong support for Morocco, as is the case with Niger and Benin. After talks with his Moroccan counterpart, the speaker of the Liberian House of Representatives, Bhopal Chambers, reaffirmed his country's support for Morocco's ECOWAS membership bid (Maroc.ma, 2018). The same applies to Benin, where the Speaker of the National Assembly, Adrien Houngbedj, reaffirmed the government's support for Morocco's bid (The North Africa Post, 2018).

In essence, while Nigeria's opposition may have stalled Morocco's bid, countries like Liberia where Nigeria's attraction is evident do differ with it on this specific issue, suggesting that political interests do trump attraction, and attraction does not connote political subserviency.[4] It is also instructive to note that despite Morocco's soft power in Nigeria stemming from long-term economic linkages and its offering of educational scholarships to Nigerians for over a decade, Nigeria isn't favourably disposed to welcoming it into ECOWAS, even if under the pretext of forging African integration.

To the extent that West African states are in support of Morocco's bid, but respect Nigeria's unwillingness to accede to its membership, the indirect effects of Nigeria's soft power are at work. However, the fact that they openly welcome Morocco's membership also demonstrates the limitation of soft power in self-interested contexts, especially when interests collide. What is, however, notable is that these disagreements are taking place in a cooperative context aided by Nigeria's foreign policy disposition. It also suggests that respect for Nigeria's leadership bears on the decision of African states to support its candidates, more often than not, within the UN and the AU. While Oshewolo (2019b) concedes this point, he argues, "this recognition has not been proportionate, in degree and extent, to Nigeria's assumed clout both continentally and globally" (p. 8). To Agbu (2009) the lack of complete support for Nigeria makes a mockery of the principle of reciprocity, which should naturally govern interstate relations, as foreign policy ought to be deemed a policy of consequences, where positive and negative dispositions are reciprocated.

Yes, there are challenges to Nigeria's leadership and influence in Africa, but if the yardstick for their determination is the rare instances where West African states have voted against Nigerian candidates for elective offices in international organizations, then the line for determining outcomes may have been drawn too thinly. The expectation that Nigeria's benevolence in its external disposition should naturally amount to complete support for its policies at every instance amounts to a level of political subserviency that is inimical to the idea of sovereignty and the self-interested nature of states. After all, the former president of Senegal, Abdoulaye Wade, is known to have said that it is preferable to have an ECOWAS that excludes Nigeria, suggesting that Nigeria's contribution to the sub-region may not have doused historical rivalries with its Francophone neighbours or Nigeria's internal contradictions are eroding its influence in the sub-region (Agwu, 2013, p. 639).

Especially in regional fora, support for Nigeria should naturally indicate responsiveness to soft power, but other states do aspire for leadership in these institutions or have competing interests and not much should be made of their unwillingness to support Nigeria at every turn, especially when it contravenes their interests. If the idea of soft power is the complete abdication of one's interest in favour of another's, then that power may not be soft after all. What this implies is that states do not make decisions because they are attracted to one another *per se*, they equally consider their interest. Perhaps this is why realists frown at the concept of soft power because it does very little to limit the choices of others, and even when it does, we are unable to tell if the changed behaviour is the result of attraction or shared interests.

However, what is clear is that Nye provides a concept that captures intangible elements of power whose meaning derives from the subjectivities of international audiences, and usefulness from their willingness to act on these subjectivities in the practice and conduct of international politics. The case of Nigeria's relations with Ghana and Liberia validates Nye's conceptualization of soft power, as it demonstrates that looking out for others, putting one's house in order, and adopting multilateral approaches to shared challenges are behaviours that attract and enhance a country's image and leadership credential. It also shows that illiberal political values erode the reputational gains of states.

As the previous section suggests, creating indirect effects, regardless of the ability of political elites to influence the foreign policy decision-making processes of others, creates an environment of friendliness where political discourse can be aired, thus, engendering the likelihood of favourable outcomes. As Nye (2011) himself notes, power is not always effective, and this appears to be the case with Nigeria when the question of direct effects is considered. In other words, in international politics aesthetics, benevolence and empathy are not always gainful, but so also is the use of force. As a senior government official in Liberia remarks, the fact that Nigeria continues to maintain support for Liberia despite instances when his country did not vote with/for Nigeria suggests that "Nigeria is flexible ... and being democratic" – qualities that are likely to enhance its influence and leadership (D. Remongar, personal communication, January 22, 2020). More importantly, it builds trust and enhances cooperation.

That Nigeria's foreign policy is unstrategic is a valid point but voting coincidence as an indicator of political influence does not prove this point. If anything, one has to look at the gap between Nigeria's foreign policy objectives and the instrumentalization of its full range of attractive sources of influence and the lack of policies to confront the negative dimensions of its influence to explain the lack of strategy in its foreign policy approach, all of which are exacerbated by the ineffectiveness of exiting public diplomacy initiatives.

Explaining the Ineffectiveness of Nigeria's Soft Power

Discussions in the preceding section suggest that Nigeria's African policy does generate indirect effects in the form of reputational gains. This has in some instances generated direct effects, in the form of foreign policy gains, when voting coincidence is used as an indicator of political influence. While this section concedes that these gains are insufficient to argue the effectiveness of Nigeria's African policy, it offers a different take from prevailing assumptions on why this is the case. It argues that the problem of Nigeria's foreign policy is not in the nature of its behaviour, but in its inability to harness its soft power capabilities in a way that advances the national interest. A major reason advanced herein is a dysfunctional domestic context marred by internal challenges and institutional inadequacies, including the usurpation of the role of the foreign ministry by the presidency, as well the accompanying deficits both in the conception and implementation of policies that keep with new trends in the exercise of influence.

A Nation in Crisis: The Domestic Impediments of Nigeria's African Policy

Nigeria's strategic retreat from its habitual overgenerous contribution to subregional and continental affairs in the face of internal challenges is a testament to the truism that domestic politics have an overbearing influence on foreign policy and, by implication, the realization of the national interest. The fact that Nigeria's foreign policy appears dysfunctional and unstrategic is in no small way due to a domestic context that suffers from institutional inadequacies both in the conception and implementation of policies and in the substance of governance. Sixty years after independence, the Nigerian state is in crisis, suffering the consequences of ill-formation or colonial arbitrariness (Agwu, 2009). From inter-ethnic tensions, and security challenges such as banditry, insurgency, and kidnapping, to governance deficits, rising poverty levels, and soaring unemployment, inflation, and debt levels, the proverbial giant of Africa offers little to be desired.

There is no gainsaying that in the current dynamics of international politics, an attractive partner is one whose domestic affairs are in order. As McClory (2015) notes, "a successful model of domestic government is an

192 Foreign Policy Outcomes as a Measure of Soft Power Capability

important feature of a nation's overall attractiveness" and has the potential to drive investments, tourism, and, broadly speaking, economic gains (p. 21). The fact that perceptions in Liberia and Ghana reveal strong negative sentiments not just towards the values espoused in the practice of politics in Nigeria but also its overall governance system is a worrying sign for Nigeria's influence in Africa and exposes a glaring contradiction between its foreign policy posture and domestic politics. It is this reality that prompted Tella (2018) to remark that "Nigeria does not have the legitimacy to lay claim to a model of democracy in Africa and lacks the moral authority to promote it" yet continues to do so (p. 385).

The foregoing, to some extent, erodes Nigeria's attractive influence, and glaring contradictions of this nature put into contestation its overall ability to take advantage of the opportunities its military, economic, and cultural attractions offer in a complex regional and international system where competition remains brute. Beyond this, the dysfunctional nature of the domestic context also affects the mobilization of consensus towards what the country's national interest should be and how the resources required for their realization are to be channelled. The consequences are that an array of soft power resources is lying untapped, while the country's internal politics, which Campbell and Page (2018) aptly capture as the "means by which competing and cooperating elites divide up the country's wealth" (p. 86), excludes competent hands from participating in their location and instrumentalization towards the national interests. This is evident in the usurpation of the role of the foreign ministry by the presidency, thus, placing the burden of foreign policy conception in the hands of unqualified politicians.

In the words of G. Rose (2021), foreign policy ought to "emerge piece by piece, bottom-up from departments and the field, rather than spring from the head of some scribbler [...] who thinks he knows where history is going." The context of G. Rose's writing may differ, but it fits seamlessly with the Nigerian case where career diplomats rarely feature in foreign policy decision-making processes. Africa is the centrepiece of Nigeria's foreign policy and West Africa is its sphere of influence, but diplomats have more to say about Nigeria–US relations or Nigeria–China relations than Nigeria's relations with Benin or Togo. This suggests the lack of a coherent strategic framework in Nigeria's relationship with West African states. Take for instance the poor record of implementing existing agreements.

This sentiment is not new by any chance. For instance, Uhomoibhi (2012) and Gambari (2012) attribute the major challenges confronting Nigeria's foreign policy to the absence of a coherent, result-driven, and dynamic strategic framework. To quote Salui (2013), "Nigeria's Afrocentric foreign policy is the worst reflection of the apparent lack of coordination in the formulation and execution of ... foreign policy" (p. 189). It is the absence of a strategic framework that explains the glaring gap in the ability of the state to make the best of its power resource lying in unofficial circles or even track the effectiveness of its public diplomacy initiatives as will be discussed subsequently.

The Gap between Governments and Transnational Non-State Actors

In September 1977, the second World Black and African Festival of Arts and Culture, otherwise known as Festac 77, was co-hosted in Lagos by the Nigerian government and UNESCO to showcase diverse African or black cultural expressions to the world. This month-long event, which witnessed the participation of over 16,000 persons from Africa, including the African diaspora, is the last of its kind in the history of Nigeria, even though it inspired the establishment of the National Council for Arts and Culture (NCAC), an institution dedicated to the promotion of the country's arts and culture. For clarity, the occasional carnivals organized by some select states of the federation during the Christmas season do not compare to this.

Despite strong cross-border cultural relations between Nigeria's cultural actors and their sub-regional counterparts, the fact that the mission statement of the NCAC on its website makes no mention of their external utility but emphasizes their use for internal political purposes such as national integration and unity illustrates the gap in the instrumentality of non-state actors in the conduct of foreign policy (NCAC, 2021). More importantly, it speaks to a pattern where politicians use cultural actors like Nollywood stars, musicians, and religious actors to serve mostly domestic political purposes such as propping up their images amongst unsuspecting local electorates (Njoku, 2010).

When France lost the Franco-Prussian War in the late-19th century, the government of the time set up the French cultural diplomacy outfit, *Alliance Française*, to promote French culture as well as restore the pride of the nation. In the same vein, at the height of the first World War, the US government convinced Hollywood practitioners to make movies that sought to portray their country positively to foreign audiences (Rosenburg, 1982). Nye (2011) notes the contribution made by the head of Hollywood studios, as well as corporate and advertising executives to create an enabling environment in Europe by selling American culture and values through their products. The myth of invincibility currently enjoyed by the US Armed Forces is one which has been reinforced in no small way by the projection of extraordinary gallantry and heroic displays of American soldiers in Hollywood motion pictures.

While Nigeria is lacking in political values, its cultural values are attractive, even more than they were when the quest for the formation of ECOWAS saw the active participation of non-state economic actors in mobilizing similar organizations from West African states. What this gap suggests is, simply put, the absence of an active effort to create soft power through culture at least since the 1980s despite a dwindling global and regional image, FDIs, and tourism. If the AU can recognize the power of Nollywood as an instrument to promote the AU Agenda 2063, why then has Nigeria been unable to apply it strategically to advance its value objectives in Africa?[5] In today's world, it is difficult to find a state that has successfully achieved some level of development without the proactive promotion of the essential components of its culture. Referring to the importance of culture, Johanna Odonkor Svanikier, a former Ghanaian Ambassador to France and Portugal, decried its neglect in Africa as a "potential for increasing GDP, creating jobs and improving standards of living" (McCormick, 2019).

Other than culture, the neglect of the role of citizens in Nigeria's African policy is obvious. NIDCOM was set up in 2019 – in recognition of the importance of the diaspora community – to bridge the gap between Nigerians in the diaspora and the homeland, as well as supplement the embassies in catering to their welfare. However, its efforts need to extend beyond the evacuation of stranded Nigerians and the occasional publicization of successful Nigerians in the diaspora. As Chapter 7 reveals, while Nigeria's most attractive sources of influence lie in the purview of non-state actors, the same source constitutes the most potent challenges to its influence, and topping this list is the Nigerian diaspora, whether as cultural, religious, or economic actors. The fact that a section of this group generates strong negative sentiments may, in the long term, pose an insurmountable challenge to Nigeria's soft power if unaddressed. As Nye (2011, p. 101) notes they may arouse such negative sentiments amongst the foreign public and governing elites alike that openly cooperating with Nigeria may become "a local political kiss of death," thus, preventing Nigeria from meeting certain foreign policy objectives.

Already data presented in the previous section suggest that culture, where the Nigerian diaspora features prominently, trumps other power categories as a source of attractive influence. Losing this dimension of influence because of the actions of a few may be detrimental to Nigeria's regional standing. Not incorporating those exemplary ones in its foreign policy may also prove detrimental. While the NTAC and the NTCF have already launched this process, the next section suggests that their effectiveness is limited by the lack of a global communication strategy.

Nigeria's Public Diplomacy Drive: An Exercise in Futile?

Active efforts by Nigeria to create soft power through public diplomacy initiatives may not be having the desired effects, as very few Ghanaians and Liberians are even aware of these initiatives. As Tables 8.4 and 8.5 suggest, only 33.2% of respondents in both countries have heard of the VON, Nigeria's

Table 8.4 The Popularity of the VON

| | | Country | | Total | Percent | Cumulative Percent |
		Ghana	Liberia			
Heard of VON	Yes	96	90	186	33.2	33.2
	No	205	170	375	66.8	100.0
Total		301	260	561	100.0	

Table 8.5 Impact of VON on Perceptions of Nigeria

| | | Country | | Total | Percent | Cumulative Percent |
		Ghana	Liberia			
If yes, what impact on your perception of Nigeria	Very positively	14	21	35	18.8	**18.8**
	Somewhat positively	37	45	82	44.1	**62.9**
	Somewhat negatively	7	6	13	7.0	**69.9**
	Very negatively	6	4	10	5.4	**75.3**
	No effect	32	14	46	24.7	**100.0**
Total		**96**	**90**	**186**	**100.0**	

tightly controlled medium of international broadcasting. In what appears to be a positive development and a suggestion that if properly calibrated it may serve as an effective instrument of foreign policy, of this number 62.9% agree that it has positively shaped their perceptions of Nigeria, while 24.7% note that it did not affect their perception of the country.

While it remains unclear in what ways VON shaped perceptions of Nigeria, what this finding suggests is that broadcasting remains an important medium of public diplomacy, especially in the internet age, where new channels of digital communication are emerging by the day. However, the fact that only a third of respondents are even aware of the VON may not be unconnected with another fact that its programmes are solely targeted at the Nigerian diaspora, specifically those residing in Western nations, whereas Africa remains the centrepiece of Nigeria's foreign policy. It is contradictions of this nature that give rise to questions about Nigeria's foreign policy approach.

As Nye (2011) aptly remarks, "the lines of communication are no longer a straight bar between two governments, but more like a star that includes lines among governments, publics, societies, and non-governmental organizations" (p. 102). This is true and poses a significant challenge for the Nigerian government, where information churned out through its broadcasting channels are steadily countered by its citizens on social media platforms, independently run media organizations, and non-governmental organizations. That the Nigerian government fails to understand that communication is power and that this form of power is no longer the monopoly of governments, once again speaks to the disconnect between the Nigerian state and the changing dynamics of international politics and global communications.

To the extent that news from Nigeria's official broadcasting channels is not in conformity with the prevailing narratives of the citizens or other news outlets, it is safe to say that this not only undermines credibility, a crucial source of attractive influence, but also Nigeria's global reputation. This lends credence to the popular saying that "the best form of propaganda is no propaganda at all," which simply implies that telling the truth about one's

Table 8.6 The Popularity of the NTAC

		Country		Total	Percent	Cumulative Percent
		Ghana	Liberia			
Heard about NTAC	A lot	14	22	36	6.4	**6.4**
	Some	31	41	72	12.8	**19.3**
	Not very much	58	88	146	26.0	**45.3**
	Nothing at all	198	109	307	54.7	100.0
Total		301	260	**561**	100.0	

Table 8.7 The Popularity of the NTCF

		Country		Total	Percent	Cumulative Percent
		Ghana	Liberia			
Heard about NTCF	A lot	9	19	28	5.0	**5.0**
	Some	29	34	63	11.2	**16.2**
	Not very much	58	96	154	27.5	**43.7**
	Nothing at all	205	111	316	56.3	100.0
Total		301	260	**561**	100.0	

challenges may even generate attraction and invite the help of others. This is what Nye (2011) refers to as meta soft power, that is, the ability of a state to introspectively criticize itself and acknowledge its flaws.

Similar to VON, other public diplomacy initiatives by the Nigerian government such as the NTAC and the NTCF are also not known by a lot of Ghanaians and Liberians (see Tables 8.6 and 8.7). This is even as Nigeria still expends millions of dollars on these programmes.

That Ghanaians are not too familiar with these programmes is not surprising at all as the preceding analysis already suggests, but the fact that very few Liberians are aware of them, despite being one of the major beneficiaries, once again illustrates the absence of synergy between Nigeria's public diplomacy initiatives and its communication strategy. One would assume that programmes of this nature would be readily broadcasted to the African public to demonstrate Nigeria's commitment to the region and shore up its leadership aspirations, but this is not the case. This exposes, once again, the lack of strategy in Nigeria's African policy.

Soft Power and the Future of Nigeria's African Policy: The Way Forward

Having discussed the challenges inhibiting the effective use of soft power in Nigeria's foreign policy, in this section, I argue that much more can be made of Nigeria's soft power assets through a skilful combination of the tools of government and non-state actors in a strategic framework that first addresses the image of the country and moves towards an approach to public diplomacy that is dialogic and digital.

The Imperative of a Renewed Approach to Foreign Policy

The context of West African politics is such that the overt use of force by one state against another is "almost" inconceivable regardless of disparities in power capabilities. This is due to the nature of regional priorities, which since independence have revolved around integration, trade, security, domestic challenges to juridical sovereignty, internal political instability, and development deficits. The fact that these issues are mostly addressed through a collaborative approach within ECOWAS, albeit with minor discords, is indicative of a sub-regional context where interstate relations are cordial and the utility of force almost unnecessary. This context makes the use of soft power, especially for regional leaders like Nigeria, practicable and the ultimate means to success.

Despite its realist undertone, Nigeria's foreign policy behaviour is liberalist in nature, suggesting that Abuja recognizes the imperative of soft power but is unable to bridge the gap between its policies and attractive resources. This calls for a renewed approach to foreign policy that begins with taking actionable steps towards addressing the domestic impediments of foreign policy, both at the levels of state administration and the conception and implementation of strategies. Specifically, Nigeria has to shelve the "illusion of grandeur," which has informed its foreign policy and come to terms with the reality that its global standing hinges on addressing its pressing domestic challenges and revamping its global image (Agwu, 2009, p. 174).

In January 2020, Nigeria's minister of foreign affairs announced a new foreign policy approach in the Trumpian model, "Nigeria first," which caters specifically to the country's economic vulnerabilities. Apart from the catchy slogan, the content of this pronouncement does not deviate substantially from what is discussed in Chapter 6. However, it was specific on eight areas of priority upon which bilateral and multilateral cooperation will be based – building a viral economy, energy sufficiency, expanding transport and infrastructure, protection of its citizens, enlarging agricultural output, expanding business growth, industrialization, and entrepreneurship (The Guardian, 2020). While emphasizing domestic priorities in the conduct of foreign policy is what any rational nation will do, borrowing a jettisoned Trumpian slogan that connotes nationalism, unilateralism, isolationism, and protectionism, even if as a meaningless phraseology, is not the way for Nigeria to go. The fact that Nigeria's oil-boom-financed foreign policy behaviour emerged as one of the country's attractive sources of influence in Chapter 7 suggests that it may need to maintain such disposition, although the need for a strong economy cannot be overemphasized.

As important as the economy is, the government is unlikely to get it working without addressing the myriad of domestic challenges inimical to the image, credibility, and reputation of the country. This will require creating an enabling domestic environment of enhanced security, reducing corruption, reduced poverty levels, national cohesion, and political stability – all of which are likely to boost investor confidence. The images of violence that are the hallmark of Nigeria's elections need to be addressed as they increasingly conjure up sentiments of a nation that cannot put its house in order and is stuck in the "hypocrisy trap." It is only when genuine steps are taken to address these challenges and transparently communicated in a dialogic approach that Nigeria's domestic affairs may begin to inspire confidence in its political leadership and also enhance its soft power. After all, the successful conduct of the 2015 presidential elections, culminating in the defeat of an incumbent president, reverberated around West Africa and saw the chairman of the electoral commission invited to countries like Ghana to play an advisory role in the conduct of their elections.

In the implementation of its foreign policy objectives, a coordinated approach based on a well-conceived strategic framework that mobilizes all relevant agencies of government as well as soft power assets located within the purview of the government and non-state actors is necessary. In the case of the eight priority areas, which are mainly in the economic domain, a compartmentalization strategy may be devised to situate these goals within the authority of competent agencies, all under the coordination of the ministry of foreign affairs. For instance, while NIDCOM may handle aspects of citizen diplomacy as it already does, the Nigerian Investment Promotion Commission, which coordinates Nigeria's investment drive, may collaborate with the Ministry of Industry, Trade, and Investment, and the Ministry of Agriculture to develop a strategic framework.

This may even require the formation of a committee similar to the Adebayo Adedeji-led committee established during the Murtala/Obasanjo regime, which mobilized universities, the military, mass media, and economic actors to qualitatively transform Nigeria's foreign policy from a conservative to a dynamic approach (see Agwu, 2013). It is this dynamism in foreign policy conception and implementation that is needed to make the best of the diverse attractive resources lying untapped in unofficial circles. There is no gainsaying that Nigeria's leadership aspiration should warrant the formation of a robust partnership between the government and its diaspora entrepreneurs, companies, and cross-border cultural actors towards the pursuit of its African policy. The formation of this type of partnership not only stands to increase Nigeria's global influence but also the security and prosperity of its citizens. This should be accompanied by building a national brand that improves Nigeria's image and the digitization of its public diplomacy initiatives – all of which are essential to its soft power and sustained influence in an information age.

Take for instance the GREAT campaign launched in 2011 by the UK to leverage the gains of hosting the 2012 Olympics. In addition to enhancing the UK's global image, GREAT had specific objectives of boosting businesses by £1 billion and bringing over 4 million foreign tourists to the UK. It was conceived and coordinated from No. 10 Downing Street, pooling financial and human resources from 17 government departments, including the UK Trade and Investment, Visit Britain, Culture Department, and the Foreign Office, into a coherent strategic framework (BBC News, 2011). It is important to note that over 350 private actors around the globe were mobilized for this project, with Britain's attractive attributes such as Richard Branson and the animation characters of Wallace and Gromit featuring prominently in marketing materials and advertisements. As of 2018, the GREAT campaign surpassed its objectives by bringing in over £3 billion into the UK's economy, in a sign that soft power works (Owen, 2018). This is a well-executed model that Nigeria may want to emulate if it wants to make the best of its soft power.

Also, while prioritizing the welfare of citizens is a noble endeavour, the objective shouldn't be limited to this. Rather, Nigeria should capitalize on the networks citizens have with foreign governments in such a way that channels their influence towards the pursuit of the national interest. The same applies to religious organizations and companies with strong networks around the continent. Certainly, a bank like Access, with a presence in 12 African countries, or a religious organization like the RCCG, which boasts over 20,000 parishes across the globe, has strong networks with foreign actors that may be beneficial to Nigeria's foreign policy. With cross-border linkages already in existence between these actors, especially in West Africa, the Nigerian government may want to key into these networks by sending representatives to their events or programmes. For instance, Pastor Adeboye's crusades in African states draw the participation of major Pentecostal movements in host countries as well as representatives of governments. This may even be a solution towards bridging existing divides between Francophone and Anglophone West Africa.

However, professionals trained in cross-cultural communications and armed with networks of contacts should man these public diplomacy initiatives. This is because while Nigeria has been successful in developing long-term relations with key individuals through its public diplomacy initiatives, it has been unable to steer this relationship into long-term bonds. As one respondent in Liberia decried, despite studying at Nigeria's Ahmadu Bello University, the institution has never contacted him, whereas he is in constant communication with Brown University in the US where he also studied (A. Fofana, personal communication, January 29, 2020). This is a deficiency that may be mitigated by maintaining a record of all foreigners who obtain educational or military qualifications in Nigeria.

Towards a Nation-Branding Strategy

For most people in Liberia and Ghana, the mention of Nigeria conjures images of entrepreneurial ingenuity, military, and economic pre-eminence, as well as a diverse array of exemplary cultural actors. However, these are embedded in stereotypical images of criminality, aggressiveness, corruption, illicit trade practices, and domestic governmental incompetence. Even more, local media and journalists reinforce these negative images by ascribing every heinous crime to Nigerians, as a Nigerian diplomat in Ghana noted (S. Alege, personal communication, September 3, 2019). While the impact of these perceptive contradictions at the state-to-state level appears to be minimal as cross-border political interest often transcends "these petit issues," their effect is increasingly prominent at the people-to-people level.

These perceptive contradictions shouldn't be left unaddressed, especially for a country that projects itself as the giant of Africa and hopes to bank on West Africa's support for permanent membership in the UNSC. If oil, large population size, and a history of coming to the aid of neighbouring states are all the country can boast of, its influence may wane faster than imagined. Not only has the country withdrawn considerably from its generous role in Africa, but a good number of West African states have also struck oil, including Ghana, Niger, and Senegal. This renders the need for an improved regional and global image essential not just for reputational gains but also as a potential soft power currency.

Chapter 6 discussed attempts to rebrand Nigeria's image including positioning TAC volunteers as country ambassadors, setting up the VON as an international broadcast medium, launching such nation-branding strategies as "the Heart of Africa Project," "Nigeria: Good People, Good Nation," and "Fascinating Nigeria." While these efforts had clearly defined objectives, the targets were unclear. Equally, the issues affecting the image of the country were not clearly defined, which perhaps would have better shaped the objectives of these initiatives. More importantly, these projects were not backed by empirical research on the perceptive dispositions of specific target audiences. The absence of coordination and political will was also evident in the lack of funding and deliberate efforts in addressing the root causes of Nigeria's image problem. If the effectiveness of Nigeria's soft power can only be demonstrated where it has sought to create an enabling environment for its policies, due largely to its no-strings-attached foreign policy behaviour, then it must learn to complement it by consistently selling a positive image of itself.

Nigeria does need to rebrand its image, as this study suggests, to reflect its self-proclaimed status as the giant of Africa. This implies the implementation of a deliberate strategy that builds, connects, and manages "the systemic flow from perceptions to emotion, within the scope of reality, to minimize distorted images and maximize nation brand potential to attract and appeal through a positively reinforced reputation" (Bloom Consulting, 2020).

As discussed previously, this should begin by setting up a committee of stakeholders made of state and non-state actors alike unaffected by political interests and supported with adequate and sustained funding. Perhaps, an independent institution or agency, supported by national brand consultants with proven track records, could be set up to manage such a project. An important question that follows from this, which this research has answered to some extent, is what does the African public associate with the Nigerian brand? Not only does answering this question clarify the gap between self-identity and external perception, as well as emotions associated with the Nigerian brand, it also identifies the problems associated with the country and aids in the formulation of clear-cut solutions or objectives.

While perceptions of Nigeria in this study were drawn from foreign publics, it is important to account for perceptions of the domestic audience, as this will clarify the gap between self-identity and external perceptions. An important domain of investigating external perceptions, which this book does not capture, is the digital space, as digital footprints do impact how nations are perceived. Following from this is the importance of target audiences, which was lacking in previous national branding strategies. The underlying contradictions in Nigeria's image suggest that a strategy geared towards the African public, companies, and investors is imperative. Not only are clearly defined targets important for policy conception, but it also eases the burden of measuring effectiveness.

Given Nigeria's national interest, which prioritizes the welfare of its citizens, both in security and economic terms, its actions, policies, and activities should be geared towards this objective, with measurable metrics put in place to ascertain effectiveness. Such image branding endeavours should take advantage of the appeal of Nollywood and Nigerian music, as well as take the form of a strategic campaign and the hosting or organization of symbolic events to advance government policies with foreign publics. In all of this, it is important to be consistent, act more, and talk less. However, if the need to talk arises, a dialogic approach to digital communication portends to be the best approach.

The Imperative of Digitalizing Public Diplomacy

As governments have recognized, the digital space offers a platform for a reimagined approach to public diplomacy, the affirmation of values, as well as reputation and image management. In addition to the fact that it provides a transparent and inclusive stage for policy discourse, it also brings government policies, whether domestic or foreign, closer to public scrutiny. With social media platforms the go-to for the latest news and information by global audiences, state actors have capitalized, even to the extent of engaging themselves publicly. This has engendered a situation whereby different acts of diplomacy that normally takes place behind closed doors are now open to the global public. Consequently, digital diplomacy has moved from the fringes of diplomatic studies to assume an important dimension of diplomatic statecraft (Manor, 2016; Collins et al., 2019).

Even more, platforms such as Twitter, Facebook, and Instagram provide governments with a wide audience to influence and attract by amplifying their policies and positions on contemporary global issues. Although influence is not guaranteed, a dialogic approach to communication is necessary for the hope of its occurrence. As is the case with Nigeria, most government agencies and senior officials have functioning accounts on social media platforms; however, they lack public engagement, as these platforms mostly serve the purpose of announcing offline events, such as meetings between diplomats or signing of agreements, a practice which suggests "a concession to modernity, without the risk that greater engagement of transparency entails" (McClory, 2015, p. 34).

Take for instance, the case of the former British Ambassador to Lebanon, Tom Fletcher, who is reputed to have recurrently engaged in conversations on social media. These simple acts of engagement at times prove more effective than the traditional offline means of public diplomacy that most states are accustomed to. In digital diplomacy, the most important elements are accessibility, authenticity, and credibility. As long as these elements are inherent in the use of digital platforms by government agencies and their authorized representatives, they are likely to be effective. Nye (2004) is reputed for emphasizing the importance of credibility in international politics. While international politics still revolves around the military and economic capabilities of nations, the importance of information and, by implication, communication cannot be overemphasized in an age where social media has become an arena for the contest of credibility not just between state actors, but between governments and non-state actors, including citizens, foreign publics, and transnational organizations.

Witness the #ENDSARS protest in Nigeria, which culminated in what is now referred to as the Lekki Massacre of October 20, 2020. It is not the fact that these protests were mobilized and coordinated using digital platforms such as Facebook, Twitter, and WhatsApp that is instructive, rather, it is the contest of credibility playing out between the Nigerian government, protesters, and transnational organizations, in a bid to frame interpretations of events that culminated in the killing of unarmed protesters at the Lekki tollgate by the Nigerian Army. The protesters exposed a glaring gap in Nigeria's nonchalant approach to communication – that is, the unwillingness of the government to engage with its citizens on important social and political issues until the international media places a spotlight on them.

It is this approach to digital communication that Nigeria must jettison if it hopes to sustain its leadership position in the affairs of West Africa. The fact that estimates from 2020 reveal the presence of 475 million mobile Internet users in sub-Saharan Africa, of which one-fifth is Nigerians suggest that Nigeria is not making the best of the unfiltered access digital platforms offer to convey its domestic and foreign policies directly to African publics

(Global Systems for Mobile Communications, 2020). While the MFA has an established presence on Facebook and Twitter, its approach to digital communication lacks direct interaction. As of the writing of this book, the MFA has just over 12,000 followers on Facebook, 22,000 followers on Twitter, and 5,000 on Instagram; however, it never reacts to comments under its post, even when important enquiries are made or messages about the welfare of Nigerian citizens passed across.

In sum, while Nigeria recognizes the importance of creating a digital identity, its digital diplomacy strategy if what is practised can be labelled as such, misses important elements of daily and strategic communication that need to be addressed. First, it ought to move beyond tweets or Facebook posts that fail to expatiate the domestic and external significance of diplomatic engagements. Second, Nigerian diplomats ought to approach public diplomacy as a two-way dialogue that elevates citizens and the foreign public alike to the status of co-creators of communication (Nye, 2011). They may even promote interactions through Q&A sessions on social media platforms, as a means of demonstrating credibility, accessibility, and, ultimately, authenticity. Finally, Nigerian citizens represent the country's biggest foreign asset, not because of the weight of their remittances but because they represent the country abroad and their perceptions matter significantly. As one Ghanaian remarked, Nigerians always speak ill of their country (Nii-Dortey, personal communication, August 30, 2019). Maybe if the government takes the opportunities offered by digital platforms to communicate with its diaspora and restore their confidence, this group of Nigerians will speak well of the country and restore its waning image.

Conclusion

This chapter set out to ascertain the extent to which Nigeria's attractive qualities and attributes, as well as its foreign policy behaviour, have amounted to tangible foreign policy benefits. It also sought to ascertain the extent to which negative perceptions of Nigeria have affected the pursuit of its African policy. To these ends, two levels of effectiveness or outcomes were contemplated: direct and indirect. In both levels of outcomes, the preceding discussions suggest that Nigeria may lay claim to a level of efficacy in its soft power approach to foreign policy. This is based on favourable perceptions of its leadership, influence, and a concomitant will for enhanced cooperation with Nigeria by elites in Ghana and Liberia. Certainly, Nigeria's contribution to integration efforts, regional peace and security, and democratic consolidation rub off positively on Ghanaian and Liberian elites in a way that influences their perception of its leadership credentials. Even when the direct effects of Nigeria's strategic disposition in Africa, specifically on questions of policy, are scrutinized, the evidence suggests that more time than not, West African states have sided with Nigeria. This is evident in the number of times Nigerian-backed candidates in regional and global multilateral fora have gained the support of West African states.

That discussions in this chapter make the case for Nigeria's soft power in West Africa or the effectiveness of its soft approach to foreign policy does not suggest that its overall foreign policy approach in Africa has been effective. While this finding reflects a point of convergence with prevailing scholarly assumptions about Nigeria's foreign policy, this chapter offers a different take. It finds that the ineffectiveness of Nigeria's foreign policy results from a dysfunctional domestic context marred by internal challenges and institutional inadequacies, including the usurpation of the role of the foreign ministry by the presidency, the inability of the Nigerian state to make the best of its attractive resources, especially those aspects lying within the purview of non-state actors, and deficits in the conception and implementation of policies that keep with new trends in the exercise of influence.

However, these challenges can be mitigated by a renewed approach to foreign policy that skilfully combines the tools of government and non-state actors to advance the interests of Nigeria. This may entail a coordinated approach that mobilizes all relevant agencies of government and technical expertise to implement strategies that are geared towards repairing the country's dwindling international reputation. Perhaps, a national branding strategy that truthfully communicates the domestic challenges of the country and the various strategies adopted to address them may help in this regard. These may be further aided by a digital diplomacy strategy that emphasizes a communication-centric approach that is dialogic and makes the best of Nigeria's increasingly influential diaspora community.

Notes

1 A press release by the Ghana High Commission in July 2021 to debunk disparaging remarks, purportedly made by President Akufo-Addo about Nigeria and its leadership, appears to validate this point. In this press statement, the Ghanaian government describes Nigeria as a "very strategic partner" and, as is increasingly the norm, a "brotherly" country (Thisday, 2021).

2 It is important to note that Hadiza Mustapha, Nigeria's former ambassador to Cameroun, is the current Advisor, Peace, Security and Governance to the Chairperson of African Union. But for lack of records on the composition of the Executive Council prior to 2013, one may even find that Nigerians have been regularly elected.

3 It is instructive to note that in the US News and World Report Power Rankings for 2020, which ranks countries according to their political influence, economic influence, strength of international alliance, leadership and military strength, Canada ranked 12th in the world, whereas Norway ranked 23rd and Ireland did not feature on the list of 73 countries (US News & World Report, 2020).

4 Estimates from 2019 value trade relations between Morocco and Liberia at $3.38 million (Trading Economics, 2019). This is in addition to Morocco providing educational scholarships to Liberian students.

5 In a visit to Abuja in 2018, Moussa Faki Mahamet expressed the willingness of the AUC to use the medium of Nigerian films and Nollywood actors to promote the AU Agenda 2063. According to Mahamet, "the Nollywood brand is a tool that should be used to popularize [the] African agenda because it is well-known all-over Africa and beyond" (Vanguard, 2018).

References

Affa'a-Mindzie, M. (2012, July 19). *Fierce battle over AU Commission Chair ends in South Africa's favor. IPI Global Observatory.* Retrieved March 26, 2020, from https://theglobalobservatory.org/2012/07/the-election-of-the-african-union-com mission-chairperson-a-fierce-battle-for-a-clear-win/

African Courier. (2020, May 27). *Why the US opposes Akinwumi Adesina's re-election as African Development Bank's president.* Retrieved September 26, 2020, from www.theafricancourier.de/special/business/why-the-us-is-opposed-to-akinw umi-adesinas-re-election-as-african-banks-president/

Agbu, O. (2009). Nigerian foreign policy under President Umaru Musa Yar'Adua: Challenges and prospects. In O. C. Eze (Ed.), *Citizen diplomacy* (pp. 41–61). Nigerian Institute of International Affairs.

Agwu, F. A. (2009). *National interest, international law, and our shared destiny.* Spectrum Books Limited.

Agwu F. A. (2013). *Themes and perspectives on Africa's international relations.* University Press PLC.

Akinboye, S. O. (2013, July 17). *Beautiful abroad but ugly at home: Issues and contradictions in Nigeria's foreign policy* [Paper presentation]. The 9th Inaugural Lecture of the University of Lagos, Lagos, Nigeria.

Akinterinwa, A. B. (2012). Overview of Nigeria's foreign policy, 1960–2010: Challenges and recommendations. In E. Anyaoku (Ed.), *Review of Nigeria's foreign policy: Issues and perspectives* (pp. 15–34). Nigerian Institute of International Affairs.

BBC News. (2011, September 22). *London 2012: David Cameron launches "Great" campaign.* Retrieved April 6, 2021, from www.bbc.co.uk/news/uk-15019587

Bloom Consulting. (2020). *14 steps to nation branding.* Retrieved May 18, 2020, from www.bloom-consulting.com/journal/bloom-consulting-14-steps-to-nation-branding/

Brand Finance. (2020). *Global Soft Power Index 2020.* Retrieved May 18, 2020, from https://brandirectory.com/globalsoftpower/

Campbell, J., & Page, M. T. (2018). *Nigeria: What everyone needs to know.* Oxford University Press.

Collins, S. D., DeWitt, J. R., & LeFebvre, R. K. (2019). Hashtag diplomacy: Twitter as a tool for engaging in public diplomacy and promoting US foreign policy. *Place Branding and Public Diplomacy, 15*(2), 78–96.

Doss, A. (2020, September 29). *Safeguarding democracy in West Africa.* Africa Centre for Strategic Studies. Retrieved December 22, 2020, from https://africacenter.org/spotlight/safeguarding-democracy-in-west-africa/

Fabiani, R. (2018, March 28). *Morocco's difficult path to ECOWAS membership.* Carnegie Endowment for International Peace.

Freedom House. (2019). *Freedom in the World Report 2019: Democracy in Retreat.* Retrieved May 18, 2020, from https://freedomhouse.org/report/freedom-world/2019/democracy-retreat

Gambari, I. A. (2012). Nigeria at the United Nations: Prospects and challenges. In E. Anyaoku (Ed.), *Review of Nigeria's foreign policy: Issues and perspectives* (pp. 49–62). Nigerian Institute of International Affairs.

Gambia Armed Forces. (2018, March 6). *President Adama Barrow receives Commandant and Faculty staff of National Defence College of Nigeria.* Retrieved December 28, 2020, from https://gaf.gm/index.php/2018/03/06/president-adama-barrow-receives-commandant-and-faculty-staff-of-national-defence-college-of-nigeria/

Global Systems for Mobile Communications Association. (2020). *The Mobile Money: Sub-Saharan Africa 2020.* Retrieved August 1, 2020, from www.gsma.com/mobileeconomy/wp-content/uploads/2020/09/GSMA_MobileEconomy2020_SSA_Eng.pdf

International Civil Aviation Organization. (2013a, November 18). *ICAO Council elects new president.* Icao.int.

International Civil Aviation Organization. (2013b, October 1). *ICAO assembly elects new council for three-year term.* Icao.int.

Jobson, E. (2012, July 16). *African Union chooses first female leader. The Guardian.* Retrieved March 26, 2020, from www.theguardian.com/world/2012/jul/16/african-union-first-female-leader

Koundouno, T. F. (2018, November 9). *African diplomat: "Nigeria is key to Morocco's ECOWAS aspirations". Morocco World News.* Retrieved March 27, 2019, from www.moroccoworldnews.com/2018/11/257307/nigeria-key-morocco-ecowas-aspirations/

Landler, M. (2017, December 20). *Trump threatens to end American aid: "We're watching those votes" at the U.N. The New York Times.* Retrieved from January 22, 2020, from www.nytimes.com/2017/12/20/world/middleeast/trump-threatens-to-end-american-aid-were-watching-those-votes-at-the-un.html

Manor, I. (2016). *Are we there yet: Have MFAs realized the potential of digital diplomacy?* Brill. https://doi.org/10.1163/9789004319790

Marc, A., Verjee, N., & Mogaka, S. (2015). *The challenge of stability and security in West Africa.* World Bank Publications.

Maroc.ma. (2018, January 22). *Liberia reaffirms support for Morocco's request to join ECOWAS.* Maroc.ma. Retrieved March 28, 2020, from https://maroc.ma/en/news/liberia-reaffirms-support-moroccos-request-join-ecowas

McClory, J. (2015). *The soft power 30: A global ranking of soft power.* Portland.

McClory, J. (2017). *The soft power 30: A global ranking of soft power.* Portland.

McCormick, M. (2019, July 9). *Could heritage and culture become as important to Ghana's economy as fashion is for france? Forbes.* Retrieved September 26, 2020, from www.forbes.com/sites/meghanmccormick/2019/07/09/could-heritage-and-culture-become-as-important-to-ghanas-economy-as-fashion-is-for-france/

Munshi, N. (2019, January 24). *Morocco's Ecowas bid sparks African fear and suspicion. Financial Times.* Retrieved March 27, 2021, from www.ft.com/content/f17bf958-f96b-11e8-a154-2b65ddf314e9

National Council for Arts and Culture. (2021). *Mission statement.* Retrieved March 30, 2021, from www.ncac.gov.ng/about-us/mission-statement/

Njoku, B. (2010, November 5). *I'll act Majek better than Fashek – Francis Duru.* *Vanguard News.* Retrieved March 18, 2019, from www.vanguardngr.com/2010/ 11/i%E2%80%99ll-act-majek-better-than-fashek-francis-duru/

Nye J. S. (2004). *Soft power: A means to success in world politics.* Public Affairs Books.

Nye J. S. (2011). *The future of power.* Public Affairs Books.

Ogbonna, N. C., & Ogunnubi, O. (2018). Rethinking the Role of Nigeria's Technical Aid Corps as Soft Power: Rough Diamond or Fools' Gold. *African Journal of Peace and Conflict Studies, 7*(2), 121–141.

Olagunju, D. (2021, February 11). *The long road to free trade and beyond. Foreign Policy.* Retrieved March 21, 2021, from https://foreignpolicy.com/2021/02/11/the-long-road-to-free-trade-in-nigeria-and-beyond/

Oshewolo, S. (2019a). A reconsideration of the Afrocentric principle in Nigeria's foreign policy framework. *GeoJournal, 86,* 1–8. https://doi.org/10.1007/s10 708-019-10114-1

Oshewolo, S. (2019b). Major contentions on Nigeria's Afrocentric policy. *India Quarterly, 75*(3), 1–15.

Owen, J. (2018, September 25). *Seventh anniversary of the GREAT campaign: Three billion reasons to be cheerful.* PRWeek. Retrieved April 6, 2021, from www.prw eek.com/article/1494006/seventh-anniversary-great-campaign-three-billion-reas ons-cheerful

Rose, G. (2021, March 15). *Foreign policy for pragmatists. Foreign Affairs.* Retrieved March 30, 2021, from www.foreignaffairs.com/articles/united-states/2021-02-16/ foreign-policy-pragmatists

Rose, S. (2018, May 4). *Linking US foreign aid to UN votes: What are the implications?* Centre for Global Development. Retrieved March 24, 2020, from www.cgdev.org/ publication/linking-us-foreign-aid-un-votes-what-are-implications#ftn2

Rosenburg, E. (1982). *Spreading the American dream.* Hill and Wang.

Saliu, H. A. (2013). New options for Nigerian foreign policy. *Nigerian Journal of International Studies, 38*(1&2), 167–200.

Singh, J. P., & MacDonald, S. (2017). *Soft power today: Measuring the influences and effects.* Edinburgh: The Institute for International Cultural Relations, The University of Edinburgh.

Tella, O. (2018). Is Nigeria a soft power state? *Social Dynamics, 44*(2), 376–394. https://doi.org/10.1080/02533952.2018.1492833

Temin, J., & Linzer, I. (2020, March). *West Africa's democratic progress is slipping away, even as the Region's significance grows. Freedom House.* Retrieved April 22, 2020, from https://freedomhouse.org/article/west-africas-democratic-progress-slipping-away-even-regions-significance-grows-0

The Guardian. (2020, February 3). *That "Nigeria First" foreign policy initiative. The Guardian Nigeria News.* Retrieved April 1, 2021, from https://guardian.ng/opin ion/that-nigeria-first-foreign-policy-initiative/

The North Africa Post. (2018, February 22). *Benin National Assembly reaffirms support for Morocco's ECOWAS bid. The North Africa Post.* Retrieved March 28, 2020, from https://northafricapost.com/22377-benin-national-assembly-reaffirms-support-moroccos-ecowas-bid.html

Thisday. (2021, July 26). *Ghana debunks alleged Akufo-Addo's disparaging comment on Nigeria.* Retrieved September 7, 2021, from www.thisdaylive.com/index.php/ 2021/07/26/ghana-debunks-alleged-akufo-addos-disparaging-comment-on-nigeria/

Torres, C., & Van Seters, J. (2016). *Overview of trade and barriers to trade in West Africa: Insights in political economy dynamics, with particular focus on agricultural and food trade* [Discussion Paper, No. 195]. European Centre for Development Policy Management.

Trading Economics. (2019). *Morocco exports to Liberia – 1993–2019 Data.* 2021 Forecast. Retrieved December 16, 2020, from https://tradingeconomics.com/moro cco/exports/liberia

Uhomoibhi, M. (2012). An overview of Nigeria's foreign relations: A practitioner's perspective. In E. Anyaoku (Ed.), *Review of Nigeria's foreign policy: Issues and perspectives* (pp. 1–14). Nigerian Institute of International Affairs.

United Nations. (2020b, October 15). *Past presidents, General Assembly of the United Nations. UN.org.* Retrieved December 25, 2020, from www.un.org/pga/73/ about/past-presidents/

United Nations Security Council. (2021, February 11). *Countries elected members. UN.org.* Retrieved March 25, 2021, from www.un.org/securitycouncil/content/ countries-elected-members

United States Department of State. (2018). *Voting practices in the United Nations, 2017.* Retrieved April 5, 2020, from www.state.gov/voting-practices-in-the-united-nations-2017/

US News & World Report. (2020). *The most powerful countries in the world. USnews.com.* Retrieved March 27, 2021, from www.usnews.com/news/best-countr ies/power-rankings

Vanguard News. (2018, October 27). *Nollywood set to promote AU Agenda 2063.* Retrieved March 30, 2021, from www.vanguardngr.com/2018/10/nollywood-set-to-promote-au-agenda-2063/

World Bank. (2020c, July 27). *The African Continental Free Trade Area.* Retrieved September 21, 2020, from www.worldbank.org/en/topic/trade/publication/the-afri can-continental-free-trade-area

9 Conclusions

The Promise of Nigeria's Soft Power in West Africa

For over three decades, soft power has been widely studied in international relations scholarship, as more states embrace diplomatic approaches associated with the concept in their interactions with others. The geographical disparity in prevailing assumptions about the operationalization of the concept informed the need to interrogate Nigeria's soft power capabilities in West Africa; a sub-region that presents a conducive socio-economic, cultural, and political context that creates a permissive environment for the exercise of soft power. By and large, the use of brazenly coercive posturing in the sub-region is a rare occurrence, as relations between West African states have evolved cordially since independence, albeit amidst subtle rivalries. Regardless of these rivalries, the overall disposition of states in the sub-region towards each other has been shaped by variables such as shared colonial experiences, cross-border cultural ties, geographic contiguity that facilitates cross-border movements, and regional challenges that require a collaborative approach to their resolution.

At the heart of some of these challenges are gun-wielding non-state actors challenging the juridical sovereignty of states and terrorist networks that operate transnationally. However, they are not the only non-state actors with outsized influence on the dynamics of West African relations. While the destructive effects of colonialism on West African states, especially in its aftermath, cannot be minimized, it created culturally heterogeneous societies with transnational cultural ties and networks that have facilitated cross-cultural interactions and the emergence of cultural actors, including religious leaders, movie practitioners, and diaspora communities, that are increasingly influential in foreign policy decision-making. In addition to these are economic actors such as MNCs and diaspora entrepreneurs whose business activities beyond their home countries have given rise to networks of economic actors with influence over the economic policies of states.

Equally associated with colonialism is the unifying role it played in forging an African consensus towards the herculean task of reducing Western influence in the continent and deepening integration. In West Africa, this

DOI: 10.4324/9781003396628-9

culminated in the formation of ECOWAS, which not only provided a forum to bridge the divide between French and Anglophone West African states, but also the institutional mechanisms to address a range of security, economic, and political challenges. Some of the security challenges include the rise of trans-border fundamentalist movements, narco-trafficking, maritime piracy, and the proliferation of SALW. West African states still have huge problems caused by poverty and underdevelopment, which is in no small way due to governance and democratic deficits, lack of transparency and accountability, weak state institutions, and political instability. Also notable is the fact that trade relations remain protectionist and low in volume, as most states still rely on extractive commodities for revenues.

While these challenges do not necessarily apply uniformly across the sub-region, no one state has been able to resolve them on its own. In other words, a positive-sum approach informs the strategic disposition of West African states towards their resolution. This essentializes the utility of soft power and suggests that for a regional leader like Nigeria, which has since independence carried the burden of ECOWAS, soft power is the best approach to mobilize consensus towards resolving some of these challenges. Take Ghana and Liberia's relations with Nigeria for instance. While both countries have occasionally locked horns with Nigeria, it is the collaborative approach between them, under the auspices of ECOWAS, that brought an end to the Liberian civil wars. Certainly, relations between these states and Nigeria have benefitted from linguistic similarities; however, a history of collaboration and brotherly relations has facilitated cultural and economic interactions between citizens of these states and Nigeria that suggest the effectiveness of an approach to foreign policy that relies on the tools of soft power.

However, for Nigeria to wield soft power it has to possess resources susceptible to generating attraction. A critical analysis of Nigeria's power resources revealed potentially attractive elements as well as contradictions that may inhibit their effectiveness. For instance, despite possessing the largest economy in Africa, Nigeria's overall economic competitiveness is challenged by tepid growth rates, high indebtedness, souring poverty levels, high inflation levels, and corruption. The same goes for Nigeria's military superiority, as its combat proficiency, derived from a reputation of gallantry in intra- and extra-regional peacekeeping efforts, has not translated to the domestic realm where the AFN struggles with containing extremist groups such as Boko Haram. What is clear is that these security challenges are tied to a domestic political context that continues to suffer from the flaws of a federalist framework that has entrenched a democratic system that is at best flawed, both in the practice of political contests and governance. Even Nigeria's rich cultural diversity that promises an array of potentially attractive resources has served as domestic political tools to sow mistrust and divisions, thereby exacerbating ethno-religious tensions, and promoting a climate of political contest that is ethnically charged, violent, corrupt, and to some extent authoritarian.

Notwithstanding these contradictions, there exist some positive attributes that may constitute attractive sources of influence. Economically, the Nigerian government maintains a policy of coming to the aid of neighbouring states through economic aid and technical assistance. Beyond the purview of the government lies transnational economic linkages centred around MNCs and the diaspora. Equally notable are the size of Nigeria's market, its entrepreneurial culture, and its innovative capacity in the realm of popular culture and tech. The same can be said of Nigeria's military capabilities, as security alliances within the sub-region have led Nigeria to instrumentalize its military resources to come to the aid of West African states. These alliances are largely informed by a foreign policy posture that espouses such universal values as multilateralism, peaceful coexistence, the principle of good neighbourliness, and the promotion of democracy. Beyond these are cultural resources such as a budding entertainment industry – movies, music, and comedy. Emerging from Nigeria's large Christian population and diaspora is a charismatic brand of Pentecostalism that currently attracts huge followership in the region. These cultural expressions are also embedded in cultural actors who hold sway in the continent and possess the ability to instigate social change.

However, whether in their latent or active forms, these cultural resources have featured sparingly in the foreign policy of Nigeria, as the country relies on its military and economic resources to advance its strategic objectives. Apart from the pursuit of the national interest, which involves protecting the welfare of Nigerians, all other objectives suggest the need to create an enabling environment to sustain its influence. It is not that they do not serve Nigeria's interest, it is that they serve the collective interest of West African states. While there appears to have been some coercive posturing in Nigeria's quest to meet its objectives, as sanctions imposed on Ghana and Liberia illustrate, Abuja has mostly relied on economic aid, technical assistance, cash gifts, development assistance, peacekeeping, and to some extent peace enforcement, targeted at governments and foreign publics alike, to advance its strategic objectives, geared towards its leadership aspiration.

What is clear is that Nigeria's overall disposition in the continent has not gone unnoticed. Prevailing attitudes in Ghana and Liberia suggest that Nigeria's foreign policy behaviour is favourably perceived in Ghana and Liberia, suggesting that its foreign policy disposition constitutes an attractive source of influence. Notable aspects of Nigeria's external disposition that generates positive sentiments include its role in advancing the cause of peace and regional integration, technical and humanitarian assistance, and contribution to the decolonization struggle. However, culture emerged as Nigeria's most attractive source of influence, of which Nollywood, the diaspora, and music emerged as the most attractive components. These are in addition to Nigerian Pentecostal churches, pidgin English, fashion, and literary icons. While Nollywood stood out for its propagation of African values and culture, the character traits of Nigerians, especially their business acumen and aggressiveness, stood out for the Nigerian diaspora. The relatability and quality appeared to be influential factors in perceptions of Nigerian music. Beyond their cultural influence, the Nigerian diaspora also features as the country's strongest source of economic attraction, surpassing other economic variables such as Nigerian banks, the government's economic assistance programmes, and informal trade links between Nigerians and their West African counterparts.

Similarly, the AFN emerged as an attractive source of influence due to its involvement in personnel exchange programmes and training exercises. The decisiveness of the AFN during the civil wars in Liberia and Sierra Leone, as well as its perceived strength were appealing to Ghanaians and Liberians. However, their penchant for violating UN laws guiding the conduct of peacekeepers and unending struggle with curtailing the rising threat of Islamic fundamentalism in Nigeria are perceived unfavourably. Also, much of Nigeria's internal political dynamics, especially the violent nature of politics in the country and deficits in governance are perceived unfavourably even if Nigeria's decentralized system of administration, steady democratic transition since 1999, and its rotational presidency along ethnic and religious lines are perceived favourably and deemed worthy of emulation. As a sign of their strong influence, cultural elements like the Nigerian diaspora, Nollywood, and Nigerian churches also aroused strong negative sentiments. Negative perceptions of the diaspora in Ghana and Liberia are mainly due to their involvement in illicit practices while negative perceptions of Nigeria's economic interactions stem from its protectionist and mercantilist policies.

What these findings suggest is that Nigeria does have attractive power resources in Ghana and Liberia, although they appear to resonate more strongly in the latter. The question then becomes the extent to which these attractive components of Nigeria's influence have amounted to tangible foreign policy outcomes, whether direct or indirect. As long as Nigeria's strategic objectives are designed to create an enabling regional context and shore up its influence, Nigeria may lay claim to a level of efficacy in its soft power approach to foreign policy. This is based on favourable perceptions of its leadership, influence, and a concomitant will for enhanced cooperation by elites in Ghana and Liberia. Even when the direct effects of Nigeria's strategic disposition in Africa, specifically on questions of policy, is scrutinized, the evidence suggests that more times than not, West African states have sided with Nigeria. This is evident in the number of times Nigerian-backed candidates in regional and global multilateral fora have gained the support of West African states.

In as much as the case for Nigeria's soft power in West Africa or the effectiveness of soft power as a tool of statecraft is made, this does not suggest that Nigeria's strategic disposition in the sub-region has been entirely effective. While this finding reflects a point of convergence with prevailing assumptions about the un-strategic nature of Nigeria's foreign policy, discussions in this book have shown that the ineffectiveness of Nigeria's foreign policy results from a dysfunctional domestic context marred by internal challenges and institutional inadequacies, including the usurpation of the role of the foreign ministry by the presidency, the inability of the Nigerian state to make the best of its attractive resources, especially those aspects lying within the purview of non-state actors, and deficits in the conception and implementation of policies that keep with new trends in the exercise of influence.

These challenges may be mitigated by a renewed approach to foreign policy that skilfully combines the tools of government and non-state actors alike to advance Nigeria's strategic objectives. This may entail a coordinated approach that mobilizes all relevant agencies of government and technical expertise to implement strategies that are geared towards repairing the country's dwindling international reputation. Perhaps, a national branding strategy that truthfully communicates Nigeria's domestic challenges and the various strategies adopted to address them may help in this regard. These may be further aided by a digital diplomacy strategy that emphasizes a communication-centric approach that is dialogic and makes the best of Nigeria's increasingly influential diaspora community.

Realism, Soft Power, and the West African Experience

I began the empirical discussions in this book with a definition of soft power that draws on a relational understanding of power, where attraction does not derive from the tangibility of resources, but from the behaviour a state exhibits in its interactions with others. Consequently, I argued that interrogating an agent's soft power capability requires an account of the context within which relations between the agent and subject(s) are embedded, the resources available to the agent, the foreign policy objectives and behaviour of the agent, perceptions of the subjects of power, and the changed behaviour of the subject as a result of the attractiveness of the agent. In this section, I evaluate the extent to which these assumptions conform with, or contradict the major points discussed in the empirical sections.

Do soft power work only where cooperative relations exist between the agent and subject of power? This book theorized this question in the affirmative, as it assumes that for soft power to go into operation, there has to be some level of friendliness, trust, credibility, and cooperativeness between the agent and the subject of power. This is because the absence of these factors may distort the flow of policies and cultural outputs to their intended target. In other words, where conflictual relationships exist, soft power is unlikely to be effective. As the findings conveyed in this book suggest, West African states have maintained a consistent level of cooperative relations under the framework of ECOWAS which may explain why Ghanaian and Liberian elites are positively disposed to Nigeria's soft power. The role of intersubjective variables such as shared colonial experiences, language similarities, and cultural compatibility permeating this regional relational dynamic corroborates a constructivist position that the nature of social interactions between states affects their preferences and how they interact with each other. It is also worth noting that the nature of issues in contention, which requires a collaborative approach to their resolution, may also explain why relations are mostly cordial.

The fact that most West African states are culturally heterogeneous with cultural and language ties that extend beyond traditional state boundaries may explain why Nigeria's cultural outputs resonate positively in Ghana and Liberia. Already we know that Africa's diaspora in the Western world is mainly responsible for the global consumption of cultural outputs – Nollywood, Afrobeats, charismatic Pentecostalism – from Nigeria. What this implies is that the context of relations between the agents and subjects of power is particularly important in understanding the workings of soft power. Perhaps, if the case studies included Francophone West African states like Cote d'Ivoire and Senegal, with historical animosities with Nigeria, this assumption would not hold, but, yet again, barring the Nigerian civil war, these states do not demonstrate any overt hostility towards Nigeria. Even the supposed animosity has not prevented these states from working with Nigeria on several fronts when their interests align.

This brings to the fore the compatibility of interest as an essential condition in understanding the workings of soft power. In other words, does attraction trump interests or vice versa? This book assumed that states act on their interest and where these interests collide between the agent and subject(s), attraction is likely to be ineffective. But, where the issues in contention reflect the shared or collective interests of states, soft power is likely to be effective. Although Nigeria's national interest prioritizes the safety and welfare of its citizens, its external disposition has been largely geared towards actualizing the shared aspirations of West African states, in a bid to create an enabling environment for the exercise of its influence. These aspirational goals include eradicating colonialism, promoting regional peace and security, and promoting a just economic order. While this explains why a collaborative approach has mostly informed their actualization, it also explains why Nigeria's leadership role in their actualization is perceived favourably in Ghana and Liberia. What this suggests is that the pursuit of milieu goals tend to neutralize competing interest and engender attraction for regional leaders; however, one cannot conclusively say that interest trumps attraction or vice versa.

What is clear is that where states are pursuing self-interested goals, where interests tend to collide, the evidence suggests that they do not act against their interest because they like another state. Nigeria's unilateral decision to close its borders did anger a lot of Ghanaians, and true to this sentiment shops owned by Nigerian traders were closed in retaliation, with the backing of the government, for engaging in retail businesses. The deportation of Nigerians from Ghana is another example where relations of cordiality, attraction for Nigerian citizens, and ultimately the existence of the Free Movement Protocol among West African states did not deter Ghanaian authorities. Even more revealing is the fact that despite strong bilateral relations and strong attraction for Nigeria, Liberia supports Morocco's ECOWAS membership, which Nigeria does not support. What these findings suggest is that state actors may be attracted to another state, but this does not mean that they will negate their interests in favour of another's.

What does the West African context reveal about the sources of attraction? Certainly, context does inform how resources and behaviours are perceived. As the findings of this book suggest, despite contradictions such as protectionist economic policies, rising debt levels, and pervasive poverty, Ghanaian and Liberian political elites did find Nigeria's diaspora entrepreneurs, Nigerian banks, the competitiveness of the Nigerian economy, and Nigeria's economic assistance programmes attractive. While prevailing assumptions suggest that the competitiveness of a state's economy and economic assistance programmes are likely to be attractive, all other attractive components of Nigeria's economic power are context-specific and are simply the result of interactions between non-state actors. While it remains unclear if the attractiveness of these variables extends beyond these countries, one can assume that Western audiences are unlikely to find Nigeria's economy attractive as it suffers challenges that are unworthy of emulation. Perhaps, Nigeria's economic superiority may explain why Ghanaians and Liberians find it attractive, but what is clear is that most of the challenges bedevilling the Nigerian economy cut across the sub-region and may also explain why certain negative elements do not affect their overall perception of Nigeria's economic competitiveness.

While the foregoing suggests that economic resources can be attractive, military resources can constitute a source of attraction also. As the findings of this book suggest, the participation of the AFN in personnel exchanges and joint military exercises, its decisiveness in regional conflicts, and its perceived invincibility in situations of regional conflicts, specifically Liberia and Sierra Leone, did emerge attractive in Liberia and Ghana. This tends to confirm prevailing assumptions on the attractive potential of military resources and Morgenthau's postulation that intervention in peace support missions or the use of military force when morally and legally justified can be a source of attraction power. Also, this validates a behavioural approach to soft power where the way states apply their resources dictates how such resources are perceived, as opposed to the tangibility of resources. This underlines the attractiveness of a state's external disposition or foreign policy. As this book corroborates, a state's foreign policies are likely to be attractive if they appear legitimate and espouse multilateralism.

While states cultivate attraction through their behaviours, there is a tendency to limit this to the external realm. How a state behaves within its boundaries also matters. Nigeria's internal political dynamics were not particularly appealing to Liberian and Ghanaian elites who are averse to prevailing illiberal and anti-democratic practices. These are in addition to the fact that a seemingly rich country, with huge oil reserves, cannot put its house in order by providing for its citizens. What these findings suggest is that globalization has facilitated the flow of information about the internal happenings of states that inform the perceptive disposition of international audiences, and these audiences are averse to states who are unable to put their domestic affairs in order and espouse illiberal political values. This tends to affirm that a country's reputation for success can enhance its influence and, as Morgenthau submits, the quality of society and government is, evidently, a source of power.

What can also be drawn from this is that Africans want a well-functioning system of democratic governance and states that can get it right are likely to be influential. Also notable is that these findings tend to validate Nye's assumption about the attractiveness of American political values and their universalism. As perceptions of Nigeria's political values suggest, its decentralized system of government, which draws from the American political system, is a model Ghanaians and Liberians would want to emulate as it decentralizes governance and administration. There is no gainsaying that the West African public is increasingly influenced by the constructive aspects of Western-style democracy and would want states in the sub-region to espouse such values. However, what is unique about the sub-region is that successive transition from one "democratically" elected government to another, a rare occurrence in the continent, is perceived favourably even when electoral outcomes are heavily contested. Equally notable is that the ethnic and religious diversity of African states presents unique challenges that present opportunities for states that are able to effectively manage the destructive effects of this diversity, especially in the contest for power.

In as much as the findings of this research suggest that the activities and actions of states do generate soft power, much of soft power resources are in the purview of non-state actors, specifically the cultural sector. It is no wonder scholars synonymize soft power with cultural power. As the findings of this book affirm, Nigeria's cultural sector accounts for the most attractive components of its power resources. And in what is suggestive of the fact that the sources of soft power are not universal across cultural variables, Nigeria's cultural attractions present unique qualities that make them alluring to Ghanaians and Liberians. Notable among them is the portrayal of African values and social practices. However, as was theorized, most states find them difficult to wield and Nigeria is no different in this regard as the government has sparingly wielded these resources for foreign policy gains. Regardless, they appear to be Nigeria's most potent soft power resources.

Do outcomes-based studies provide more certainty about the operationalization of soft power in foreign policy? Does soft power work in international relations? While the case of Nigeria suggests that soft power can be effective where the goal is to create an enabling environment for the exercise of influence, on self-interested objectives, its effectiveness can be called into question especially when decision-makers are likely to act in the interest of the state should the need arise. Where a state is driven by the need to shore up its influence and leadership credentials, as the case of Nigeria suggests, cultivating attraction can be an effective foreign policy strategy. The fact that this study cannot uniformly identify the workings of soft power where states are pursuing "self-interested" objectives, even if voting preferences do provide a useful generic proxy, reveals why states find it difficult to wield and aren't too inclined to rely on soft power. The problem is that apart from prescribed behaviours associated with the use of economic and military resources, and the reputation that derives from how a state manages its internal affairs, the attraction that stems from cultural variables or intersubjective elements of power cannot be fixed into clear-cut categories of influence that states can rely on for specific purposes.

Perhaps, further research in this regard may help, but what is clear is that outcomes-based approaches to soft power encourage an account of the context within which power relations are embedded, the resources available to states that may cause attraction, how these resources serve the purpose of foreign policy, how a state's resources and behaviour are perceived, and, importantly, the reasons behind prevailing perceptions. Where it falls short is that it is challenging to isolate the impact of specific attractive variables on specific foreign policy outcomes. However, it does highlight the constitutive effects of ideational factors such as Pan-Africanism, shared colonial experiences, and African value systems on the subjectivities of Ghanaian and Liberian elites. And the fact that Nigeria, in different forms, champions and espouses these ideals in its African policy in no small way positively affects perceptions of its leadership and influence – a long-held aspirational goal.

This is where constructivist scholarship can assume some theoretical primacy over classical realism in explaining the operationalization of soft power. Specifically, how intersubjective understandings and expectations arising from African values affect how states perceive others within the system. Liberals may also lay claim to the fact that liberal values like democracy, multilateralism, and institutionalism are dispositions that make states attractive in international politics. But, by accounting for all of these variables, in addition to material resources, as sources of power in a two-way relationship between an agent and subject, classical realism provides a theoretical core towards a holistic understanding of attraction within power relationships – albeit insufficient. Theoretically, realist interpretation of the operationalization of soft power is not robust; it leaves gaps that constructivists may account for. Ideas, values, and norms, both in their constitutive and restrictive forms, involve a process of transmission that constructivist perspectives capture. However, these variables have not evolved into a concrete concept of power with policy implications. Rather they have formed the bases of realist and constructivist debates on the deterministic effects of anarchy on the behaviour of states.

What the findings of this research suggest is that a theoretically neutral approach to soft power may suffice given that the concept does not fit neatly into any of the grand theories, exposing the researcher to criticism of incoherent usage. However, following this path may obscure critical junctures in the operationalization of soft power. For what it is worth soft power does complement realist assumptions about the centrality of power in international relations. And as the findings of this book reveal, states must leverage the opportunities policies like public diplomacy, international broadcasting, and strategic communications offer in altering the perceptions of the global public and creating an enabling environment for the exercise of influence, especially when power is the ultimate goal of foreign policy.

Appendices

Appendix 1: Demographic Features of Respondents

Although demographic considerations did not influence the collection of qualitative data for this book, given the positional and reputational criteria that influenced the collection of data, the questionnaires were distributed bearing two important demographic variables in mind: gender and age. Gender and age were factored into the study to ensure an adequate spread.

Gender

Overall, 327 (58.3%) of sampled respondents were male, while 234 (41.7%) were female. When broken down, Ghanaian respondents include 169 (56%) males and 132 (44%) females, whereas Liberian respondents constitute 158 (61%) males and 102 (39%) females. The data in Liberia are mostly skewed in favour of men due to bias towards educational qualifications, which favours men by almost two to one. Liberia boasts of a 48.3% literacy rate, with men making up 62.7% of this group and women 34.1%.

Age

Overall, 94% of the total respondents sampled in Ghana and Liberia were between the ages of 18 and 54 while only 6% were above 55 years of age. In Ghana 86 (29%) respondents were between the ages of 18 and 24, 119 (40%) were between the ages of 25 and 34, 86 (29%) were between the ages of 35 and 54, and 10 (three percent) respondents were over the age of 55. In Liberia, 72 (28%) respondents were between the ages of 18 and 24, 67 (26%) respondents were between the ages of 25 and 34, 100 (38%) respondents were between the ages of 35 and 54 and 21 (8%) respondents were over the age of 55.

Appendix 2: List of Interviewees[1]

S/N	Name	Office/Institution	Designation
1	Ambassador George W. Wallace	Ministry of Foreign Affairs, Liberia	Special Adviser to the President of Liberia on Foreign Affairs
2	Ambassador Dennis Remongar	Ministry of Foreign Affairs, Liberia	Director, Foreign Service Institute of Liberia
3	Shedrick Jackson	Ministry of Foreign Affairs, Liberia	Assistant Minister on International Cooperation and Economic Affairs
4	Dr. Abraham Fofana	University of Liberia	Lecturer in Political Science
5	Prof. Sekou Kone	University of Liberia	Acting Chair, Political Science Department and Dean, Liberal College of Social Sciences and Humanities
6	Dr. Thomas Jaye	University of Liberia	Deputy Director of Research, Kofi Annan International Peacekeeping Training Centre
7	Abou Sherif	Fabric FM	Broadcast Journalist, governance and politics
8	Prof. Al-Hassan Conteh	Embassy of Liberia, Nigeria	Ambassador Extraordinaire and Plenipotentiary of Liberia to the Federal Republic of Nigeria, Benin, Equatorial Guinea, and Permanent Representative of ECOWAS
9	Prof Augustine Konneh	African Methodist Episcopal University, Liberia	Dean, Graduate School of International Studies
10	Nyene-Yaba Freeman Thompson	Ministry of Foreign Affairs	Assistant Minister, Bureau of International Organizations Affairs
11	Roseline Tomah	University of Liberia	Coordinator of Student Services, Research Assessment, and Evaluation
12	Albert Tse-Tse	University of Ghana	Lecturer

S/N	Name	Office/Institution	Designation
13	Dr. Benjamin Amakye-Boateng	University of Ghana	Lecturer
14	Richard Mensah	Citi TV, Ghana	Director of Television
15	Dr. Moses Nii-Dortey	University of Ghana	Lecturer
16	Ambassador Henry Hanson-Hall	Former Ghanaian Ambassador to Israel	Career Diplomat
17	Dr. Senyo Adjei	University of Cape Coast, Ghana	Lecturer in Music
18	Ambassador Paul King Aryene		Former Ghanaian Ambassador to Germany with concurrent accreditation to Estonia, Latvia, and Lithuania
19	Dr. Joshua Alfred Amuah	University of Ghana	Head of Department, Music
20	Philip Attuquayefio	University of Ghana	Senior Research Fellow
21	Ali Baba		Comedian
22	Ben Adam Shemang	Voice of Nigeria	Director, Training
23	Chinenye P. Ihuoma	Federal Ministry of Information, Culture, and Tourism	Director, Public Communications
24	Dr. Francis A. Odey	Federal Ministry of Foreign Affairs	Deputy Director, Policy Planning
25	Dorothy I. Duruaku	Federal Ministry of Information, Culture, and Tourism	Deputy Director, Domestic & Eco-Tourism Promotion and Control Department
26	Dr. Guy Fineman	National Assembly	Assistant Chief Administrative Officer
27	Dr. Matthew Oguche	National Open University	Lecturer
28	Dr. Joshua Bolarinwa	Redeemed Christian Church of God	Director of Research
29		Directorate of Technical Aid Corps	
30	Francis Duru		Nollywood Actor
31	Geraldine Yop Kim-Aku	Institute for Peace and Conflict Resolution	Researcher
32		Federal Ministry of Finance	International Economic Relations Department
33	Kanayo O. Kanayo		Nollywood Actor
34	Kelechi C. Nwogu	Nigerian Institute of International Affairs	Research Fellow
35	Micah Godbless	Niger Delta University	Lecturer

S/N	Name	Office/Institution	Designation
36	Aishatu Morido Yanet	Centre for Strategic Research and Studies, National Defence College	Research Fellow
37	Wasa Festus	Federal Ministry of Defence	Deputy Director Policy Planning
38	Shina Alege	Nigerian High Commission, Ghana	Minister
39		Nigerian Tourism Development Commission	Director, Policy Research and Studies
40	Prof. Charles Dokubo	Nigerian Institute of International Affairs	Former Director, Research and Studies
41	Prof. Fred Aja Agwu	Nigerian Institute of International Affairs	Director, Research and Studies
42	Prof. Barclays Ayakoromo	University of Africa, Toru-Orua	Head of Department, Theater Art
43	Segun Akintoye	Directorate of Technical Cooperation in Africa	Chief Admin Officer, Monitoring and Evaluation
44	Tony Olonwu	Federal Ministry of Foreign Affairs	Assistant Director, African sub-Regional Organization Department (ASROD)

Note

1 Sources who preferred to remain anonymous are not included in this list.

Index

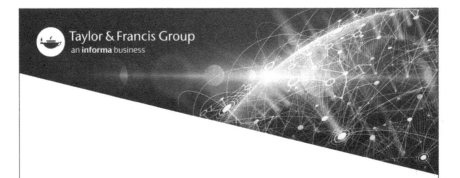